WITHDRAWN

COMPLEMENTARY MEDICINE
AND THE LAW

Complementary Medicine and the Law

JULIE STONE
MA, LLB, Barrister
Research Associate, Hempsons

and

JOAN MATTHEWS
LLB, MRQA
Complementary Health Practitioner
Tokyo, Japan

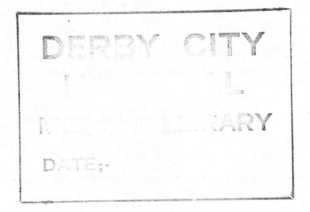

OXFORD UNIVERSITY PRESS

Oxford University Press, Great Clarendon Street, Oxford OX2 6DP

Oxford New York
Athens Auckland Bangkok Bogota Buenos Aires Calcutta
Cape Town Chennai Dar es Salaam Delhi Florence Hong Kong Istanbul
Karachi Kuala Lumpur Madrid Melbourne Mexico City Mumbai
Nairobi Paris São Paulo Singapore Taipei Tokyo Toronto Warsaw

and associated companies in
Berlin Ibadan

Oxford is a trade mark of Oxford University Press

Published in the United States
by Oxford University Press, New York

First published 1996

British Library Cataloguing in Publication Data

Data available

Library of Congress Cataloging in Publication Data
Stone, Julie.
Complementary medicine and the law / Julie Stone and Joan
Matthews.
p. cm.
Includes bibliographical references and index.
1. Alternative medicine—Law and lesiglation—Great Britain.
1. Matthews, Joan, LLB. II. Title.
KD3395.S76 1996
334. 41´041—dc20
[344.1044] 96–259
ISBN 0–19–825970–0 (cloth).—ISBN 0–19–825971–9 (paper)

3 5 7 9 10 8 6 4 2

Printed in Great Britain
on acid-free paper by
Biddles Ltd, Guildford and King's Lynn

Contents

PART III A MODEL FOR ETHICS-LED REGULATION

Acknowledgements

We are immensely grateful to the following people who have given us so much generous support during the writing of this book: John Barkworth DOMRO, Chairman of the Ethics Committee of the General Council and Register of Osteopaths; Stephen Gordon, MCH., RSHom., Chairman of the Council for Complementary and Alternative Medicine; Joseph Goodman, NDDO, Dr Ac., F.Ac., AFCO, MCrOA, Chairman of the British Acupuncture Council and Cranial Osteopathic Association; Dr George Lewith, MA, DM, MRCP, MRCGP, Honorary Senior Lecturer, Department of Medicine, University of Southampton and Director of the Centre for the Study of Complementary Medicine, Southampton; Sato Liu, Executive Director of the Natural Medicines Society; Michael Endacott, Anthony Baird, and Jane Foulkes of the Institute for Complementary Medicine; Graeme Millar, Editor of the *Journal of Alternative and Complementary Medicine* and Chairman of the British Complementary Medicine Association; Jane McWhirter, McTimoney Chiropractor, MA, MC, MMCA; Dr Xu Hua, of Chinese Herbal Health Consultants, London; Kate Williams, Cert. Ed., ITEC, Reg. Mem. AMP; Sarah Wise, BSc. RGN; Dr David Morgan of the Scientific Affairs Department of the British Medical Association; Professor Patrick D. Wall, FRS, DM, FRCP; Michael Webbern, Administrative Director of the British Holistic Medical Association; Steve Wright, MBE, RGN, MSc, Director of the European Nursing Development Agency; Dr Chris Worth, Director of Public Health, West Yorkshire Health Authority; Victoria Conran; Celia Manson, Adviser in Nursing Practice, Royal College of Nursing; Janet Richardson of Lewisham Hospital NHS Trust Health Services Research and Evaluation Unit; David Dickinson, Editor of *Which? Way to Health*; Oliver Rugen; Roger Worthington, DO, MGO, former Chairman of the Health Practitioners Association. Deepest thanks to our editor, Richard Hart for his support and enthusiasm and to Hempsons Solicitors for their encouragement and advice, with particular thanks to Jo Wright and Karen Scott for their invaluable assistance in tracking down research materials. This is a controversial and political subject and the views in this book are the authors' alone.

Joan Matthews writes: I would like to thank the staff of the Law Department at the School of Oriental and African Studies, London University, for the intellectual challenge and unique perspective of so much of the teaching that I was privileged to enjoy as a student there. In particular, I would like to acknowledge the guidance and encouragement of Francois du Bois, my supervisor over two years of research into the legal aspects of complementary medicine. I should also like to thank Professor David Arnold and Dr Chris Cullen of the History Department at SOAS for a most stimulating and helpful introduction to the history of disease and medicine in Asia. To Gabriel Mojay, Director of Studies at the Institute of Traditional Herbal Medicine and Aromatherapy, I remain lastingly indebted for the quality and enthusiasm of his teaching and for so expertly introducing me to the fascination of holistic aromatherapy. My thanks too, to Dr AnneRose Akaike for giving me the opportunity to work in her general practice in Tokyo, and for sharing her wisdom and insight into the nature of healing.

   A heartfelt thanks to all my friends who have supported me over the two years this book has taken to write. I would particularly thank my friends John and Eunice Rourke, for lovingly providing my children with a second home during times of high stress and domestic crisis, for being among the first to submit themselves to my fumbling therapeutic ministrations during the early days of my training, and for the many hours of philosophical and political discussion over the best steak and kidney pies in the world. Finally, my deepest love and gratitude to my family: to my husband Darryl who, electrical skills notwithstanding, has helped me in so many practical ways to write this book, to my son James, for his technical expertise and for helping to rescue my computer from the flames and to my daughter Jessica, for her tea and sympathy.

Julie Stone writes: I would like to recognize the input of three people who have so shaped my academic development: Professor Margot Brazier, a constant source of inspiration, and for her ongoing role, ten years later, as my personal tutor; Professor Ian Kennedy, whose intellectual rigour and inspired teaching on the MA course in Medical Law and Ethics at King's College stretched me utterly and opened enthralling new vistas, and whose frequent appeal not to start sentences with 'certainly', 'surely', or 'obviously' has been firmly in my mind throughout writing this book; and finally, the late

Dr John Dawson of the BMA, with whom I had the privilege of working, albeit for a short time—a truly visionary man whose influence lives on. I would also like to thank the many students I have taught over the years at St Mary's Hospital, St George's Hospital, and the John Radcliffe Hospital, Oxford, for giving me the opportunity continually to refine my own thoughts on medical ethics and the law.

On a more personal note, words cannot adequately describe my gratitude towards friends for their love and encouragement during this long and challenging period, and for reminding me that there is life outside this book. Their willingness to engage in debate, often into the small hours, has made a tangible difference to the text. My thanks, in particular, to my sister Lucy, role model *par extraordinaire* in the art of pushing oneself to the limit; to my precious Joe and, latterly, Benjamin, for showing no interest in this project whatsoever; to Simon, for his eagle eye; to Christina, for her superb proofing, her extreme kindness and for picking me up off the floor; to Ali, for putting up with me day in day out with indefatigable patience and good humour; and most of all, to my mother, with thanks, for a lifetime's love and chicken soup.

Foreword

The growth and popularity of complementary medicine in Britain is one of the most prominent and influential developments to occur in health care over the past ten years. The enhancement of its status and credibility is such that complementary medicine is now being taken seriously by orthodox health care professionals, and its methods and practices are increasingly being introduced or incorporated into mainstream medicine. These developments have gained pace amid a rising clamour that complementary medicine should be subjected to the same stringent regulatory controls that govern orthodox medicine. To date, the regulatory debate has been blighted by an uncritical assumption that the 'medical model' is the most appropriate form of regulation for those therapies requiring formal control. We challenge this notion and offer an explanation as to why medical-style regulation will not work for many holistic therapies.

We examine the wider background to the debate in an attempt to expand the discussion beyond the often artificial rationale of 'consumer protection'. We look at the ways in which the common law presently affects the practice of complementary medicine, and ask how effective statutory regulation and voluntary self-regulation in its current form might be at regulating holistic complementary therapies. We argue that the highly individualized, intuitive, and whole-person approach central to holistic complementary therapies is not amenable to the degree of certainty, objective assessment, and quantification required for the efficient operation of existing legal mechanisms. We argue further that the participatory nature of the therapeutic relationship which characterizes complementary therapies raises quite distinct issues which need to be taken into account when formulating the most appropriate regulatory response to complementary medicine.

Our solution focuses on the need for a more dynamic commitment to the role of ethics in training and practice. We describe a system of ethics-led regulation which is responsive to the holistic dimension of complementary medicine, and which promotes and enhances the patient-centred values which are so much at the heart of holistic therapies. We recognize the radical nature of our proposals: however, to continue to ignore the very real legal problems inherent in trying to squeeze holistic therapies into a regulatory model designed for scientific medicine will result either in regulation which does not work, or in complementary medicine being stripped of its most valuable characteristics.

Table of Cases

Table of Legislation

Table of Legislation

Introduction

The astonishing growth of complementary medicine over the past decade is now so well documented as to be beyond dispute. Recent surveys have revealed that as many as one in four of the United Kingdom population may now use complementary therapies,[1] a statistic which would appear to be broadly paralleled throughout many of the industrialized countries of the West. A major survey estimates that one in three American adults used some form of complementary therapy during 1990.[2] To meet increased public demand, the number of complementary health practitioners in Britain has been increasing at an estimated rate of 10 per cent in each year since the mid-1980s.[3] This demonstrable public confidence and support for non-conventional medicine has encouraged a number of more well-established therapies to initiate or renew efforts towards achieving legislative recognition of their status. The Osteopaths Act 1993 and the Chiropractors Act 1994 have recently conferred the benefits of statutory registration of title on these two therapies, and in doing so, have provided other complementary therapies with a potential model in their drive towards formal statutory recognition.

The growth of unorthodox therapies in the past five years is particularly remarkable for the extent to which it has expanded beyond the confines of the private sector. Hospitals and general practitioners are showing considerable interest in both the methods and the practices of complementary medicine. An example of one of the most recent initiatives is the Complementary Therapy and Research Centre established in 1994 at the Lewisham Hospital in London. A survey of local general practitioners carried out before the Centre was authorized

---

[1] A 1989 survey carried out for *The Times* by MORI revealed that 27% of the respondents had used non-orthodox medicine. This is a figure broadly in line with a 1991 Consumers Association survey which showed 25% of their members used complementary therapies.

[2] D. M. Eisenberg *et al.*, 'Unconventional medicine in the United States: prevalence, costs and patterns of use' *New England Journal of Medicine*, **328** (1993), 246–52.

[3] Fulder, S. and Monro, R., *The Status of Complementary Medicine in the United Kingdom* (Threshold Foundation, London, 1982).

showed that 92 per cent would refer patients to a complementary therapy unit.[4] While the idea of complete 'integration' may never be more than a mirage on the horizon, it can sensibly be predicted that complementary medicine will increasingly be regarded as a significant part of the health care of the future. Prince Charles' famous remark, that 'today's unorthodoxy is probably tomorrow's convention'[5] is showing every sign of being realized at a pace far faster than practitioners of either orthodox or complementary medicine ever expected.

This expansion in consumer usage has inevitably led to an escalation in the debate on regulation for complementary medicine. The direction of developments in this arena is heavily influenced by the activities of two major groups—those whose opinions are focused on issues of consumer protection, and those whose primary concern lies in the furtherance of the interests of complementary medicine. The unregulated state of most complementary therapies is largely assumed by both groups to be an undesirable state of affairs, albeit for different reasons. Consumer protectionists, in whatever guise, point to the lack of uniform training standards, inadequate disciplinary procedures, and to the fact that patients harmed by incompetent or negligent complementary practitioners are often left with no effective form of protection or redress save that provided by the common law. The absence of effective registration systems has prompted calls for 'tighter' regulation, often uncritically assumed to be statutory control.

Within the past decade, many complementary health practitioners and their representative organizations have expanded their political ambitions towards the achievement of some form of statutory recognition. This impetus towards a legislative solution is fuelled by fears of medical 'colonization' by orthodox health care providers, and especially by the prospect that European 'harmonization' might destroy the common law freedom to practise that has long characterized the British approach to alternative medicine. Complementary health practitioners have recognized, and are responding to, the perceived linkage between the achievement of statutory recognition and the need to demonstrate competence. Much more emphasis is now being placed on qualifications, and degree and diploma courses are

[4] *Complementary Therapy Centre Report* (Lewisham Hospital Trust, 1994).
[5] Extract from the valedictory address given by Prince Charles as President of the BMA (1983).

proliferating. Training standards are being raised and the length and content of many courses is being re-evaluated.

It is, therefore, part of the purpose of this book to evaluate whether these calls for greater regulation are well founded, and, if so, to examine what sort of regulation best serves both the public and practitioners. We analyse the spectrum of healing modalities that are currently understood as being within complementary medicine, and argue that certain therapies bear many of the hallmarks which characterize orthodox medicine. We conclude that such therapies would be more appropriately regulated along the lines of the current medical model. However, the majority of complementary therapies do not fall into this category, and for such therapies, formal statutory regulation would be unworkable, untenable, and unnecessary.

The view that complementary medicine should be better regulated is often conjoined with an assumption that some form of statutory intervention is the only satisfactory route to regulatory control. We shall seek throughout this book to challenge this proposition. We base our argument on two main grounds: first, we argue that reliance on statutory regulation will not necessarily result in better controls or in greater consumer protection; secondly, we consider that the regulation of complementary medicine requires an entirely new paradigm which reflects and accommodates the holistic nature of the therapies involved and the very different therapeutic relationship between therapist and patient from that characterizing the conventional doctor/patient model. We shall argue that the present 'medical model' of regulation is too heavily centred on the maintenance of professional self-interest at the expense of the interests of the consumer. For this reason alone, significant reservations should be expressed about holding the medical model up as the regulatory standard to which complementary medicine should aspire.

Our argument, however, extends beyond this position. We take the view that much of what is integral to the holistic therapeutic approach is beyond the reach of formal statutory mechanisms and that the interests of both consumer and practitioner can be best served by a regulatory approach which takes account of the holistic perspective. The 'whole' approach to regulation we describe recognizes the role played by the common law, litigation, codes of practice, and complaints mechanisms, but emphasizes a more dynamic and systematic use of flexible ethical codes rather than a statutory approach grounded in prescriptive, self-protective legislation.

It is perhaps no accident that the escalation of interest in the theories and practice of complementary therapies should coincide with a heightened concern with the legal and ethical problems of mainstream medicine. It has long been appreciated that part of the explanation for the success of complementary medicine can be found in patient dissatisfaction with certain aspects of orthodox medicine.[6] We take the view that this criticism of orthodox medicine is better understood as a criticism of medical *regulation*. Regulation provides the framework for, and to some extent determines the nature of, the medical encounter. If it is seen not to work, then public confidence in doctors, and the system within which they work, will plunge.

Public dissatisfaction with orthodox medicine is not just about iatrogenic disease (i.e., conditions caused by medical treatment either as an unforeseen or inevitable side-effect), impersonal therapeutic procedures, and uncommunicative doctors. It is also about a profession that is too often seen as being insufficiently accountable, operating within a regulatory system that has long been criticized for its over-zealous protection of the profession it is meant to regulate.[7] More specifically, it is about the lack of adequate grievance procedures and about the absence of mechanisms whereby consumers of medical services can have their views more fully represented. It is about disciplinary procedures that are widely perceived to be outmoded and ineffective, the shortcomings of which leave the injured and aggrieved patient to a hazardous litigation process that is, in any case, only a realistic option for either the very rich or the very poor. In other words, many of the perceived problems within orthodox medicine are about *regulatory malfunction* rather than the *practice of medicine*.

This inter-connectedness between the perceived failure of orthodox medicine and the apparent success of complementary medicine has legal and ethical implications which are, as yet, largely unexplored, but which can already be seen to be operating to bring about change in both conventional and non-conventional medicine. The more assertive complementary therapies become in making their therapeutic claims, the more strident will be the demand that they provide evidence of efficacy. As evidence-based medicine becomes a priority

[6] See Taylor, R., 'Alternative Medicine and the Medical Encounter in Britain and the United States', in Warren Salmon, J. (ed.), *Alternative Medicines: Popular and Policy Perspectives* (Tavistock Publications, 1984).

[7] See Kennedy, I., *The Unmasking of Medicine* (Allen and Unwin, London, 1981).

in orthodox medicine, so increasingly will calls be made for complementary medicine to provide scientific validation of its claims. Furthermore, the existing discrepancy between an intensely regulated orthodox profession and the formally unregulated position of most complementary therapies will become increasingly difficult to justify. Mainstream medicine is, today, one of the most highly regulated of all social and economic activities. With this firmly in mind, and at a time when so great an emphasis is being placed on consumer rights in health care, on what basis are we able to defend a situation in which so much of complementary medicine remains apparently unregulated? On the face of it, it is not only illogical, but hazardous.

Clearly, current concerns about the legal and ethical aspects of health care can no longer exclude those arising in complementary medicine. However, there are significant difficulties in viewing the regulation of complementary medicine primarily from the perspective of orthodox medicine: we argue that holistic therapies require more than just minor adjustments to the set of regulatory priorities that govern orthodox practice. As we shall see, the very discourse of medical law and ethics has been shaped by the prevailing doctor/patient relationship in which the doctor is the expert and the patient the passive recipient of treatment. Such a model cannot be readily transposed to a relationship based on mutual responsibilities and commitment in which information, and thus power, is shared.

It is ironic that having criticized orthodox medicine for decades, the orthodox regulatory model is still the approach to which many complementary therapies aspire. The wisdom of uncritically adopting the 'medical model' as the standard for the regulation of complementary medicine has been openly questioned by some within complementary medicine. But the debate, while rightly pointing to the flaws in the 'medical model', has rarely extended to the question of whether, in fact, holistic medicine is actually *capable* of being formally regulated in any meaningful sense.

The holistic approach which is so fundamental to complementary medicine is not amenable to measurement and objective assessment in the same way as scientific medicine. These difficulties have frequently been debated in the context of the problem of research in complementary medicine. There has been a failure to appreciate that these same difficulties also have legal and ethical implications which may complicate and frustrate the operation of conventional statutory regulation and the common law.

Complementary medicine differs from orthodox medicine in a much more profound way than theoretical disagreement over disease causation. In fact, it might more accurately be said of many complementary therapists that looking at *disease* is not their primary focus. Central to the practice of many complementary therapies is an understanding of patients and their health problems within the context of their experiences as human beings. Complementary therapists believe that health is critically determined by individuals' relationships with their total environment, their work, and their home, and by their interpersonal relationships. Complementary therapists thus see the social, emotional, and spiritual context as being central to the issue of health and disease. Put in simple terms, this patient-centred medicine is primarily focused on relationships and on the concept of healing, rather than on disease mechanisms and technological intervention.

This patient-centredness goes beyond an understanding of the importance of the social environment to an individual's health problems —it extends to the nature of the therapeutic relationship itself. Arguably, the holistic approach is at its most distinct with regard to the therapeutic dynamics between therapist and patient. The relationship is usually of a very different order to that which characterizes modern medical practice. In many complementary therapies, respect for autonomy is not merely an abstract ethical principle, but a therapeutic prerequisite. It will be argued that the greater degree of patient participation, the emphasis on self-responsibility, and the highly individualized therapeutic approach are just some of the features which create very particular problems when trying to devise workable regulation for holistic medicine.

In much the same way as orthodox medicine requires scientific proof of efficacy, the operation of law and regulation demands a level of evidence and certainty to a degree that many complementary therapies will never be able to provide. We shall argue that certain aspects of the practice of complementary medicine are simply not amenable to proof and hence may be *beyond the reach of existing legal mechanisms*. Indeed the growth of medical ethics has arisen in part because of a realization that whilst doctors are capable of making decisions about the technical aspects of their work, they cannot profess to have particular expertise on the medical–moral issues arising out of what they do. This problem is exacerbated by adopting an holistic approach to medicine, in which the quantifiable, technical aspects of healing assume far less significance than responding to the patient on an emotional and intuitive level.

There is increasing recognition of the fact that the solutions to many of the diseases which beset modern civilization may lie outside the narrow confines of biomedicine (i.e., the body of knowledge derived from the life sciences and influenced by the Cartesian principle of the separation of mind and body). Likewise, it may be necessary to re-evaluate the means by which we seek to regulate the emerging holistic model for medicine. If we ignore the full significance of what is involved in the shift to a more patient-centred, holistic approach to health care, then we are likely to transfer to complementary medicine the regulatory problems which presently frustrate both consumers and some practitioners within orthodox medicine. To force holistic medicine into an incompatible regulatory mould must result either in laws which do not work, or in regulation which strips holistic medicine of much that is of real value.

This then, is the essence of the tension in the debate about regulation for holistic medicine: how to control the practice of unorthodox therapies safely and effectively without destroying entirely their potential contribution to future health care needs. Equally important is the need to take into account the perceived strengths of complementary medicine for its capacity to enlighten and inform any future attempt at reforming certain aspects of mainstream medical practice. This suggestion is not as improbable as it might seem. The medical profession is now in the process of seriously re-evaluating the purpose of medicine and its role as a key provider of health care.[8]

Regardless of whether moves towards a more patient-centred approach within orthodox medicine have been prompted by the challenge posed by the popularity of non-conventional medicine, some of the pronouncements coming out of this debate are couched in terms which sound strikingly similar to the central concerns of complementary medicine. In particular, the need for medicine to become more patient-centred and holistic in orientation is now openly and often sympathetically discussed within mainstream medicine. In a recent article, Dr Kenneth Calman, the Government's Chief Medical

---

[8] In Nov. 1994, a major medical conference was convened entitled 'Core Values in the Medical Profession in the 21st Century'. Its purpose was to consider the way in which changes in society, demography, health care organization, patients' expectations, and techniques of medical care were challenging doctors' traditional role and core values.

Officer, called for the need to re-examine the concept of the profession and recommended, 'the need for a holistic approach':

Making a diagnosis is not simple and straightforward even when the name of the 'disease' is well recognised. Social and family implications are crucial, emphasising the holistic nature of the concept and of patient care. It is a person with an illness, not just a label, and the wider implications of the 'diagnosis' need to be emphasised . . .[9]

His recommendations as to the 'key values' expected of doctors include, alongside the more familiar demands for improved research and continuing professional development, high standards of ethics, a concern with health as well as with illness, improved communications skills, and the requirement that the profession be 'patient and public focused'.

The greater willingness of the medical profession to recognize the limits of modern medicine and to appreciate the potential contribution of non-conventional therapies, particularly in relation to chronic and degenerative health problems, is likely to lead to a growth in the integration of complementary medicine within the National Health Service. Should the holistic approach become more widely acceptable within conventional medicine, it will almost certainly be linked to a greater acknowledgement of the contribution of the paramedical professions, and especially that of nurses. Moves in this direction are already apparent, particularly with the introduction of growing numbers of nurse practitioners.

It has sometimes been forgotten that the politics of the complementary health movement encompass issues which extend far beyond a dispute about disease causation and the safety and efficacy of non-conventional therapies. Recently, it has more readily been recognized that the holistic approach of complementary medicine draws much of its support and strength from the fact that it is in tune with more profound movements within society.[10] It can be seen as evidence of commitment to a philosophy of life that is focused on such issues as the desire for a greater sharing of knowledge, and with involvement and participation in environmental matters and other aspects of society which are now understood to have a critical impact on health.

While the core of this book is focused on the problem of regulation for complementary medicine, it is both our intention and hope that

[9] Calman, K., 'The Profession of Medicine', 309 BMJ 1140–1143 (1994).
[10] See, generally, Capra, F., *The Turning Point* (Flamingo, London, 1982).

some of the issues discussed will also be of value to those interested in working towards a more holistic approach to health care within mainstream medicine.

II. TERMINOLOGY

It seems an almost universal requirement that all books on complementary medicine begin by explaining and apologizing for the unsatisfactory nature of the terminology at the disposal of the authors. We too must justify our terms.

It is often remarked that the diverse therapies embraced by terms such as 'complementary' or 'alternative' medicine have little in common apart from their exclusion from the official health sector. A number of these therapies have never considered themselves to be 'alternative'; many of them are not particularly 'natural', and a few of them are not convincingly 'holistic'. The preferred terminology of the British Medical Association is 'non-conventional therapy' which makes for laboured reading and is pedantic in its avoidance of the word 'medicine'. The French, possibly, have the best description in *'médicine douce'*, but its translation, 'gentle medicine', is not a term in common usage in Britain.

Most of the available labels say rather more about the political stance of the writer than they do about the therapies concerned. The term 'complementary medicine', being now the most politically acceptable term, is the one we use most frequently, but we shall also use all the above terms throughout the book interchangeably. We shall, however, make a distinction in the use of the term 'traditional' medicine, which we shall restrict to those few therapies such as herbalism, Ayurveda, acupuncture, and shiatsu which predate modern scientific medicine by many centuries and are still an important part of the traditional health culture in many countries.

The definition of the term 'holistic' is rather more critical to the nature of our discussion. A word used with less than precision in much of the literature, it generally refers to 'an understanding of reality in terms of integrated wholes whose properties cannot be reduced to those of smaller units . . . '.[11] It describes an approach that considers the whole picture rather than the function of small fragmented aspects in isolation from one another. The term 'synergy',

[11] Ibid., p. 21.

with which holism is sometimes confused, describes an action or effect in which the whole is more effective than the sum of the individual fragmented parts.

The term 'holistic' is perhaps most familiar in connection with medicine, though the concept is being increasingly used in other contexts. The commonly understood meaning of holistic medicine refers to the notion that problems of ill-health involve the mind, body, and spirit of an individual. The term 'holistic medicine' is thus used to describe a therapeutic approach which aims to treat the whole person. Pietroni writes 'Holistic medicine is indeed about whole-person medicine but its strength and vitality lie in the fact that its definition of what constitutes a "whole" person is drawn from a number of different disciplines and not solely the biological sciences . . .'.[12] In practice, this can mean a number of different things. It must mean that a doctor or healer will have regard for the patient's whole life pattern and the spiritual, emotional, and physical dimensions of the health problem. However, while some practitioners may adhere to a therapeutic approach that seeks to treat *all* levels of a patient's problem, this is not usual. More common is the understanding that a therapeutic intervention on one level will have a beneficial effect at other levels.

The British Holistic Medical Association, an organization of doctors and medical students established in 1983 lists, as its principles, that 'whole person care' depends on:

(1) Responding to a person as a whole within their environment and seeing that person as mind, body, and spirit.

(2) Being open to a wide range of approaches, not only drugs and surgery, but also education, communication, self-help, and complementary therapies.

(3) Returning power and responsibility to patients wherever appropriate, encouraging self-awareness and the capacity for self-healing.

(4) Recognizing that the carer is also a whole person, needing care, support, and the chance to develop and grow.

Just as there is an argument for a holistic approach to therapy, so there could be an argument favouring a holistic approach to *regulation*. This would rest on the notion that 'regulation' encompasses far more than formal statutory regulation. The common law, codes of practice, complaints procedures, and ethical guidelines all have a role

---

[12] Pietroni, P., *The Greening of Medicine* (Gollancz, London, 1991), p. 25.

to play in controlling and regulating economic and social activities. We would argue that just as in medicine, the balance in favour of the scientific and measurable has got out of hand at the expense of other more 'human' qualities, likewise, in the regulation of medicine, too much reliance has been placed on statute or code-based regulation to achieve ends that are beyond the scope of these modes of regulatory control.

Much that is involved in the healing act, whether in orthodox or complementary medicine, is not amenable to any form of objectively verifiable measurement. A healing act which is founded upon the notion of the importance of treating the whole person in mind, body, and spirit, is one in which two aspects of treatment are beyond the kind of assessments that characterize the therapeutic procedures of modern, technological medicine. Thus, to consider one very simple example, how might it be possible to establish that damage has been caused if measurement of that damage is incapable of assessment? How can one prove harm has been suffered if there is, in any case, significant doubt that the therapeutic intervention in question has any efficacy at all? We argue that a holistic approach to the regulation of complementary therapies is necessary in order to devise systems that work to the satisfaction of consumers and to do justice to the perceived strengths of complementary medicine itself. This 'whole' approach will require a heightened emphasis on the role of ethics as an integral part of the spectrum of regulatory control, and an understanding that dynamic, ethics-directed solutions may have far more to offer the emerging patient-centred, holistic models of medicine than can ever be achieved by reliance on conventional, statute-based regulation.

At this point we must also explain, and perhaps defend, our use of the term 'patient'. Despite the paternalistic overtones the word conveys and the pejorative implications that all clients are sick and need looking after, we use this term since it is that most commonly used within complementary medicine itself.

For similar reasons, we acknowledge similar problems with the use of the term 'consumer protection', even though it is one which we shall employ from time to time as shorthand for concerns relating to public safety. We use the term with some hesitation, because it automatically introduces a value-laden perspective implying that patients need protection from something intrinsically harmful and it generalizes patients as a homogenous, vulnerable group, who need the State to protect them from harmful practitioners. To counterbalance these

ideas, we must remind ourselves that the decision to consult an alternative practitioner rather than an orthodox doctor is almost always
a carefully considered choice; such a choice is often informed and
prompted by the knowledge that the patient will be asked to take a
more active interest in their treatment than would be the case if they
were to see an orthodox doctor. Thus, it might be reasonable to
import a degree of self-responsibility into the relationship. Also, we
recognize that whilst some complementary therapies carry certain
risks, most are considerably safer than orthodox medicine.

Of considerable importance to our argument is an understanding
of the fundamental principles underlying complementary therapies,
whether they would describe themselves as being, variously, 'holistic',
'traditional', 'complementary', or 'natural'. Central to our discussion
is the notion that complementary therapies are so profoundly different from technological, scientific medicine that the same regulatory approach cannot merely be transferred from one system to the
other. Clearly, an understanding of these differences is basic to our
argument.

The principles listed below are by no means universally held across
the spectrum of complementary medicine, but they form a core of
ideas that are integral to the practice of many such therapies.

A. 'Only nature heals'

Almost all complementary therapies espouse some version of a belief
in the healing power of nature. This is expressed in varying ways and
with varying degrees of sophistication, but some such notion is almost
universal. It may incorporate the idea of a vital force, of life energy,
such as the '*chi*' or '*ki*' concept of Chinese and Japanese traditional
medicine. More often it refers to the belief in a self-regulating
capacity which is seen as inherent in all living beings. This self-
regulating capacity requires the harmonic functioning of the physical,
emotional, and spiritual dimensions of an individual. Disease thus
occurs when this harmonic balance becomes overburdened and is
seen as the body's attempt to restore balance and proper function.
Thus, as Simon Mills writes, 'This means seeing illness as more "soil"
than seed. . .'.[13]

[13] Mills, S., *The Essential Book of Herbal Medicine* (Arkana, London, 1991),
p. 8.

B. Individualized treatment

The holistic understanding of the nature of illness requires an approach to health problems that is quite different from the approach of orthodox medicine. It is probably fair to say that in general, there is less emphasis on *symptoms* in the complementary approach than there is in orthodox medicine, but this contention cannot be upheld uniformly across all therapies.

It is, however, very characteristic that the treatment is usually *highly individualized*. Whether the mode of therapeutic intervention is herbs, essential oils, homeopathic remedies, or acupuncture treatment, the choice will be influenced by such factors as the patient's personality and lifestyle as much as it will by the presenting symptoms and perceived patterns of disorder. Thus it would be quite normal for three people suffering from the same disorder, who would be treated with the same prescription drug by an orthodox doctor, to be given three quite different remedies were they to see a herbalist or a homeopath.

C. Patient participation

As more illness is acknowledged to be lifestyle-related and linked to stress, diet, lack of exercise, alcohol and tobacco consumption, so the importance of patient participation is increasingly acknowledged within orthodox medicine. In complementary medicine, this participation factor has *always* been a fundamental feature of the therapeutic approach.

It follows from an understanding that a person's lifestyle may contribute to, or even cause, a health problem, that the active involvement of the patient is seen as being of critical importance. There is commonly an explicit understanding that improvement will be critically determined by the degree of the patient's own participation. Therapists often see themselves as acting primarily to facilitate the release of the patient's own will to recover. Whether one considers this viewpoint as being justified or not, one important consequence is that the balance of power within the relationship of healer and patient is significantly different from that which pertains between doctor and patient. With the exception of the more medicalized group of therapies, such as osteopathy, the complementary practitioner does not possess the knowledge base held by the scientifically trained doctor. Often, claims to be able to help are not based on any kind of superior intellectually acquired knowledge at all. Despite the fact that both doctor and complementary practitioner are engaged in activity aimed at curing or alleviating 'disease', this should not obscure the fact that the expertise involved, the therapeutic approach, and the healing encounter itself are often profoundly different in nature.

However, this is not invariably the case. A number of the more well-established therapies show signs of more closely resembling orthodox medicine. These are the therapies which have been classified as 'whole systems' or 'discrete clinical disciplines', and which, more than most complementary therapies, are amenable to a greater degree of quantifiable assessment and measurement.[14] Their characteristic modes of therapeutic intervention are the same as that of scientific medicine: ingestive remedies, invasive procedures, or external manipulation. Their training is extensive and, increasingly, based on a knowledge of the biological sciences. For a number of such reasons, we argue that these therapies would be more appropriately regulated along the lines of the current medical model. Furthermore, these are the therapies in which there appears to be a greater interest in the achievement of statutory recognition. We suggest that these are the therapies which will be most tempted to trade the holistic and traditional base of their therapy for the perceived gains of the certainty and measurability of both science and regulation.

III. STRUCTURE OF THIS BOOK

The tripartite division of the book reflects the separation of the discussion into the three major areas on which we focus. Part I deals with the background details essential to a full understanding of the regulation debate. It attempts to untangle and analyse some of the arguments surrounding the debate on regulation for complementary medicine. This section of the book is written to highlight the point that much medical regulation is determined more by political, historical, economic, and cultural factors than it is by what might be called therapeutic factors. Health care policies are inextricably linked to political power bases; as has become all too clear, those setting the

---

[14] See BMA, *Complementary Medicine: New Approaches to Good Practice* (OUP, Oxford, 1993), pp. 60–3.

agenda for health are not exclusively concerned with therapeutic outcome or even with patient needs.

The history of much professional regulation shows that it is often determined from within the profession itself, and is principally focused on the enhancement and maintenance of professional self-interest. In particular we seek to demonstrate that many of the issues now being discussed as if they were somehow new or novel, have in fact, been the subject of controversy for centuries. The dispute is grounded in issues which are as old as medicine itself.

In Part II we examine the regulatory structures which are currently in place. We shall focus our attention on the three main regulatory options, namely statutory regulation, the common law, and voluntary self-regulation. We shall explore the interrelationship between overlapping systems of regulation, noting the centrality of ethics to all three. As well as a description of how each of the above applies to the practice of complementary medicine, we shall be attempting to evaluate each of these systems. In particular, we shall be trying to analyse why there are difficulties in applying each system, as they currently operate, to the complementary therapeutic relationship.

In Part III we shall attempt to synthesize the issues identified in Part I with the problems highlighted in Part II which arise when we try and apply existing regulatory mechanisms, designed entirely with the doctor-patient relationship in mind, to complementary medicine. The differences between the complementary practitioner/patient relationship, and the doctor/patient relationship, demand a different regulatory approach. We shall formulate a patient-centred, ethics-led approach to regulation capable of ensuring the high standards of practice needed to maintain public confidence and promote good health and well-being.

Finally, we would urge readers to appreciate that this book requires a shift of emphasis in that it is attempting to design regulation which is responsive to an holistic approach to medicine. We have attempted to explore new paradigms for applying law and ethics to complementary medicine and have not allowed the medical model to determine the parameters of the debate.

PART I

*An Overview of
Complementary Medicine*

1

Why History is Important

A brief account of the historical development of the regulation of both mainstream and non-orthodox medicine provides one of the most instructive starting-points from which to analyse the factors which shape regulation. Among the complex, interrelated components which help to determine regulation, historical factors can be particularly significant: the original regulatory system imposed when controls were first established will tend to continue to exert an influence on future patterns of regulation in the same field.[1] The historical approach encourages us to adjust our perspective and to appreciate that modern medicine has only dominated medical practice for the past one hundred years. It also serves to remind us that medical theory is transient, a fact rarely given sufficient weight in the heat of debate. In particular, the historical perspective helps to illuminate certain aspects of the regulation of medicine that are not always adequately appreciated or understood. We do not wish to exaggerate the importance of history. We regard it as simply a useful perspective, an acknowledgement that when asking how something *ought* to be done, it is sensible to examine how it has been done in the past. As Joe Jacob states: 'Law and regulation generally are largely understandable only from a viewpoint grounded in a wider social and political understanding of the past. Quite simply, history will not go away . . . '.[2]

In the analysis below, we shall be asking whether there was a rationale behind the choice of one policy approach over another. We are not so much interested in presenting a detailed chronological outline as we are in trying to identify and assess certain key themes which seem to have been a consistent feature of the political debates surrounding the issue of the regulation of medicine.

Before the twentieth century, major legislation to regulate the medical profession was largely concentrated within two main periods:

[1] Moran, M. and Wood, B., *States, Regulation and the Medical Profession* (Open University Press, Buckingham, 1993) p. 29.
[2] Jacob, J. M., *Doctors and Rules: A Sociology of Professional Values* (Routledge, London, 1988).

1512–42 and 1815–58. It is notable that the practice of unorthodox medicine has only once been the direct object of regulation, in the Herbalists' Charter of 1542 (commonly referred to in the literature as the 'Quacks' Charter'). The main historical landmarks which we shall discuss are:

(1) The Medical Act 1512
(2) The Herbalists' Charter 1542
(3) The Medical Act 1858

We shall first look briefly at the factual background to these Acts before going on to discuss the relevance of these events to the current situation.

One important point is worth making at the outset. Readers may be surprised to learn how many of the central issues still being contested today have been the source of conflict for hundreds of years. Organized medicine has expended considerable energy over the centuries in an attempt to eliminate unorthodox therapies. The language of consumer protection has invariably been invoked to mask blatant professional self-interest. Conversely, the rhetoric of non-orthodox medicine, in attacking the medical monopoly, has often been based on an appeal to the common man to take up his right to improved health and greater self-determination.[3] In English history, the essence of the dispute between the medical élite and lay practitioners of non-orthodox medicine, has been conducted in language which has a history of use going back at least five hundred years.

This point is important, not least because of the tendency within the orthodox profession to present alternative medicine as a passing fad, an untried and untested phenomenon taken up by the gullible public. The 1986 British Medical Association Report *Alternative Therapies*, for example, concluded: 'While we have a duty of fairness to the practitioners of alternative therapies, our long-term duty to our patients is not to support what may be passing fashions, but to ensure for them the benefits of medicine in the future . . . '.[4] It is important

---

[3] Examples of practitioners who recognised the political appeal of unorthodox medicine include the Puritan and Parliamentarian Nicholas Culpeper 1616–54 and Albert Isaiah Coffin 1798–1866. Coffin, who introduced the Thomsonian physio-medicalism to England in 1838, deliberately focused his work among the urban working-class populations of Leeds, Manchester, and London. See Griggs, B., *Green Pharmacy: A History of Herbal Medicine* (Robert Hale, London, 1981).

[4] BMA Report *Alternative Therapies* (BMA, Chameleon Press, 1986) p. 76.

to remember that many of the well-established unorthodox therapies such as acupuncture, herbal medicine, homeopathy, and, arguably, even osteopathy, have origins which long precede modern medicine. Herbal medicine is one of the oldest methods of healing known to mankind. The archaeological finds at Shanidar in the Zagros mountains are a strong indication that even Neanderthal man practised some form of herbal medicine.[5] Not only has every civilization made use of plant medicine, but some cultures, notably that of China and India, developed a highly refined and scholarly tradition of botanic medicine which included extensive written texts on the subject.

Plant-based remedies have been the principal source of medicines in healing traditions throughout the world and, as the World Health Organization is at pains to remind us, 80 per cent of the world's population still depends primarily on plant medicine.[6] Similarly, techniques such as massage and hand-healing have been part of almost all medical cultures, in one form or another for centuries. It is for these reasons, that many practitioners dislike the use of the term 'alternative' medicine. As the herbalist, Simon Mills says: 'It is genuinely arguable whether herbal medicine really belongs in the category of "alternative medicine". It is too close to the heart of history for that . . . '.[7]

In other words, we shall need to consider that what may be threatening to the orthodox profession about unorthodox medicine has, in reality, had very little to do with a concern that alternative therapies are in any way new, capricious, or ephemeral. Of course, some of them are just that; but most of the major unorthodox therapies have been around for far longer than scientific medicine. And here lies the real source of the tension: non-orthodox therapies never really were just about treating sick people with therapies that organized medicine did not recognize. One of the most instructive lessons that history teaches is that healing has always been so closely associated with political power in society that those who claim the knowledge to heal will often find themselves having to defend that right in a philosophical and political arena, and in terms that have changed hardly at

[5] Stockwell, C., *Nature's Pharmacy* (Century, London, 1988) pp. 27–31.

[6] WHO/UNICEF Meeting Report. *Primary Health Care; Report of the International Conference on Primary Health Care* (WHO, Geneva, 1978).

[7] Mills, S., *The Essential Book of Herbal Medicine* (Arkana, London, 1991) p. 21.

all over the centuries. There is startlingly little that is new in the essence of the regulation debate.

I. THE MEDICAL ACT 1512

The activity of regulation in Britain has a long history. The Tudor and Stuart periods were notable for the unprecedented degree to which regulation was used as a means of economic and social control. Ogus has recently drawn attention to this, the 'first period of extensive regulation in English legal history'.[8] This period was characterized by a highly interventionist approach which included the use of economic instruments such as licensing mechanisms combined with sanctions which were, at best, inefficiently or spasmodically enforced.

Ogus argues that this penetration of regulation into the economic and social life of Tudor and Stuart England produced fundamentally the same kind of tensions that are the subject of so much analysis today. He describes two rival conceptual models of the origins of regulation which he terms the 'public interest' and the 'public choice' models. Ogus's categorization is useful here because it represents, in a simple form, one of the most pivotal features of regulation. The 'public interest' approach explains regulation as a mechanism by which economic and social activity is controlled in the interest of what is perceived to be the good of society. The contrasting 'public choice' approach broadly represents regulation as a commodity which is obtained from the governing and administrative establishment by competing interest groups within society who wish to secure regulation in order to protect their own interests.[9] We shall argue that the history of medical regulation up to and including the 1858 Medical Act was one in which the 'public choice' theory of regulation can clearly be seen to dominate.

The emergence and eventual predominance of the professional physician class in England was not achieved without considerable political struggle. From time immemorial, until well after the emergence of modern, scientific medicine in the late nineteenth century, healing has been practised by many different groups within society. As is still the case outside the industrialized, developed countries of

[8] Ogus, A. I. (1992) 'Regulatory Law: Some Lessons from the Past', *Legal Studies*, 1: p. 4.
[9] Ibid., p. 2.

the West, lay practitioners shared in the practice of medicine along-side members of the élite medical profession. The high sickness levels and high mortality rates characteristic of pre-industrial Britain resulted in a strong demand for a wide variety of healers of all persuasions including orthodox medical practitioners.[10] In practice however, the majority of the population was precluded from seeking the attentions of a professional physician by the high cost of such treatment. Medicine was, therefore, primarily a domestic matter, with resort to lay and professional healers only if necessity so required.[11] In short, until well into the nineteenth century, there was a pronounced culture of medical pluralism: it was standard practice to go outside orthodox medicine in search of relief.

The first attempt to secure control of medical practice came in 1421 when Henry V was unsuccessfully petitioned to pass an Act restricting the practice of medicine to those who possessed a university degree.[12] By 1512, the monarchy would appear to have become more amenable. The first Medical Act made it an offence to practise physic or surgery unless the practitioner was a university graduate or had been licensed by the bishop of the diocese wherein he resided. Justification for the Act is found in the Preamble where much is made of the increased numbers of ignorant persons practising medicine, 'in which they partly use sorcery and witchcraft to the grievous hurt, damage and destruction of many of the King's liege people . . . '.[13]

The 1512 Act was followed by a spate of regulatory legislation, mainly in the form of licensing agreements in various guises. In 1518, the Company of Physicians was established by Letters Patent, eventually to become the Royal College of Physicians in 1551. The Company's charter empowered it to license physicians throughout the realm, to ensure the purity of drugs sold by apothecaries, and to control the practice of medicine within a seven-mile radius of London.[14] The surgeons were quick to follow in the physicians' footsteps. Thomas Vicary, who was appointed surgeon to Henry VIII, obtained the King's consent in 1540, to establish a union of all the surgeons'

[10] Porter, R., *Health for Sale: Quackery in England 1660–1850* (Manchester University Press: Manchester, 1989) Ch. 2.
[11] Thomas, K., *Religion and the Decline of Magic* (Penguin, London, 1971) pp. 12–13.
[12] Cartwright, F. F., *A Social History of Medicine* (Longman, London, 1977) p. 44.
[13] Preamble to the Medical Act 1512. Quoted in ibid., p. 44.
[14] Ibid., p. 45 .

guilds in England. Their charter granted the Union Company of Barber-Surgeons a number of rights, among which was the right to impose fines on unlicensed surgeons in London.

These regulatory devices can be seen as part of the wider development of the medieval practice of control by self-regulation under the craft guilds endowed with powers granted in charters of incorporation. The evidence strongly suggests that such measures were introduced primarily at the demand of professional interest groups to serve as barriers to entry thus maintaining high fee levels.[15] Despite the high moral tone of the Preamble to the 1512 Act, it is clear that the avowed purpose of public protection was little more than a smoke screen for restrictive legislation promoted essentially in the cause of professional self-interest.

II. THE HERBALISTS' CHARTER 1542

Fortunately for the majority of the population who could not afford physicians' fees, the ambitions of the newly-organized medical profession were not to be realised quite so easily. At first glance, the Herbalists' Charter appears to be something of a royal U-turn. Attributed to, or at least supported by, Henry VIII, the Preamble now castigated surgeons for, 'minding only their own lucre', and for allowing many to 'rot and perish to death for lack of help'.[16] The Act went on, in a seemingly remarkable policy reversal, to exempt from the penalties of the 1512 Act those lay practitioners of herbal medicine who charged only for the supply of the herb itself:

it shall be lawful for every person being the King's subject, having knowledge and experience of the nature of Herbs, Roots and Waters, or the operation of the same, by speculation or practice within any part . . . of the King's dominions, to practise, use and minister in and to any outward sore, uncome, wound, apostemations, outward swelling or disease, any herb or herbs, oynments, baths, pultres, and amplaisters, according to their cunning, experience and knowledge in any of the diseases, sores and maladies before-said, and all other like to the same . . . without suit, vexation, trouble, penalty, or loss of their goods . . .[17]

[15] Ogus, op. cit. (above n. 8), p. 18.
[16] Statutes of the Realm, 34–35 Henry VIII, c 8. Cited in Griggs, B., *Green Pharmacy: A History of Herbal Medicine* p. 61.
[17] Ibid., p. 61.

Thus the Act had the effect of legalizing lay practitioners of herbal medicine, providing their advice was given free. Those who charged for their advice and help could be, and frequently were, prosecuted in actions brought by the Royal College of Physicians.

It is difficult to know what to make of this regulatory volte-face. It has been suggested somewhat unconvincingly that while the 1512 Act served to organize the medical trade, it subsequently became apparent that there were not enough doctors to meet demand.[18] This view, that the problem in medieval England was one of inadequate *supply*, quite ignores the fact that the majority of the population could never have afforded their fees anyway. A more plausible suggestion is related to the contrast between the symbolic, moralistic tone of much of Tudor regulation and the ineffectiveness with which many provisions were enforced. 'Much of the legislation must have served a symbolic purpose, appeasing those aggrieved or responding to political demands, rather than fulfilling the apparent instrumental goals . . . '[19] There is, however, some evidence to suggest that an important objective of the physicians in their pursuit of licensing regulation may well have been to defend their professional territory against others in the orthodox medical hierarchy. The immediate effect of the 1512 Act appears to have been litigation on the part of the physicians to prevent surgeons from practising medicine, while the surgeons, in their turn, were engaged in action against the barbers for practising surgery.[20] It is, therefore, likely that the 1542 Act may have been enacted in order to confine the battlefront to demarcation disputes within the hierarchy of regular medicine. Orthodox medicine was, as yet, a long way from being powerful enough to attempt to assert a monopoly over the practice of medicine, and the 1542 Act remained largely unchallenged for the best part of three hundred years.

III. THE MEDICAL ACT 1858

The political aspirations of the British Medical Association, which was effectively founded in 1832, under the name of the Provincial Medical and Surgical Association, are essential to an understanding

[18] Cartwright, F. F., *A Social History of Medicine* p. 45.
[19] Ogus, A. I. (1992) 'Regulatory Law: Some Lessons from the Past', *Legal Studies*, 1: p. 15.
[20] Griggs, B., *Green Pharmacy*.

of the developments which led to the enactment of the Medical Act 1858.

Pressure for reform of the medical profession had built up from a number of sources. The increasingly affluent middle classes were beginning to require greater numbers of better-educated doctors. More urgently, the disastrous epidemics associated with urban industrial expansion concentrated the attentions of the Government on the provision of more reliable and effective medical and public health services. However, despite these trends, it is clear that the real focus for reform was centred within the medical profession itself.

At the beginning of the nineteenth century, physicians were an embattled and powerless occupational group, plying their services in competition with hosts of unqualified practitioners of varying skill levels, often only barely able to make a living in a rapidly expanding economy where the easy availability of mass-produced remedies added to the pressures of professional survival. Describing the social position of doctors at this time, Steve Watkins writes: 'Surgeons were craftsmen, physicians were domestic servants of the rich and apothecaries were tradesmen. . . .'[21] These three occupational groups were eventually to emerge as the modern medical profession, but not without considerable infighting in the process.

In 1800, the Company of Surgeons had become the Royal College of Surgeons. A private agreement was reached between the College of Surgeons and the Society of Apothecaries whereby surgeons could acquire their own diploma by following the Apothecaries' regulations and supplementing these studies with additional courses in surgery and a period of practical training on hospital wards. In this way, it became standard practice for the more ambitious medical students to seek the dual qualification of Membership of the Royal College of Surgeons and the Licence of the Society of Apothecaries. Doctors so qualified were to become the general practitioners of the future.

The Apothecaries Act 1815 was an innovation in licensing, and the first of a series of Acts aimed at regulating and reforming the medical profession. The old corporations of Tudor and Stuart England were empowered to exercise control only within London: outside London, the practice of medicine was largely unregulated. The Act empowered the Society of Apothecaries to control the licensing of apothecaries throughout the country. As of 1815, all apothecaries were required to

[21] Watkins, S., *Medicine and Labour: The Politics of a Profession* (Lawrence and Wishart, London, 1977) p. 15.

be licensed after serving a five-year apprenticeship and passing the prescribed examinations. While the 1815 Act was far from an unqualified success, the extent to which the licensing system was accepted is revealed in the numbers who began to acquire the licence. In the two years between 1842 and 1844, only 53 licences were issued by the universities and the Royal College of Physicians. By contrast, during the same period, some 953 licences were granted by the Society of Apothecaries and the Royal College of Surgeons under the new amalgamated scheme.[22] It was the graduates of this new, more rigorous licensing system who were to become the spearhead of the medical reform movement.

This new generation of educated, qualified general practitioners included in their ranks activists such as Thomas Wakely and Charles Hastings. Wakely founded *The Lancet* in 1832, a journal dedicated, in its early years, to a vigorous campaign for the reform of medical practice. Hastings was to establish the Medical and Surgical Society in 1816, which, under its new name of the Provincial Medical and Surgical Society, held its first annual convention in 1832. It was this organization that developed into the British Medical Association by 1855.

Agitation for reform was closely associated with both *The Lancet* and the BMA. The new class of general practitioner sought to limit the influence of two very different groups: the unlicensed, untrained quacks and the Royal College of Physicians which had exercised a stranglehold over the organization of the medical profession for centuries. The advocates of reform argued that licence-holders qualified under the new regulations were better educated and more competent than the physicians who had qualified via the academic training available at Oxford and Cambridge.

Seven Bills to reform the medical profession were promoted during the period 1832–58, all largely drafted by the BMA. When the 1858 Act finally reached the statute book, many of its provisions had been substantially influenced by the opinions and recommendations of the BMA. The aspirations of the medical profession were assisted in no small way by the crisis precipitated by the outbreak of major epidemic disease which helped to persuade the Government of the need for some way of distinguishing between qualified and unqualified medical practitioners. The success of the BMA in its endeavours to secure regulation was also related to its ability to extend its influence

[22] Cartwright, F. F., *A Social History of Medicine*, p. 53.

from advising the Government on scientific and public health issues to becoming, as Jacob describes it, 'a part of the machinery of government'.[23]

The Medical Act 1858 established a State-sanctioned system of self-regulation. It provided that all existing licensing bodies should be placed under the control of a General Medical Council (GMC) whose duty it was to compile a register of qualified practitioners. More importantly, the GMC was empowered to control the educational training of doctors and was thereby able to restrict entry to the profession to those who had followed the approved courses. The Act was, in essence, a form of contract between the State and the profession, in which control of medical practice was delegated to the profession itself. The GMC, in turn, came to function as the State advisory body on health issues. By separating the overtly trade unionist activities of the BMA from the regulatory functions of the State-sanctioned GMC, the 1858 Act immeasurably strengthened the authority and status of the medical profession in a way that purely independent self-regulation could never have achieved.

Despite agitation by the profession to introduce clauses restricting practice to those medically qualified, the Act did not give the medical profession a monopoly; it did, however, make it illegal for the unqualified to describe themselves as being qualified. However, because the State would henceforth only employ those practitioners who were duly qualified and registered, and because the GMC ensured that medical training screened out any unorthodox practices, non-conventional medicine was effectively marginalized.

The historical importance of this, the first modern Medical Act, to the future course of professional regulation has been summed up by Moran and Wood: 'Unlike some countries where direct regulation by the state prevails, in the UK a tradition of government–profession contract creating a legal regulatory body and hence legitimizing self-regulation was, and still is, the preferred approach. . . .'[24] The system of State-sanctioned regulation still dominates the practice of medicine and has become the model for the regulation of other paramedical professions, including some of the more well-established complementary therapies.

---

[23] Jacob, J. M., *Doctors and Rules*, p. 104.
[24] Moran, M. and Wood, B., *States, Regulation and the Medical Profession*, p. 37.

IV. KEY FEATURES OF MEDICAL REGULATION

A number of themes and features emerge from an analysis of the historical development of medical regulation which can be considered still relevant to the regulation issue today. We shall now turn to examine some of these themes and consider what influence such issues might have on the future course of regulation for complementary medicine.

A. Consumer protection *v.* consumer choice

The first theme concerns the way in which consumer protection has been consistently invoked over the centuries to justify the political positions of both orthodox and unorthodox medicine. As we have seen, the 1512 Act was passed with the specifically stated aim of protecting the public from charlatans and unskilled practitioners. However, the same justification, that of protecting the public interest, was also used to explain the enactment of the Herbalists' Charter 1542. The propagandists behind the promotion of the 1858 Medical Bill similarly made much use of the need to protect the public from charlatans and quacks. While it can quite legitimately be argued that public interest was at stake in the need for a more rigorous and standardized licensing system, the GMC was 'essentially created to protect doctors, not the public. . . .'[25]

Beyond the rather obvious point that the language of consumer protection has often been little more than a convenient veneer to mask more self-interested goals, the most interesting aspect of the dispute between regular and irregular medicine is the divergent interpretation, given by the two parties, of what constitutes the public interest in health matters. It is a distinction which is still very apparent in the modern context.

The orthodox profession has tended to take the paternalistic view that the general public needed protection from unlearned and unskilled healers who would inevitably wreak harm if allowed to practice unrestricted. The Charter of the Royal College of Physicians explicitly ruled that a member physician should not reveal to the population either the names of medicines, or the use to which such medicaments could be put. Unorthodox medicine has, likewise, always represented itself as protecting the people against a self-seeking profession whose economic interests were preserved, not only by charging exorbitant fees for their work but also by deliberately seeking to withhold and obscure medical knowledge from the general public. The apothecary and herbalist Nicholas Culpeper (1616–54) was fiercely attacked by orthodox physicians, for his translation of several medical works from Latin into English. His *Physicall Directory* was described by his opponents as being the product of, 'two yeeres drunken Labour . . . '. Culpeper, a Puritan and Parliamentarian, had some wry things to say about the policy of College of Physicians: 'It seems the College had a strange opinion that it would do an Englishman mischief to know what the herbs in his garden are used for'.[26]

Since time immemorial, the capacity to heal has been associated with the acquisition of specialized knowledge and therefore, power. In primitive societies, the line between magic, religion, and healing was always obscure: knowledge of the most potent plants was invariably kept a secret within the early priest-physician class. In medieval England, it was primarily the Church that claimed the right to control and determine healing in society.[27] The Church was determinant of the early development of the professionalization of medicine. The alliance of the medical and ecclesiastical establishment was rooted in a shared concern to control the power associated with the claim to heal. As Oakley points out: 'male medicine was highly theological and anti-empirical: hence its acceptability to the Church . . . '.[28]

During those times in history when practitioners of unorthodox medicine have been drawn into a more overtly political stance, they have often sought to justify their own position by challenging the secrecy surrounding the practice of medicine, and championing the right of access of ordinary men to medical knowledge and greater self-determination. This association between unorthodox medicine and populist political movements gained increased momentum during the early nineteenth century, when non-conventional medicine became

---

[26] Culpeper, N., *London Dispensatory* (1653) cited in Griggs, B., *Green Pharmacy*, p. 96.

[27] See Oakley, A. 'The Wisewoman and the Doctor' in Saks, M. (ed.), *Alternative Medicine in Britain* (Clarendon Press, Oxford, 1992). The negative appellation 'witch' was fostered by the medieval Church, to whom disease was a God-given affliction, and thus a phenomenon which had to be under strict religious control.

[28] Ibid., p. 41.

more consciously anti-elitist and radical, emphasizing self-reliance, participation and free access to knowledge. The early Victorian period saw a growth of alternative health movements, often drawing overt support from other philosophical and political movements such as Chartism, the Friendly Societies, and vegetarianism. These medical movements resembled contemporary alternative approaches to health in that they all avowed allegiance to a medical creed entirely at odds with that of allopathic medicine (the system of medicine in which the use of drugs is directed to producing effects that directly oppose the symptoms of a disease).[29] Porter writes:

ideology, philosophy, and morality moved centre stage. These were movements that had designs on men's minds more than their pockets. Preferring the pamphlet to the pill, activists prided themselves on being the moral vanguard, expounding emancipated doctrines upon health, advancing popular physiologies as a somatized religion of life, and holding out hope, both personal and social.[30]

Unimpressed with the professed importance that orthodox medicine placed on consumer protection, unorthodox medicine preferred to see the public interest being served by a system which allowed for a much greater degree of self-responsibility and participation.

More recently, the connection between the erosion of the status of the orthodox profession, the rise of non-orthodox therapies, and the 'proletarianization' of knowledge and power has been more generally accepted. Dr Patrick Pietroni, in his book, *The Greening of Medicine*, states:

The professions, including medicine, have experienced serious erosions of their status over the last ten to fifteen years. A number of different factors have contributed to this process not least the decentralising or proletarianisation of knowledge and power ... In the context of the 'greening process' such influences in medicine can be interpreted as a consequence of the knowledge revolution, the self-help and consumer movement, the rise of the ancillary medical professions, especially nursing and midwifery, and including the 'alternative' professions of osteopathy, chiropractic etc.[31]

Users of alternative medicine thus tend to have political and social

---

[29] See Porter, R., *Health for Sale*, p. 15, and ch. 8.
[30] Ibid., p. 233.
[31] Pietroni, P., *The Greening of Medicine*, p. 74.

opinions which echo their concerns about autonomy and self-determination in other areas. Mary Douglas has identified the deeper implications behind the choice to use complementary medicine:

> To understand their [the general public's] liking for a spiritual medicine we need to set it in the whole context of their other preferences and attitudes to authority, leadership and competition ... If they have made the same choice for gentler, more spiritual medicine, they will be making the same choice in other contexts, dietary, ecological as well as medical. The choice of holistic medicine will not be an isolated preference unco-ordinated with other values upheld by the patient ...[32]

This point is often missed by doctors, many of whom would be far more comfortable were the debate about the availability of complementary medicine more closely confined to the issue of scientific validity. It is worthwhile reminding ourselves that the issues which are so central to non-orthodox medicine have always involved much more than a question of efficacy; behind the rhetoric are some very ancient arguments which have as much to do with the linkage between power and knowledge in society as they have to do with whether therapy X can cure 'disease' Y.

B. Gender issues

Closely related to the issue of the accessibility of medical knowledge, is a second feature which has re-emerged with some intensity in recent years—that of the alliance of male élites in both the medical profession and the Church, often to a common end, namely the suppression of female healers within society. Despite the fact that women were legally barred from entering university to study academic medicine, healing was still largely a domestic activity administered by the women of the household using traditional herbal remedies. Should the severity of the sickness be beyond the skills of the housewife and her simple herbal preparations the village 'wise woman', with her more specialized knowledge of herbs, would often be brought in.

The publication of the treatise *Malleus Maleficarum* (1486), the Witchcraft Acts, and the subsequent burning of thousands, and possibly millions of women across Europe, have come in for much conflicting interpretation among scholars. Some feminist historians claim

[32] Douglas, M., 'The Construction of the Physician' in Budd, S., and Sharma, U., *The Healing Bond* (Routledge, London, 1994), pp. 35–6.

to have identified a connection between the Witchcraft Acts and an attempt by both the Church and the medical establishment to eliminate the women who held specialized knowledge of healing plants, but this interpretation is far from being generally accepted.[33] 'These were crimes against one-half of humanity that guaranteed that all women who chose healing as a vocation would be placed in the limelight of suspicion. The church fathers had predetermined much earlier that witchcraft was a woman's crime. . . .'[34]

It is hard to ignore entirely certain coincidences of time: most notably, the printing and distribution of large numbers of popular herbals during this period, and the fact that the first English Witchcraft Act was passed in the same year as the Herbalists' Charter, 1542.[35] Certainly the *Malleus Maleficarum* was chillingly explicit on the central point: 'If a woman dare to cure without having studied, she is a witch and must die'. Moreover, during the medieval witch trials, the 'expert' witness called in by the Church to help determine the issue was, almost always, a male physician.

Whatever the interpretation of the involvement of the Church and the medical profession in the prosecution of the Witchcraft Acts, official medicine undoubtedly benefited from this persecution of the old women who performed so much of the healing in sixteenth and seventeenth-century England. From that point on, to heal exposed one to the potential charge of witchcraft. Thus the dictates of Christian theology and the laws governing the academic study of medicine ensured that women were doubly barred from any legitimate role in healing. The relevance of this issue today is that it highlights the tenacity with which the medical profession has attempted to determine and preside over the conditions under which other groups in society may practise healing. Historically, one of the most obvious ways medicine controlled entry to the profession was by barring women from access to medical training. Today, the regulation of other healing professions in society is still closely scrutinized and influenced by the orthodox profession. It is largely true to say that

[33] See Thomas, K., *Religion and the Decline of Magic*, Chs. 14–18. See also Achterberg, J., *Woman as Healer* (Rider, London, 1990) for a view of witchcraft which identifies the Church's role as being instrumental in the movement to eradicate female healers.

[34] Achterberg, J., *Woman as Healer*, p. 82.

[35] The first herbal in the English language, *The Grete Herbal* was published in 1526. A number of other herbals followed, notably William Turner's *Herbal* published in 1551.

regulation for these groups can only be achieved at the price of some degree of subordination to the medical profession.[36]

The sexual politics of healing is an issue which will assume an even greater significance in the future of orthodox medicine. There is a groundswell of feeling among the nursing profession of the need for a greater recognition of the healing potential of the more personal, 'human', touch-based skills of nursing.[37] It is perhaps no accident that a resurgence in the demand for a more dynamic role for the nursing profession has coincided with a considerable interest among nurses in many of the complementary therapies.[38] All such developments, in both orthodox and complementary medicine, may be seen as indicative of a desire to redress the balance away from the impersonal, mechanistic style of much modern medicine towards the more personal, nurturing, gentle bias that is characteristic of the 'feminine' approach to healing. The question still to be determined is: to what extent will these adjusted priorities be reflected in the way the medicine of the future is organized, financed, and regulated?

C. The influence of unorthodox medicine

In what ways did unorthodox medicine influence the development of the regulation of the orthodox profession?

A case could possibly be made for the argument that regulation for orthodox medicine has been most strenuously pursued by the medical profession when the threat from unorthodox therapies has appeared to be particularly strong. It can only remain conjecture, but perhaps it is no coincidence that the first Medical Act in 1512 followed, not only in the wake of the printing of popular herbals, but also at a time when élite medicine had to contend with competition from the proliferation of other types of practitioners—the barber-surgeons, surgeons, and

[36] See also Larkin, G., *Occupational Monopoly and Modern Medicine* (Tavistock Publications, London, 1983).

[37] See, e.g., Denise Rankin Box's article 'Innovation in Practice: Complementary Therapies in Nursing' in *Complementary Therapies in Medicine* (1993) 1, pp. 30–3.

[38] The Royal College of Nursing now has a professional interest group for complementary therapy. Its Statement of Beliefs says that 'ALL patients and clients have the right to be offered and to receive complementary therapies either exclusively or as part of orthodox nursing practice'. It advocates that registered nurses who are appropriately qualified to carry out a complementary therapy must agree to work locally agreed protocols for practice and standards of care (RCN, October 1994).

apothecaries. Certainly the 1858 Medical Act was enacted against a backdrop of the growing commercial success of the irregular practitioners, many of whom were now advertising and marketing mass-produced nostrums aimed at supplying the needs of the newly affluent urban classes.[39] Pressed on the one side by the threat of cheap, mass-produced remedies, and on the other by the radical philosophies of the alternative health movements, élite medicine made a bid for the only option left to it: to professionalize.

History seems to indicate that, despite the apparent segregation of orthodox and unorthodox medicine, unorthodox medicine has often been instrumental in effecting change within its rival. In respect of the nineteenth century, some historians have written convincingly on the manner in which the challenge of homoeopathy was dealt with by the orthodox profession, who simultaneously barred homoeopaths from practising medicine while at the same time quietly incorporating a number of their tenets and remedies into their own practice.[40] Current developments in acupuncture practice within the medical profession might indicate a similar movement towards 'colonization', as it is sometimes called.[41] It is entirely possible that the support and encouragement that non-conventional therapies have enjoyed over the past decade will function as a catalyst within the more progressive elements of the orthodox profession to effect reform and review of its own methods and procedures.

D. The initiators of regulation

A final and important feature of the history of medical regulation up to 1858 is the way in which regulation has been enacted largely at the instigation of the party seeking to be regulated. While a better trained and organized profession has undeniably been in the public interest, the regulation which brought it about was primarily designed to benefit the status and position of the profession itself. A historical perspective teaches us that regulation for complementary medicine, when it

[39] Porter, R., *Health for Sale*, p. 43.
[40] Nicholls, P., 'Homeopathy in Britain after the Mid-Nineteenth Century' in Saks, M. (ed.) *Alternative Medicine in Britain* (OUP, Oxford, 1992) 'In response to the presence of homoeopathy, and its popularity, regular practitioners had abandoned heroic therapy, and covertly turned to the *materia medica*, and even principles, of their rivals. . . .'
[41] See Saks, M. 'The Paradox of Incorporation: Acupuncture and the Medical Profession in Modern Britain' in Saks, M. (ed.) *Alternative Medicine in Britain.*

comes, is more likely to be brought about by pressure from within the complementary health movement itself. The medical profession and consumer organisations will all have their stake in the debate and may influence the outcome, but the impetus is likely to be generated from within complementary medicine. It is here that we come back to the 'public interest' and 'public choice' models of regulation, and the tension between the two largely conflicting facets of regulation: regulation as a source of restriction, and regulation as a means of economic opportunity.

Within the profession of medicine, it is hard to escape the conclusion that 'the public choice' rationale of regulation has dominated regulatory development. In other words, regulation was promoted by doctors for reasons that had more to do with professional closure and self-protection than with the protection of consumer interests. While such regulation undoubtedly benefited the public indirectly as a consequence of the raised training standards such legislation enforced, nevertheless, this bias has a number of implications which should be considered.

The most important of these considerations, is that when regulation is initiated and achieved primarily as a consequence of the active pursuance of the party seeking to be regulated, features such as consumer rights and accountability tend to be ignored or treated less than rigorously. One would hope that those therapies currently set on the achievement of autonomous statutory legislation will be particularly circumspect about appreciating the importance of accountability and consumer protection as primary aims of self-regulation. Without the certainties of science, or the formal rigour of modern medical training, complementary medicine *must* be able to demonstrate its commitment to the consumer if it is to retain its popular support which is the sole base of its power.

2

Regulation of Health Care

If regulation can be defined in simple terms as the means by which control is exercised over the exchange of goods and services in society, then the practice of medicine has been regulated for centuries. Today, medicine is one of the most highly regulated of all economic and social activities in Britain. By contrast, and despite the Osteopaths Act 1993 and the Chiropractors Act 1994, there is still an almost total absence of formal statutory regulation in relation to complementary medicine. In Britain, while the practice of medicine is coming under increasingly close control as a consequence of the reforms of the National Health Service, regulation of the profession is still largely in the hands of the profession itself, through the General Medical Council (GMC). The issue of regulation for complementary medicine has intensified at a time coincident with a heightening of the perceived need to reassess the regulation of the orthodox profession, and when the power of doctors to determine the political outcome of the debate is weaker than in the past.

Because the State-sanctioned self-regulation of the medical profession is the primary model to which emergent complementary health professions appear to aspire, this chapter will focus on an examination of the reason why orthodox medicine is regulated in this way. It will also discuss some of the problems and criticisms associated with the 'medical model' and open the question as to whether this regulatory approach would work for complementary medicine.

I. GOVERNMENT ROLE

Health care issues are invariably given a high priority by the governments of most developed countries. The regulation of doctors long predates modern medicine, but, apart from times of epidemic crisis, health care has only assumed its present importance since the development of urban-based industrial economies. Critical to the economic and social stability of industrial economies is a healthy and

productive workforce, and it was appreciation of this fact that per-
suaded the British Government in the nineteenth century of the
merits of an interventionist approach to public health legislation
which was quite at odds with the 'hands-off' position that characterized their attitude towards the professional regulation of doctors.
Thus, there are economic and social reasons why governments
usually see the need to regulate both the practice and the profession
of medicine. However, as society's health care needs and preferences
change, so do the political dynamics which determine regulatory
outcomes.

In contrast to many other developed countries, the British Government is, for the time being at least, committed to a National Health
Service which has resulted in a single, dominant system of health care
marked by a high degree of central control. Moreover, the Government also has to resolve, often by legal means, the tension between
protecting consumers and allowing individuals to exercise freedom of
choice in health care. It is therefore bound, not only to the provision
of a National Health Service, but also to ensuring that the State
Service so provided is of a high standard and includes legal arrangements for the compensation of those individuals harmed by medical
accidents. In Britain therefore, the existence of the National Health
Service frames the political agenda for the regulation of medicine in a
very critical way.

The Government's commitment to the provision of a National
Health Service involves policy decisions in three main areas critical
to health service planning, which will impact on the regulation debate.
The major areas of concern are the cost of health care, access to
health care and the quality of the service and treatment so provided.
A number of groups in society now have an interest in the way health
care is regulated. The priorities of the Government, the health care
professionals who work within it, and the public who use its services
do not necessarily coincide. Both the policy decisions and the regulation which results will inevitably be a compromise based on many
different kinds of factors including the availability of resources and
the relative political muscle of the parties involved.

Some activities are deemed to require more regulation than others,
particularly activities that pose risk to the safety and security of individual citizens. Because of the cost of medical error to the individual,
the standards of the medical profession are expected to be of the highest order. One of the primary criticisms of complementary medicine

is the potential danger it presents to consumers if left in its current unregulated state.

Largely as a consequence of the key social functions they perform, doctors are a powerful professional group. As the main agents in providing health care they also play an important role in the operation of certain aspects of the welfare state. Clearly, they have their own stake in decisions which affect the health service policy and the way the practice of medicine is regulated. The regulatory method chosen by a State for the regulation of medicine is intimately connected with the relationship that the dominant system of medicine has with the State in that society.

In contrast to the role of the Government in regulating the health service, the medical profession itself is still largely self-regulating through the working of the GMC. Whilst the British Medical Association is locked in almost daily conflict over organizational aspects of doctors' terms and conditions of service, the GMC, until recently, has been given almost unfettered discretion to determine issues relating to professional self-regulation. Its shortcomings in this respect have been well documented, and there is no doubt that the recent introduction of performance review procedures, increases in the Committee's lay membership[1] and proposals for reform of the medical undergraduate curriculum are in direct response to vociferous criticism of the functioning of the GMC.

Notwithstanding its shortcomings, the GMC is the model which is most frequently held up as that to which complementary therapies should aspire. We shall examine why this is the case, in particular, whether complementary therapies can avoid being subject to the same criticisms which have beset the GMC, and what therapists believe are the advantages in pursuing this regulatory route.

In addition to government and professional agendas, individual electors also place a great value on health, ensuring that health issues are placed high on the domestic political agenda. However, as chronic degenerative diseases and life-style-related health problems become more determinant of the nation's health than the bacterial infection and diseases of poverty of earlier years, notions of health are also beginning to change. Definitions of 'health' are increasingly going beyond the notion of a simple absence of disease, and are beginning more closely to resemble the once-derided approach of the World

---

[1] Lay membership was increased to 13 members by SI 1979, No. 112, and a further increase is expected shortly.

Health Organization defined fifty years ago as a 'state of complete physical, mental and social well being'. The more that is known about the linkage between health and environmental and life-style factors, the greater will be the acceleration of popular interest in the politics and regulation of health care. The popularity of complementary therapies is partly explained by the way in which they appear to fill a void not being addressed by orthodox medicine. Inevitably, these developments will also lead to a reassessment of government policies on the level of State commitment to the furtherance of these ideals.

II. ORGANIZATIONAL AND REGULATORY MODELS

What types of organizational and regulatory models are at the disposal of policy-makers in respect of the regulation of complementary medicine? Different countries make use of a wide range of arrangements in regulating their medical systems. We can think about these arrangements in two ways: first, there are the more general organizational arrangements which largely determine relationships between medicine and the State; secondly, there are the regulatory models that are chosen to operate within that general framework.

The World Health Organization has identified four major organizational relationships which characterize the provision of orthodox and traditional medicine within the State.[2] A *monopolistic* system is one in which orthodox medical practitioners have the exclusive right to practice medicine. All other forms of healing are illegal, although enforcement of this monopoly will vary from country to country. The second model is referred to as the *tolerant* system in which orthodox medicine has exclusivity within the official health service, but non-conventional medicine is still legally available outside that sector. This system most closely resembles the organizational relationship between orthodox and unorthodox medicine in contemporary Britain. The *parallel* system is one in which practitioners of both orthodox and unorthodox medicine are officially recognized. While both services are available to patients, the organizational systems controlling the two divisions of medicine remain separate. Finally, the *integrated* system is one in which the two systems of medicine are merged both for the purposes of medical education and access through the official

---

[2] Bannerman, R., Burton, J., Ch'en, W. C. (edd.), *Traditional Medicine and Health Care Coverage* (WHO, Geneva, 1983) pp. 10–11.

health services. If non-conventional therapies are to be incorporated into health care systems in the West, this will eventually entail a necessary shift to a more flexible system in which such therapies can be legalized or formally recognized by the State.

These changing organizational relationships are global in scope. A priority of the World Health Organization is to encourage a more integrated use of traditional medicine and traditional healers in the primary health care systems of developing countries. This goal has involved a number of countries in an attempt to change the current legal provisions to allow for the incorporation of traditional health practices within the official health sector. There is strong intellectual resistance in the West to the notion that the legal experience of developing countries may have anything instructive to offer developed States. While acknowledging the very different circumstances under which health care services are delivered in the West, the fundamental *legal* dimension of the problem is much the same: how to change the formal legal position to allow for a greater diversity of health care practices. The experience of both the developing countries and of much of Europe seems to suggest strongly that with regard to health care practices, the law will be disregarded if it is not congruent with people's strongly held beliefs.[3]

There are three main regulatory models used to regulate the practice of medicine. They are independent self-regulation, State-sanctioned self-regulation and direct State-administered regulation. The principle way in which they differ is in the role they assign to the State. These systems are, of course, often used in tandem with other Acts of Parliament which may regulate certain aspects of the health service and medical practice.

Independent self-regulation is now found in the fields of sports, leisure activities, culture, and religion, but is less commonly used in other areas of social and economic activity. Self-regulation without the support of statutory backing is often criticized for its lack of an ability to administer effective sanctions; accordingly, it is generally not an approach chosen to regulate the more important economic and social activities.

Direct State regulation is implemented and administered by public servants and is the approach favoured for the control of activities in which public accountability is deemed to be critical. State-sanctioned

[3] See Stephan, J., 'Patterns of legislation concerning traditional medicine' in ibid., pp. 290–313.

self-regulation is the regulatory model Britain has traditionally favoured for the control of the professions.

A number of scholars have remarked on the inclination of successive British Governments to opt for self-regulation, particularly in relation to commercial and professional regulation. In this regard, Vogel has written on the differences between American and British regulatory styles:

On the whole British regulation is relatively informal and flexible while American regulation tends to be more formal and rule-oriented. Britain makes extensive use of self-regulation and encourages close co-operation between government officials and representatives of industry. The United States does little of the former and has generally been suspicious of the latter . . . [4]

Advertising, financial services, and professional regulation are the main areas in which greater reliance is placed on self-regulation as a means of control than is the norm elsewhere in Europe. There are a number of possible explanations for this. From the Government's point of view, it is cheaper and less burdensome to allow professions to regulate their own affairs, with the State retaining only nominal control. If adequately enforced, self-regulation is more cost-effective than a Government-financed public agency. This financial argument has been particularly well received by successive Conservative Governments who have been concerned to 'roll back the frontiers of the State', by implementing schemes for deregulation and self-regulation in a number of economic and commercial areas. It has also been argued that the British preference for self-regulation reflects a desire on the part of the administrative culture not to disturb established interests. Statutory self-regulation is also a useful device for keeping politically difficult questions at arm's length, in that the regulations thus arrived at are removed from central responsibility. By giving professions the power to self-regulate, the Government allows itself to centralize credit and decentralize blame.

A useful working definition of self-regulation is that offered by the National Consumer Council in their background paper *Self-Regulation of Business and the Professions*: 'In essence, self-regulation means that rules which govern behaviour in the market are developed, administered and enforced by the people (or their direct

---

[4] Vogel, D., *National Styles of Regulation* (Cornell University Press, New York, 1986) p. 24.

representatives) whose behaviour is to be governed. . . '.[5] Many of the arguments in favour of self-regulation are relevant to the regulation of medicine and draw initially on the perceived problems inherent in the use of direct State legislation. It is frequently argued that legislation is aimed at setting minimum standards only and thus tends to foster an approach focused on compliance with the minimum standard rather than the achievement of the higher goals. Another disadvantage of legislation is the way in which it can inhibit research and innovation, largely as a consequence of the greater degree of formalization and rigidity that result from heavy-handed legislative interference. Additionally, legislation is costly for the State to implement and to enforce, particularly in the case of legislation aimed at controlling a wide range of industrial and organizational practices.

In theory at least, self-regulating professions should be able to avoid or minimize these harms. The advantage of involving a profession in drawing up their own code of practice is that the code can be refined to meet the profession's particular needs. It is argued that standards can be set significantly higher than the minimum standards safeguarded by legislation. A code can deal more effectively with matters which require subjective judgement. Self-regulation is, moreover, more flexible in application and less costly to prepare than legislation. In areas of fast change, self-regulatory mechanisms can be adapted much more quickly and with less dislocation than legislation. It is often claimed that redress of grievances is quicker and less costly than reliance upon court procedures. Finally, and most importantly, it has been argued that the codes of practice, which are the keystones of so many self-regulatory schemes, do more than merely ban detrimental conduct—they actively encourage the achievement and maintenance of high standards.[6]

III. SELF REGULATION

If the Government were to be persuaded that State-sanctioned self-regulation would work for at least some complementary therapies, then a self-regulatory system along the lines of the current medical model would be the logical choice. This is the model used for all

---

[5] NCC (1986) p. 2.
[6] In Part II we shall question whether this is true of existing codes of ethics used by complementary practitioners.

medical and paramedical professions today. Thus it would concur with both historical practice and the current political bias towards self-regulation. Additionally, larger numbers of medically qualified personnel are now training in areas of complementary medicine, and a number of therapies are becoming more widely available within general practice and NHS hospitals. In their practice of such therapies, doctors will continue to fall within the jurisdiction of the GMC, provided they maintain their registration as registered medical practitioners. It is therefore necessary to discuss some of the problems and tensions in the regulatory system controlling orthodox medicine, before going on to examine whether this model is appropriate for complementary medicine.

Both law and medicine have been represented as classic examples of professions in which self-regulation has been conferred in return for co-operation with the Government in matters of legal and medical policy. While the regulation of the medical profession has a statutory basis, now enshrined in the Medical Act 1983, the medical profession is still, to a large extent self-regulating, enjoying a high degree of autonomy. Like the legal profession, the medical profession has always insisted that self-regulation is essential to professional status, drawing on the fact that the highly technical and specialized nature of the work requires that regulation be designed and implemented largely from within the profession itself. It is argued that medical practitioners are the best equipped to recognize professional breaches and to take the appropriate remedial action. Despite the erosion of certain traditional areas of clinical autonomy which have followed as a consequence of the NHS reforms, it remains true to say that the considerable power wielded by doctors resides principally in the self-regulatory system. This system has enabled the medical profession to exert exclusive control over entry to the profession, and to command a significant degree of control over competition for patients and payment systems.

Until the passing of the Osteopaths Act in 1993, the dominance of the medical profession over other statutorily regulated health professionals seemed unassailable. As Montgomery explains:

early state intervention, in the form of a professional register, served to protect the medical profession against encroachment by other occupational groups rather than to scrutinise the quality of its practice. In such a context, medicine can be seen as a paradigm of professional power: possessing an occupational monopoly in which doctors defined both the needs of their clients and also the manner in which those needs were to be met.[7]

Following statutory regulation in 1858, doctors have managed to exert significant influence over the manner in which other health care professions are regulated. Citing Freidson (1977), Montgomery goes on to describe: 'the pattern of medical domination as a situation in which doctors are the key profession from which the legitimacy of other professions flow, and who provide the authoritative interpretation and evaluation of their contribution'.[8]

How has this control been expressed? The medical profession has exerted direct influence on the way in which other health professions are regulated, having a discernible input on the governing councils of other statutorily regulated health care professions. Statutory committees regulating nurses, midwives, and health visitors as well as professions supplementary to medicine all require the presence of registered medical practitioners. This is a critical point, as it means that the medical profession has determined which health professionals, if any, should be permitted to provide services auxiliary to their own.

We should pause for a moment to consider the political implications of monopoly service providers defining the remit of their own area of protected interest. Perhaps we can see this more clearly by leaving the health care arena for a few moments and considering the other monolithic profession—law. In the legal profession, as in medicine, a great deal of self-validation and self-justification abounds, ensuring that the *status quo* is preserved. It is thus no coincidence that lawyers tend to think that statute law and judge-made law are 'proper' law, whereas other mechanisms for dispute resolution are not given serious attention. Customary laws or religious laws, for example, are not seen as carrying much weight in any jurisdiction which is governed by formal legal mechanisms even though within indigenous communities such systems may define all relationships and transactions, and it is to leaders of the community that disputants will turn before seeking access to more formal mechanisms.

The legal profession also eschews any real attempts at empowering the public about legal rights or responsibilities, thinking this is something better handled by lawyers on a fee-for-service basis. The proportion of litigants who represent themselves is minuscule, not

[7] Montgomery, J., 'Doctors' Handmaidens: The Legal Contribution' in McVeigh, S. and Wheeler, S. (edd.) *Law, Health and Medical Regulation* (Dartmouth, 1992).
[8] Ibid.

least because they are unable to wade through the arcane practices and procedures of the legal system. The small claims court, which is the only forum where litigants can retain some sense of control over their dispute, has an extremely limited jurisdiction.[9] Likewise, law centres and free representation units who provide free access to legal advice, have always been grossly underfunded and had a very second-class status in the eyes of the profession. In short, the law surrounds itself with sufficient mystique to convince lay people that they need lawyers. This is not a criticism of individual lawyers, any more than individual doctors are to be blamed for two centuries' promulgation of the merits of supposedly objective, science-based medicine. It is simply to prove the point that professions have a vested interest in persuading the public that they are indispensable when it comes to interpreting their respective territories.

Thus, in the past, it was to the medical profession, as defenders of the public's health, to whom society deferred in determining the validity of alternative medicine. Now, however, the reduction of medical autonomy in real terms means that the medical profession is no longer able to dictate which services should or should not be provided to patients. A recent National Association of Health Authorities and Trusts Report considering the provision of complementary therapies in the NHS states: 'Reforms in the health service have offered an opportunity to reconsider the provision of health care. The separation of purchasers and providers with an emphasis on patient choice has led to a re-assessment of existing health care services'.[10] The NHS reforms, intended, in theory at least, to make health care provision more responsive to patient choice, have provided greater scope for complementary therapies to be provided within the NHS, where the views of the medical profession will still carry considerable weight, but will not, as in the past, be wholly determinative.

A. Medical Act 1983

Since the Medical Act 1983 is the model to which most statutory therapies aspire, it is worth spending some time considering the perceived shortcomings of that legislation, so that if therapies insist on following this particular route they will at least be aware of the

---

[9] Although recent reforms to the civil justice system have extended the small claim jurisdiction.
[10] *Complementary Therapies in the NHS* (NAHAT, 1993).

pitfalls of copycat regulation. In much the same way as the random-ized control trial is considered the gold standard of research, so the Medical Act 1983 is acclaimed as the gold standard for regulation of health professions.

Since 1858, a succession of Medical Acts has restricted the title 'doctor' to registered medical practitioners. This has provided doctors with a unique position as monopoly providers of medical services within the State health system. Although the law does not forbid, in general terms, the practice of surgery or medicine by unqualified persons, the Medical Act 1983 makes provisions for the registration of certain persons who possess certain medical qualifications. It is important to appreciate that medical regulation in this country does not regulate what forms of therapy may be practised by doctors who are duly registered. This means that there is no restriction on registered medical practitioners using any 'alternative' therapy, so long as they have acquired the requisite skills and/or qualifications to do so.[11] New techniques are incorporated into medicine all the time, and certainly one of the interesting trends will be to watch the extent to which those therapies whose efficacy can be demonstrated in scientific terms will be taken up and colonized by the existing health care professions.

At no stage in the regulation of medicine has medicine been defined as allopathic medicine. Historically, however, the use of non-orthodox techniques has been frowned upon by the medical hierarchy and attracted harsh comment from the GMC. This position has changed as complementary therapies have grown in popularity, and particularly in respect of those therapies that are willing and have been able to attempt to demonstrate efficacy in scientific terms. The shift is particularly pronounced in primary care with an increasing number of general practitioners either learning complementary therapies themselves, or employing therapists within their practice.

Being a registered medical practitioner confers a number of privil-eges and responsibilities on doctors, including the following:

(1) only registered medical practitioners may use the title or describe themselves as registered practitioners, or be recog-nized by law as a physician or surgeon;[12]

---

[11] The BMA's 1993 Report recommends that 'medically qualified practition-ers wishing to practice any form of non-conventional therapy should undertake training in that field approved by the appropriate regulatory body, and should only practise the therapy after registration'. *Complementary Medicine—New Approaches to Good Practice*. BMA (OUP, 1993).

[12] Medical Act 1983, s. 49. This provides that any person who wilfully and

(2) Only registered medical practitioners can recover their fees for medical attendance or advice in a court of law;[13]

(3) only registered medical practitioners can hold certain posts, such as medical officer in the forces, in prison, or in mental hospitals;[14]

(4) only full registered medical practitioners may be entered on the lists of practitioners undertaking to provide general medical services in connection with the National Health Service.[15]

(5) only registered medical practitioners can give certain statutory certificates, including the signing of birth, still-birth and death certificates;[16]

As well as the practices listed above, various statutory provisions also prevent unqualified people from performing certain medical functions. These include the practice of dentistry, the practice of midwifery and the treatment of venereal disease. Further statutory provisions prohibit the advertising of treatments for cancer and certain other illnesses, including diabetes, epilepsy, and glaucoma.[17] Also, regulations restrict advertisements which make medicinal claims to the public and prohibit advertisements which claim to treat, prevent or diagnose a variety of diseases, including malignant diseases,

falsely pretends to be or takes or uses the name or title of physician, doctor of medicine, licentiate in medicine and surgery, bachelor of medicine, surgeon, general practitioner or apothecary, or any name, title, addition or description implying that he or she is registered under any provision of the Medical Act 1983 is liable on summary conviction to a fine not exceeding level 5 on the standard scale.

[13] Ibid., s. 46. However, an unregistered person may recover charges in respect of treatment which does not amount to the performance of an 'operation': *Halls* v. *Trotter* (1921) 38 TLR 30, DC, in which the court held that an osteopath was able to recover charges for manipulative treatment.

[14] Ibid., s. 47.

[15] NHS (General Medical Services) Regs. 1992, SI 1992, No. 635, regs. 2, 4.

[16] Medical Act 1983, s. 48. In respect of statutory benefits, employers are not bound to rely solely on certificates from an employee's GP and may rely on certificates issued by complementary practitioners. Officially, however, if the certificate does not come from the person's GP, the Department of Health may appoint an independent assessor to ensure that the patient is genuinely unable to work. The Council for Acupuncture's *Code of Ethics* specifically states that acupuncturists may issue sickness certificates or make statements regarding a patient's health for state benefit or other purposes, reminding members of their professional duty to exercise great care in so doing (Traditional Acupuncture Society, *Code of Ethics*, para. B. 3).

[17] It is not an offence to treat, merely to advertise treatments. Cancer Act 1939 s. 4(1)(a).

serious neurological and muscular diseases, and sexually transmitted diseases.[18]

B. The General Medical Council

The 1858 Medical Act stipulated that all qualified doctors must be entered on a single register. It did not bar unqualified persons from practising, but it made it illegal for them to claim to be medically qualified. The General Medical Council (GMC) was empowered to set training standards, to control entry to the register, and to discipline defaulting doctors.[19]

Public concern with the role of the GMC is primarily centred on its duty to maintain the standards of registered doctors, and in particular its authorization to take action against defaulting doctors. The Professional Conduct Committee may discipline any doctor found guilty of a criminal offence or who is considered by the committee to be guilty of 'serious professional misconduct'. Doctors found guilty of serious professional misconduct may have their name erased from the Medical Register, have their registration suspended, have certain conditions imposed on them such as undergoing further training, or they may simply be admonished.

The question of what amounts to 'serious professional misconduct' and the procedures which are used in investigating complaints against doctors have recently attracted much criticism. 'Serious professional misconduct' has, until now, tended to focus on isolated errors, rather than poor standards. This has led to the criticism that the GMC 'is concerned largely with etiquette, rather than competence . . . '.[20] The procedures have been censured for requiring very high standards of proof; the charge must be proved beyond reasonable doubt. This standard is higher than the civil burden of proof, which merely requires facts to be established on a balance of probabilities.[21] Perhaps this is as it should be when a doctor's livelihood and reputation are at stake, but it is seen by the system's critics as yet another of the many obstacles lying in the path of an aggrieved patient should he or she

[18] The Medicines (Advertising) Regs. 1994, SI 1994, No. 1932.
[19] The Council was first established under the name 'The General Council of Medical Education and Registration of the United Kingdom', by the Medical Act 1858, s. 3 (repealed). The GMC is now established under the Medical Act 1983, s. 1, Sch. 1.
[20] Kennedy, I. *The Unmasking of Medicine*, p. 123.
[21] See Part II.

take on the Herculean endeavour of attempting to obtain justice via the disciplinary proceedings of the GMC.

The elaborate screening procedures, designed to filter out 'frivolous' complaints, have also been criticized for the tendency to reject complaints which should properly be heard. Those doctors who are eventually 'convicted' often receive light penalties. Margaret Brazier writes that: 'since 1970 no doctor suffered the ultimate penalty of striking off for failure to attend a patient. By contrast, between 1975 and 1984 four doctors out of ten disciplined for sexual misconduct were struck off . . . '.[22]

A doctor has the right of appeal to the Privy Council against a decision of the Professional Conduct Committee. Furthermore, the GMC has a duty to protect a doctor from malicious and vexatious complaints. If it fails in this duty, the Council may be faced with legal proceedings for judicial review of its decision. In short, the system as it presently operates, is designed so as to ensure considerable protection for the doctor whose conduct is being investigated. Conversely, it inadequately safeguards the interests of patients and its failure in this regard must be seriously evaluated by those representatives of complementary therapies interested in pursuing this approach to self-regulation

Registered medical practitioners are subject to a strict disciplinary code in relation to professional and personal conduct, overseen by the General Medical Council. The GMC has various education functions, particularly in relation to the undergraduate curriculum (other functions being oveseen by the GMC but effectively exercised through the Medical Royal Colleges). In terms of disciplinary function, the GMC has jurisdiction over all medical specialities. Unlike hospital complaints procedures, the GMC's remit extends to general practitioners. It also exercises jurisdiction over private doctors as well as doctors working within the NHS.

As well as a professional misconduct jurisdiction, the GMC has, since 1980, had a health jurisdiction which enables it to deal with doctors whose ability to practise is diminished on physical or mental health grounds. Additionally, new statutory provisions about to be introduced will give the GMC much needed powers to deal with doctors whose professional performance is seriously deficient. The

---

[22] Brazier, M., *Doctors, Patients and the Law* (Penguin, London, 1992, 2nd edn.) p. 14.

inability of the GMC to deal with cases of professional performance has been identified as one of its biggest weaknesses.

Our interest lies primarily in evaluating the Medical Act 1983 as a regulatory model. Professional accountability is determined by the effectiveness or otherwise of the GMC. The general consensus is that the GMC is at a crossroads at the present time. The persistent complaint against the GMC is that it has been too soft on doctors.

Currently, the trigger for disciplinary action is 'serious professional misconduct'. Critics have argued that this has been interpreted so as to punish only the most disgraceful examples of unacceptable conduct. The emphasis on serious misconduct has focused attention on one-off, egregious examples of behaviour, rather than addressing the potentially more damaging issue of persistently poor doctoring. Although not conclusive in itself, the proportion of complaints to the GMC which actually leads to a finding of serious professional misconduct is very small.[23]

It is frequently said that the GMC is insufficiently accountable. As the disciplinary body for the entire medical profession, the GMC is seen as remote and unapproachable. Although anyone may initiate a complaint against a registered medical practitioner to the GMC, this fact is not widely advertised, and the Council is not known for being user-friendly. Little attempt is made to inform the public as to how they can bring complaints against doctors. A procedure is about to be introduced whereby any findings which have been made against a registered medical practitioner will be marked against his or her entry on the Medical Register.

The General Medical Council has 102 members, comprising 54 members elected by the medical profession every five years, 35 members appointed by medical colleges and universities and 13 lay members appointed by the Privy Council.[24] The lack of any real lay presence on the Council has long been a contentious issue, and over the last few years, steps have been taken to improve this situation. The difficulty remains that it is not sufficient to increase the lay representation—lay representatives must be allowed to take an active role in proceedings at all levels. There is a danger that if proceedings are pitched at too technical a level, lay members will either be excluded

---

[23] In 1994, out of 1,626 complaints, only 83 cases were referred from the Preliminary Screening Committee to the Professional Conduct Committee. Source: *GMC Annual Report* (1994).

[24] This figure was increased by SI 1979, No. 112.

from having any meaningful role, or, they may themselves become 'medicalized', at which point they cease to be able to represent the voice of the people. In response to criticism, the GMC has been forced to reform its constitution, so as to substantially increase the lay membership, not just at the Professional Misconduct Committee level, but also on the Preliminary Proceedings Committee.[25] This is particularly vital, as preliminary proceedings are held in private, and it is at this stage that a significant number of complaints are weeded out.[26]

One of the very real problems facing not just the GMC, but other statutory bodies also, is that, because members are not paid to sit on committees, there is a preponderance of retired or extremely senior professionals sitting on disciplinary committees, who are removed from the day-to-day problems which beset practitioners. In the same way that judges can become jaded, members who sit on disciplinary committees for several years are likely to become cynical if they hear the same defences being put forward time after time.

In terms of improving standards of practice, one of the problems of the GMC is that cases which have been heard may not be widely publicized and may simply sink without trace, without having any impact on the rest of the profession. Unless a case has received a lot of publicity, practitioners may not be aware of the seriousness with which the GMC regards certain types of conduct. Because the preliminary proceeding committee sit in private, little is known of the types of cases which are deemed inappropriate for referral to the Professional Misconduct Committee.

1. GMC Reforms

As a result of sustained public pressure, the GMC is introducing radical reforms. These reforms are prompted by the recognition that the right to self-govern depends, critically, on maintaining public confidence. To the extent that the public feels that trust is being abused, self-regulation will be threatened. As well as the impending introduction of the new performance review procedures, the GMC is

[25] Until Aug. 31 1990, there was no requirement for a lay member to be involved in the preliminary screening of case (Rule 4(5) Procedure Rules 1988).

[26] In 1993–4, of 195 cases referred to the PPC, only 83 were referred to the PCC. This is a marked improvement on previous years. In 1991, for example, out of 126 referrals to the PPC, only 31 cases were referred to the PCC.

about to replace its existing professional guidance with a new, patient-centred code entitled *Good Medical Practice*. The code will be accompanied by guidance on the duties of doctors and on confidentiality.

As the new President of the GMC, Sir Donald Irvine concedes: 'What the public says of the medical profession at the moment is that we are not good at handling our poorly performing doctors. So we are signalling very clearly that we are doing something about that. It's our duty not only to promote good practice but to protect people from bad practice'.[27]

Nearly one hundred and fifty years after the creation of the GMC, the Medical Act 1983 is to be amended to give the GMC power to implement performance procedures. The GMC stress that the new procedures are not intended to deal with less serious cases of misconduct, but to address the problem of doctors whose ongoing standard of work is seriously deficient. If, having been assessed, the doctor's performance is found to be seriously deficient, appropriate remedial training will be imposed. A new committee will impose sanctions on doctors who fail to comply with these procedures or whose performance is not sufficiently improved through remedial training. It is rather telling that the GMC recognizes that a considerable increase in manpower is likely to be necessary to cope with the expected bulk of cases which will fall into this category. When probed as to the numbers of practitioners who would be likely to be caught by the new procedures, the President said that there would certainly be hundreds and that there was likely to be an 'iceberg effect'.[28]

The GMC, in addition to its disciplinary functions, presides over undergraduate medical education. It has been subject to fierce criticism on this front as well, with few disputing that the medical school curriculum has been overloaded, and unbalanced, concentrating on scientific subjects at the expense of other areas of training, such as communication skills, which would significantly improve the way in which doctors cared for patients. Certain changes are now being implemented as a result of the GMC's 1993 Report on undergraduate training, *Tomorrow's Doctors*. Part of the Introduction reveals a distinct shift in approach:

Whereas the focus of medical education during the present century has been mainly on the understanding of disease processes as they affect

[27] Richard Smith, 'The future of the GMC: an interview with Donald Irvine, the new president'. BMJ 1995; **310**: 1515–18.
[28] Ibid. See now Medical (Professional Performance) Act 1995.

individuals, on their diagnosis and management, there is an evident re-
awakening of the wider interest of our forbears in the health of populations, the epidemic and environmental hazards that affect them and the
means whereby diseases may be controlled or prevented. Public health,
temporarily lost from the vocabulary, has been firmly reinstated as a
priority in the planning of medical services in this country and abroad,
and the undergraduate curriculum must reflect this important change
of emphasis.

As well as urging greater recognition of a team-based approach, and
the redistribution of tasks amongst a variety of health care professionals, the Report also attempts to set 'illness' in a wider context. It
continues:

Suffering and disability, which may affect not only the individual, but also
family, friends and associates at work, are often related to psychological
disturbances or those we categorize as 'non-organic'. Medical education
must strive to comprehend all aspects of human disorder. *It must also
recognize that there is a growing demand for treatments that do not conform to
the conventional orthodoxies.* (Emphasis added.)

The Report lists communication skills and a knowledge of law and
ethics amongst the objectives of medical education, as well as the
need to develop attitudes necessary for the achievement of high
standards of medical practice. The Report should be seen as a serious
attempt to set scientific medicine in a wider context. Although the
process of implementation may be slow, the shift in emphasis should
not be overlooked.

The constitution and functions of the Education Committee have
also been reviewed. Two lay members now sit on the committee and a
medical student representative attends meetings.

Within the medical profession there has always been a sharp divide
between the doctors' regulatory body, i.e., the GMC, and the trade
union, i.e., the British Medical Association (BMA). The same pattern
is repeated in nursing, where trade union functions are performed by
the Royal College of Nursing and the Royal College of Midwives, whilst
the United Kingdom Central Council (UKCC) is the disciplinary body
set up under the Nurses, Midwives and Health Visitors Act 1992.

Until now, the GMC has exercised its disciplinary role in a reactive
way. Although it circulates ethical guidance to members at various
stages in their career, GMC staff rarely respond to requests from practitioners as to whether prospective behaviour might constitute serious

professional misconduct. Nor is it particularly forthcoming towards members of the public who approach them informally to ascertain whether certain behaviour they have experienced might give rise to a case of misconduct. The remit of the BMA is considerably wider; in addition to providing ethical advice to practitioners it exercises an increasingly political role. Indeed in recent years, the BMA has exhibited far greater willingness to broaden its horizons. Since the 1986 *Report on Alternative Therapies*, not only has it softened its stance in relation to non-orthodox therapies, but it has also produced a number of papers which look beyond the causes of illness traditionally considered as important by the orthodox medical profession.[29]

2. GMC and complementary practitioners

What then of the GMC's attitude towards practitioners of complementary medicine? Whilst no longer abjectly hostile, the GMC's *Blue Book* still states that 'a doctor persisting in unsupervised practice of a branch of medicine without having the appropriate knowledge and skill or having acquired the experience which is necessary' may risk a finding of serious professional misconduct. This would suggest that if registered medical practitioners are to practice any of the major therapies, they should receive the appropriate training from a recognized registering professional body.[30]

Similar systems of registration were introduced to cover dentists in 1956 and opticians in 1958. Nurses and midwives also have their own licensing procedures, and seven paramedical professions are registered under the Professions Supplementary to Medicine Act 1960.

C. Professions Supplementary to Medicine Act 1960

The Professions Supplementary to Medicine Act 1960 is an umbrella Act which regulates a number of professions. The seven professions currently registered are physiotherapists, occupational therapists,

---

[29] See, e.g., *The BMA Guide to Living with Risk* (Penguin, 1990) and *Pesticides, Chemicals and Health*, BMA (Edward Arnold Publishers, 1992).

[30] This is a point made by the BMA in its 1993 Report. Whilst this may be possible with the more established therapies, it is uncertain what position the GMC would take if doctors started practising more esoteric therapies, or did not have such additional qualifications.

chiropodists, dieticians, orthoptists, radiographers and medical laboratory scientific officers.[31] The Act is administered by the Council for Professions Supplementary to Medicine (CPSM)[32] which coordinates and supervises the activities of statutory boards established under the Act for providing high standards of professional education and conduct amongst the relevant professions.

Each profession is represented by a board, whose primary function is to publish and maintain a register of all qualified practitioners. Employment within the NHS is limited to State-registered professionals. Professionals who move into the private sector do not have to keep up their registration. There are no sanctions for non-registered, or indeed non-qualified, people setting themselves up and using the titles protected by the Act. Therefore, the Act only provides partial protection for patients. Currently, some 90,000 practitioners are registered under the statutory scheme.

Although dissatisfaction with the Act has mounted over several years, it is only within the last five years that the Boards have united in their attempts to press for reform. At the time of writing, the whole statutory scheme is subject to a major review. Certainly the passing of the Osteopaths Act in 1993 and Chiropractors Act in 1994 intensified the debate by raising the possibility of autonomous self-regulation for health professionals. The fact that those two therapies were given wide powers to regulate their own affairs was particularly inflammatory to certain professions, given the high degree of medical representation on the CPSM demanded by the 1960 Act.

One of the difficulties which has faced those eager for review is the disparity as between the various professions registered by the 1960 Act and their aspirations for their future. Whilst some of the seven professions might be aiming towards seeking autonomous status outside the confines of the Act, others are content with their position within the orthodox medical hierarchy. Primarily, these professions act on a referral basis, but within the seven professions are practitioners who do see patients on a self-referral basis, and who wish to promote that right. We saw earlier that the question of self-referral to NHS practitioners is apt to generate concern, given the all pervasive role of GPs as gatekeepers.

Although professional standards of statutory professionals in the NHS are perceived as high and there are very few disciplinary cases,

---

[31] Professions Supplementary to Medicine Act 1960 s. 1(2).
[32] Ibid., s. 1(1).

this could be as much a reflection of the inadequacy of the disciplinary mechanism as of the probity of the profession. According to the annual report of the CPSM for 1994–5, the Disciplinary Committee of the seven Boards heard only eight cases. None of these cases resulted in a practitioner being removed from the register.[33] The right of any professional group to self-regulate depends ultimately on its proven ability to police its own members. Shortcomings in the Act itself have called into question the ability of the CPSM to exercise its role effectively.

Political changes within the NHS are likely to influence the outcome of any review. The need for cost efficiency has led certain professions to fear that their own specialism will be replaced, or diluted, by cheaper, less skilled labour, or that, where the option exists, purchasers may opt to buy in the services of alternative practitioners who are making similar therapeutic claims. Given the attempts of complementary therapists to pursue statutory self-regulation, certain supplementary professions are feeling decidedly threatened. Additionally, the Government's current deregulatory stance and the development of National Vocational Qualifications in health care has led others to fear that their status will be downgraded.

The review will examine the current operation of the statutory bodies, their relationships with interested organizations, and the constraints on their efficiency. Although the review expects to be able to report within a year, it is highly unlikely that legislative change will be introduced during the present Government's term of office. Whilst certain professions covered by the scheme will pursue independent self-regulation, any review will probably be limited to a reworking of the primary legislation, to remove some of the difficulties listed above. Crucially, any reform must address the dangers posed to consumers by unqualified practitioners assuming a title which could possibly mislead the public and question the ability of the Boards, in a time of increased consumer expectation, to monitor the professions and provide redress in the event of mishap.

The only tangible advantage to extending the Act so as to encompass selected complementary therapies is the fact that the infrastructure for regulating a diversity of health professions is already in place. This could be seen as attractive especially for relatively young therapies, whose practitioners do not have the expertise and history of

[33] The Council for Professions Supplementary to Medicine *Annual Report* 1994–5.

voluntary self-regulation which is considered to be a prerequisite for autonomous statutory regulation. Working within the Act, therapists would at least have the benefit of some degree of protection of title. A second advantage is that therapists might see this as an entrée into working within the NHS, albeit within an orthodox biomedical framework.

Given some of the specific problems we have mentioned, however, it is highly unlikely that any therapies would seek to align themselves with this particular regulatory model at the present time. Set against the recently passed Osteopaths Act 1993 and Chiropractors Act 1994, which were modelled primarily on the 1983 Medical Act, the deficiencies of the 1960 Act become all the more obvious. A serious shortcoming of the 1960 Act is the fact that registration is only required for professionals working in the NHS, and not for those working in the private sector. Completely unqualified practitioners could, for example, set themselves up in the private sector and use the title 'dietician', thus creating only a weak protection of title. Moreover, training establishments wishing to train students solely for private practice need not apply to the CPSM for approval of its courses.

The fact that the existing disciplinary mechanism has no jurisdiction to deal with professionals suffering from physical or mental illness is a serious omission. This is a matter which the current review of the 1960 Act will no doubt address. The absence of a health procedure is in contrast to most other health care professions who have rejected a punitive approach to the problems posed by practitioners unable to perform by virtue of ill-health in favour of a more supportive role.

The inappropriate and rigid disciplinary powers under the 1960 Act mean that currently members can only be found guilty of 'infamous misconduct'. This limits the number of cases which are brought under the Act, and fails to address the issue of ongoing poor standards. This is an inadequacy in the disciplinary mechanism, in that less serious misdemeanours are more likely to go unpunished because the only disciplinary measure is expulsion from the register of qualified practitioners. Unlike the Medical Act 1983, the 1960 Act includes no powers to suspend practitioners or impose conditions on their practice, nor any mechanisms to require practitioners to retrain.

One major oversight is that the 1960 Act does not require all practitioners to be covered by indemnity insurance. In terms of accountability, this is not an insurmountable problem within the NHS, where the employing health authority or NHS Trust would be vicariously liable for the wrongful acts or omissions of its staff, providing they were acting within the scope of their employment. It is a serious problem, however, for the substantial proportion of these professionals who work in a private capacity. As the 1960 Act stands at present, the only penalty is that retrospectively, the absence of insurance can be deemed to constitute infamous conduct. This is of little comfort to an injured patient who would be advised against suing an impecunious practitioner.

Primarily, the 1960 Act is intended to apply to professions employed by the NHS and working in a hospital environment, under the control of doctors, using biomedical models. Its remit does not extend to practitioners working outside the NHS. This renders the 1960 Act inappropriate for professions which operate entirely, or almost entirely in private practice. Were the Act to be extended to complementary practitioners, clashes with the medical profession over issues of professional competence would be inevitable, especially for any therapy with an underlying alternative philosophy. Problems as to the appropriate basis for a diagnosis would arise whenever the complementary practitioner put forward an alternative hypothesis as to why the patient was ill. Practitioners working under the CPSM have always had to depend on the approval of perceived medical wisdom. To the extent this is at odds with alternative philosophies of health and disease, it is unlikely that many therapists would be prepared to work within these parameters.

For the above reasons it is highly unlikely that the CPSM model would be acceptable to many therapeutic organizations or individual therapists. Indeed, the osteopaths considered and rejected this route. The main objections to this regulatory framework are the degree of medical representation on the Council[34] and the non-autonomous status conferred on professionals registered under the 1960 Act, which does not address the fact that many registered professionals work on an independent referral basis.

All of these factors are likely to render the scheme unattractive to therapies which have exhibited the highest degree of autonomy within

---

[34] S. 10(1)(c) of the 1960 Act provides that there must be an equal number of registered medical practitioners and representatives from the professional boards on the Council, as well as the medical representation on the Boards themselves.

the private sector, on a self-referral basis, working within wholly different paradigms which would be impossible to maintain within the CPSM model. Essentially, the question is how desperately do complementary therapists want to work within the NHS, and how much professional autonomy are they prepared to sacrifice in order to do so? We suspect that most therapists think that the problems of working within the NHS outnumber the advantages.

IV. COMPLEMENTARY MEDICINE—A DIFFERENT ENTITY?

One of the most basic issues to be resolved in any discussion about regulation for complementary medicine is the extent to which holistic therapies can be seen as being 'the same as' orthodox medicine and therefore potentially subject to the same kind of regulatory control. We argue that many of the holistic therapies typical of complementary medicine are so different in their methods and in their relationships with the patient as to require a different regulatory approach. But some of these differences are more related to the different nature of the relationship of complementary medicine to the State.

The same political dynamics which have been so important in shaping regulation for orthodox medicine do not apply to complementary medicine. First, despite the recent moves to incorporate more holistic therapies into the NHS, complementary medicine is still predominantly private sector medicine. As yet, it only marginally involves the government and health service purchasers in spending decisions. Secondly, complementary medicine does not possess a unified, professional lobby such as the BMA. Although a number of the more well-established disciplines such as homoeopathy, herbalism, and acupuncture have good organizational structures, many complementary therapies have not even begun to develop the kind of organizational and political sophistication that is a primary characteristic of professional and occupational bodies.

With no strong economic motivation to regulate and, in the absence of pressure from professional bodies within complementary medicine, the main governmental initiative to regulate would be founded on issues of consumer protection. The Government, in deciding whether to regulate complementary medicine will face an inherent tension between individual and collective rights, and must strike a balance between allowing individuals the right to exercise their own preferences in health care and the need to protect citizens from harm.

We need to ask first whether the paternalism reflected in orthodox medicine and its regulation is warranted in complementary medicine. The BMA now seems to take the view that only those therapies with the inherent potential to cause harm require statutory regulation. If individuals choose to place their faith in a complementary therapy, should they be prevented by law from doing so because it might cause harm? One might reasonably question whether this is a legitimate area for statutory intervention at all, or whether it falls within the realms of private choice that responsible adults should be able to make. In respect of the practice of the more esoteric therapies, it could be argued that belief in its efficacy is more closely akin to religious or philosophical considerations and beyond the legitimate realm of statutory regulation.

Equally, certain systems of traditional medicine remain popular and well-supported by ethnic communities within Britain. If the Government were to take a more proactive stance and prohibit the use of these therapies, this might be seen as unacceptable interference with the right of individuals to choose healers from their own cultural background. It could be argued that the right to cultural diversity in health care, to believe in one system of healing in preference to another, should be respected in much the same way as freedom of religion. What do we mean by a 'right' in this context? Not all rights have corresponding duties. Asserting that people have the right to believe in other forms of healing than the prevailing allopathic norm, does not necessarily mean that the Government has a corresponding duty to provide those forms of healing, although it might create a duty of non-interference. Where will the Government choose to draw the line once it begins to intervene in regulating unorthodox therapies?

In Britain, the Government has historically taken the view that freedom of choice is important. However, the medical profession has a significant interest in the extent to which other groups in society may practice medicine, and their political interests find expression most often in a criticism of the lack of scientific validation of complementary therapies and warnings of the potential such therapies have to cause harm to patients.

The more popular complementary medicine becomes with the public, the greater will be the pressure on the Government to abandon its avowed stance of 'benevolent neutrality' and declare its position. While successive Governments grapple with the policy decisions which will affect the future of complementary medicine, we shall all be reminded that medicine is an intensely political activity.

3

Regulating Complementary Medicine—Why Now?

In this chapter, we shall begin to examine why it is that after years of what could be variously interpreted as either benign tolerance or legislative neglect, regulation for complementary medicine has now become such a topical issue. Today, Britain is at the forefront of European States willing to enact legislation granting official status to certain complementary therapies; in fact, Britain is the only country within the European Union which will soon have three functioning statutory complementary medicine bodies—the General Council of Osteopaths, the General Council of Chiropractors, and the Faculty of Homoeopathy.[1]

We shall look at some of the factors behind this apparent shift in the Government's attitude towards regulation for non-conventional medicine. The question of why the regulation of complementary medicine has become such a pressing issue can be answered on two levels. The simple and immediate response is that the interest in regulating non-conventional therapies is largely derived from the significantly increased consumer usage over the past decade. When one in four of the population are using non-conventional therapies, it becomes ever more likely that the Government will feel it necessary to intervene to control these practices in the public interest.

Beyond the issue of increased consumer use, a more complex view has to take into account the political, sociological, and economic factors which play a part in determining the course of regulation. Finally, and even more critically, the dynamics of regulatory development would indicate that the vital impetus in the determination of regulation is likely to be generated from within complementary medicine itself. Many of the more respected, well-established therapies, together with a number of those that are less well-established, have

---

[1] The Faculty, which was incorporated in 1950 to train and examine orthodox practitioners in homoeopathy, does not maintain a register, but does have a limited disciplinary jurisdiction.

made it known that they intend to pursue statutory regulation for the benefits that registration and protection of title can undoubtedly bring. Thus, while increased consumer usage may have fuelled the arguments for consumer protection, it has also provided the complementary health movement with the political ammunition to insist that complementary medicine should now be taken seriously. In this chapter, we shall focus first on the issues that are the direct consequence of increased usage.

I. THE GROWTH OF COMPLEMENTARY MEDICINE

A. Private Sector

Only a recluse could have failed to notice the intense public interest in complementary medicine over the past decade; it is hard to avoid the almost incessant media coverage. Newspapers and magazines carry articles on complementary medicine, radio and television stations run regular features and documentaries, and there has been an upsurge in the publication of journals and books devoted to holistic health. Additionally, there has been a noticeable increase of shops stocking natural health products and remedies, and most local authorities now run an array of evening courses on subjects from baby massage to tai chi. Complementary medicine is fast becoming a multi-million pound industry and is recognized as being a prime growth area.[2]

This growth in complementary medicine has also been documented statistically in a number of surveys over recent years. A survey conducted by the Consumers Association in 1991 showed that one in four of the population now use unorthodox medicine. This suggests a steady increase in usage since a similar survey conducted in 1986 revealed the rate to be one in seven of the population. The number of complementary health practitioners is also estimated to have been increasing at the rate of 10 per cent each year since the mid-1980s.[3]

There is considerable interest in discovering *why* people are turning to complementary medicine in such numbers. Drawing firm conclusions from the insufficient and uneven data which currently

[2] In 1992, £30m. was spent on herbal remedies, £15m. on homoeopathic remedies and £6m. on essential (aromatherapy) oils. Source: MINTEL Market Intelligence (April 1993).

[3] Fulder, S., and Munro, R., *The Status of Complementary Medicine in the United Kingdom* (Threshold Foundation, London, 1982).

exists would be unwise, but such evidence as is available suggests that it is the middle-aged and middle-class who form the highest proportion of users of unorthodox therapies.[4] Additionally, women appear to make greater use of complementary therapies than men.

The fact that patterns of consultations appear to be different for conventional and non-conventional practitioners probably has much to do with the *cost* of complementary health treatment. With few exceptions, almost all consultations with complementary practitioners take place on a private basis, thus putting their services beyond the pocket of many. A 1989 MORI survey showed that 74 per cent of the 1,826 adults questioned would like to see some complementary therapies available under the National Health Service.[5] It is, therefore, possible that were complementary medicine to be made more widely available under the NHS, usage figures among the population would show a wider social mix.[6]

The findings in relation to women have led to the speculation that it is women who are the most dissatisfied with the way that orthodox medicine deals with many of their ill-health problems. The use of complementary therapies and self-help treatment among women may reflect a genuine distaste for the way a largely male-dominated profession deals with female health issues. That a high proportion of both practitioners and consumers of complementary medicine are women is surely significant. The feminist challenge to the male medical culture has been afoot for some twenty years. Initially unrelated to complementary medicine, the two movements share much common political ground. This was demonstrated to dramatic effect during the Wendy Savage case in 1985, which was rightly represented as a battle against the medicalization of childbirth and a demand that women be given the right to a say in the birthing process. Pietroni writes: 'In the same way as the feminist movement influenced society's attitudes towards nuclear warfare through its much publicized campaign at Greenham Common, so it has begun to shape medical approaches to the understanding of women, health and illness . . . '[7]

Surveys such as the 1986 *Which?* survey show that the most popular therapies include osteopathy, herbalism, acupuncture, chiropractic,

---

[4] Thomas, K. J., *et al.* 'Use of non-orthodox and conventional health care in Great Britain' 302 BMJ 207–10 (1991).

[5] MORI Poll, *The Times*, 12 Nov. 1989.

[6] See Sharma, U., *Complementary Medicine Today* (Routledge, London, 1992) p. 19.

[7] Pietroni, P., *The Greening of Medicine*, p. 123.

and homoeopathy. A more important aspect of the pattern of consumer use however, relates to the *way* in which a patient uses complementary medicine. Research carried out by Thomas showed that 64 per cent of the patients surveyed who were seeking treatment from non-conventional therapies had previously received orthodox treatment or advice. Of these patients 24 per cent were receiving orthodox and complementary treatment simultaneously.[8] These findings are broadly borne out by surveys conducted by Fulder and Munro in which 33.4 per cent of patients receiving complementary therapy were simultaneously receiving orthodox treatment.[9] Fulder also cites evidence from an Australian government-sponsored survey which indicates that while a minority of young, female, health-conscious patients would use complementary medicine as a first resort, the majority (67 per cent) used both systems.[10] On the basis of our current knowledge, the predominant pattern appears to be that patients use complementary medicine, not as a substitute for, but as a supplement to, orthodox medicine.

Once this pattern of usage is more conclusively established, it may help to quell the alarmist views of some factions within orthodox medicine. Given the high levels of iatrogenic disease, it would hardly be politic for the medical profession to claim that complementary medicine is directly harmful. There would, additionally be the difficulty of sustaining such an assertion in the almost total absence of any negligence claims. Their case now tends to rest on an argument that 'the most innocuous of practices may be harmful if they prevent the patient from seeking other, more appropriate treatment . . . '.[11] Not only would the supplementary mode of usage suggest that this is less of a problem than is sometimes claimed, but, critically, the BMA *Report* entirely overlooks the fact that the majority of codes of practice within complementary medicine now have a clause which fixes therapists with an explicit duty to recommend that patients see their doctor.

A potentially more intractable problem which we will go on to

[8] Thomas, K. J., *et al.*, 'Use of non-orthodox and conventional health care in Great Britain' 302 BMJ 207–10 (1991).

[9] Fulder, S. J. and Munro, R. C., 'Complementary Medicine in the U.K.: patients, practitioners and consultations', *The Lancet* 2 (1985) 542–5.

[10] Parker, G. and Tupling, H., *Consumer Evaluation of Natural Therapies*. Parker Report No. 2, App. 11 of the *Report of the Committee of Inquiry into Chiropractic, Osteopathy, Homoeopathy and Naturopathy* (Australian Government Publishers, 1977). Cited in Fulder S., *The Handbook of Complementary Medicine* (Coronet, London, 1988) p. 37.

[11] *Complementary Medicine: New Approaches to Good Practice*, (BMA, OUP, 1993) p. 60.

discuss is the difficulty that complementary practitioners face when dealing with patients who positively do not wish to discuss the fact that they are using non-conventional therapies with their GP. The extent to which this is a problem is difficult to determine and may vary significantly according to the relationship between patient and doctor. In Sharma's survey, only a minority (30 per cent) of interviewees had told their general practitioner that they were using non-orthodox medicine.[12]

We suggest that this lack of communication is not conducive to high standards of patient safety, but that the responsibility for its improvement is something which will require the active commitment and positive support of the medical profession.

A further issue in relation to usage patterns is the question of whether patients use complementary therapies for certain types of medical problems. Fulder suggests that complementary health practitioners are more commonly consulted by patients for the treatment of musculo-skeletal problems, chronic disorders and stress-related conditions.[13] Interestingly, Ted Kaptchuk has reported a very similar pattern of usage in China where patients have the choice between traditional and Western medicine.[14]

The British Holistic Medical Association, in their reply to the BMA's 1986 *Report on Alternative Therapies* had this to say on the failings of scientific medicine:

Certainly medical science has led to many benefits. However, we face a current situation where medical science is being faced with many challenges and is found wanting. Chronic disease, asthma, diabetes, stress disorders, psychological disorder, and arthritis are not tractable to orthodox medicine. . . . The over-prescribing of medication, the ramifications of iatrogeny, the alienation of patients and the failure to provide access to health care for the poor are all factors which indicate the limitations of orthodox medicine . . .[15]

---

[12] Sharma, U., *Complementary Medicine Today*, p. 55.

[13] Fulder, S. J., *The Handbook of Contemporary Medicine* (Coronet Books, Hodder and Stoughton, 1988).

[14] See: Kaptchuk, T., *Chinese Medicine: The Web that has no Weaver* (Rider, London, 1983) p. 20: 'My observations in clinical situations in China and in reading the literature points to a rough tendency to use Western medicine in acute and emergency situations and Chinese medicine in chronic situations. Often, however, the choice is left to patients, and also commonly both systems are used simultaneously . . .'.

[15] British Holistic Medical Association, *Report on the British Medical Association Board of Science Working Party on Alternative Therapy* (1986).

Thus the *supplementary* manner in which patients use complementary medicine may well reveal a pattern of choice among consumers which is quite logical—they are using complementary medicine to deal with the kinds of health problems which orthodox medicine is not especially good at treating. Much more research is needed before any definitive conclusion can be reached, but the pattern that is emerging is, without doubt, one of an increasingly pluralist approach to health care. It is not unduly cynical to suggest that it is precisely the likelihood of this fact emerging that has prevented the Department of Health from investing significant sums of money on research into complementary medicine.

The proliferation of self-care approaches to well-being can also be seen as part of the private health care sector. A very important part of the philosophy of the holistic approach to health is the emphasis it places on self-responsibility. Parallel to the growth in complementary therapies, there has been a corresponding increase in self-care techniques: yoga, relaxation, tai chi, and baby massage courses have become available in evening courses throughout much of the country. This growth in self-care has also extended to an increased use of natural medicine products, health foods, and home remedies. An example of the extent to which alternative remedies have infiltrated mainstream culture is that Boots the Chemist recently launched a range of homoeopathic remedies for sale over the counter. Vitamin supplements, herbal remedies, and essential oils are now routinely on sale throughout many chemists in the United Kingdom. The natural health business has become a multi-million pound industry in Britain alone.[16]

So significant is this growth that complementary medicine can be said to have substantially changed the way many people now respond to their own physical, emotional, and spiritual well-being. Arguably, this interest in complementary medicine and self-care activities is not only indicative of the way people are now thinking about their own health, but has also changed expectations of the treatment people would like to receive from orthodox health care professionals. The popular health movement, linked as it is to a disaffection with technological medicine, is being interpreted as realignment away from the traditional disease-based model to one which is focused more on positive health, participation, and a 'whole person' approach.[17] Of necessity such a reorientation requires doctors to be able and willing

---

[16] Mintel statistics.
[17] See, e.g., Pietroni, P., *The Greening of Medicine*, p. 179.

to move away from the paternalistic therapeutic relationship which has characterized the clinical transaction of biomedicine to date.

The growth of complementary therapies and self-care techniques involves doctors in assessments and decisions for which they are frequently unprepared. Techniques such as yoga and relaxation have earned the respect of the medical profession, but the majority of doctors would appear to have little understanding of most complementary therapies. [18] This should not necessarily be seen as a reflection of orthodox hostility; as the BMA's 1993 Report points out, there is a real problem in obtaining reliable information about both the therapies and the practitioners. While some of the reluctance of doctors to discuss complementary therapies with their patients stems from suspicion, ignorance, and hostility, an overriding factor must be the legal uncertainty which still surrounds the issue of the clinical accountability of doctors in referring/delegating to complementary health practitioners.

B. Within the NHS

The dramatic expansion of complementary medicine on the scale of the past fifteen years could not fail eventually to have an impact on orthodox medicine and on the NHS. Initially interest was shown by individual doctors, notably general practitioners. Surveys suggest that there is a marked increase of interest in complementary medicine among GPs. A 1986 survey showed that 38 per cent of the respondents had received some training in non-conventional therapies and an additional 15 per cent expressed an interest in doing so in the future.[19]

A number of organizations have been established for doctors qualified in non-conventional disciplines: in addition to the Faculty of Homoeopathy, there is now the British Medical Acupuncture Society, the British Osteopathic Society and the British Society of Medical and Dental Hypnosis. The British Holistic Medical Association, founded in 1983, serves as a forum for all doctors with an interest in the holistic approach. These organizations are a reflection of the main areas of interest in complementary therapies among doctors. There are still no very reliable statistics of the numbers of doctors practising

[18] See *Complementary Medicine: New Approaches to Good Practice*, BMA, p. 148.
[19] See Wharton, R. and Lewith, G., 'Complementary Medicine and the general practitioner', 292 BMJ p. 498–500 (1986).

non-conventional therapies but Fulder and Munro's estimate of 2,000 is probably not far out.[20]

As more general practitioners become supportive of, and qualified in, complementary therapies, it is possible that initiatives such as the Marylebone Health Centre will become more widespread. The Marylebone Health Centre, which opened in 1987, offers non-conventional therapies in addition to the more familiar orthodox treatment associated with general practice. An important part of the service provided by the centre is the educational programme of courses ranging from yoga to relaxation and music therapy. In Pietroni's words, the aim of this programme of activities 'is to enable patients to take control of their own health and well-being . . .'.[21]

Assessing the extent to which non-conventional therapies are now available in hospitals is even more problematic. Initiatives tend to be isolated and related to the interests of individual doctors. Many of the London teaching hospitals now employ complementary practitioners, or use the skills of nurses who have qualified in complementary therapies.

The National Health Service Acts impose few direct legal constraints on the provision of unorthodox medicine under the NHS. While the Secretary of State has a statutory duty to provide a comprehensive health service, nowhere in the Acts is the term 'medicine' defined in such a way as to preclude unorthodox therapies. Furthermore, in 1949 the Minister of Health gave an 'absolute guarantee' that homoeopathy would continue to be available within the NHS as long as there was a demand. However, the exclusively orthodox nature of all medical training has ensured that, with the exception of homoeopathy, non-conventional medicine was unavailable under the NHS until very recently.

It is interesting to consider why homoeopathy, which in terms of its therapeutics is most at variance with orthodox medicine, should have received sufficient support from the Government to be able to maintain a number of specialized hospitals. Currently there are five such hospitals in the public sector, in London, Liverpool, Bristol, Tunbridge Wells, and Glasgow. Part of the explanation must lie with the fact that homoeopathy was able to gain the interest of a number of orthodox doctors shortly after its introduction to England in the early

[20] Fulder, S. J. and Munro, R., *The Status of Complementary Medicine in the United Kingdom.*
[21] Pietroni, P., *The Greening of Medicine*, p. 194.

nineteenth century. A Faculty of Homoeopathy was established as early as 1844 to train doctors in homoeopathic medicine. Homoeopathy enjoyed the advantages of an influential clientele, including the royal family; it also commanded the support of a number of active campaigning and fund-raising groups. Thus, while the State has given little positive financial encouragement to homoeopathy either by way of the provision of facilities or grants for training, it has tolerated its existence ensuring that State medicine in Britain was never entirely closed to unorthodox medicine.

Greater integration of complementary medicine into the NHS could have a number of consequences which practitioners may not anticipate. Were there to be widespread integration, an element of formality would become more likely, and although practitioners might strive to retain their freedom to provide an individualized service, more of a conveyor-belt system would be inevitable, given the number of patients a practitioner would probably be seeing.[22] The highly personalized elements of the therapeutic relationship might be lost, due to constraints on the practitioner's time. This could lead to similar dissatisfactions currently expressed by patients in relation to orthodox practitioners. An unfortunate corollary of greater integration might be an increase in legal actions brought against complementary practitioners. Critically, if complementary practitioners were to be employed by the NHS, then, in the event of a mishap, the public would feel not that they were suing an individual, in whom they had put their faith, but that they were suing a faceless NHS Trust.

Within the NHS, certain regulatory pressures would inevitably be brought to bear as a result of integration. Primarily, this is because where therapists are employed by a health authority or NHS Trust, the health authority or NHS Trust will assume contractual liability for the therapists. Health authorities and NHS Trusts, as corporate bodies, are legally liable for the negligent acts of their employees in the course of their NHS employment.[23] Alternatively, if practitioners were working in the NHS on a self-employed basis, health authorities and NHS Trusts would only accept practitioners whose professional organization required them to have indemnity insurance, so that they could, if appropriate, seek a contribution in the event of negligence.

[22] A pilot scheme at the Central Middlesex Hospital in which patients have access to osteopaths or physiotherapists whilst they are on the waiting-list to see an orthopaedic specialist has 20-minute appointment slots for osteopathic treatment (including changing time).
[23] See HC (89) 34.

Either way, it will be in the interests of the NHS to insist that they are only using properly qualified therapists who belong to a responsible professional organization with a strong code of ethics.[24]

It is important to appreciate that although osteopathy and chiropractic have become statutorily regulated, this does not necessarily mean that these therapies will ever be available under the NHS. Equally, the *availability* of complementary medicine under the NHS does not *per se* signify integration. Since the enactment of the Osteopaths Act 1993 and the Chiropractors Act 1994, the existence of a statutory register may make it easier for doctors to recommend a practitioner with confidence, and some of them may do so, but this does not necessarily mean osteopathic services have become integrated within the NHS. In fact, the Osteopaths Act 1993 is noticeably silent on the subject of the availability of osteopathy within the NHS. This is not integration, but perhaps it is only a matter of time before the integration of osteopathic services comes on the political agenda.

Full integration would be a situation in which a number of therapeutic modes were made available to patients within the NHS. While integration is a much-discussed issue within complementary medicine, there is little real chance that rapid integration will take place in the near future. However, the more complementary medicine is made available within the NHS, the more likely it is that integration issues will influence the course of regulation.

Health service managers are beginning to take an increased interest in complementary therapies. This is partly in consequence of a recognition that there must be significant unmet demand; many patients are asking for complementary therapies to be made available, and are unable to obtain them privately because of the cost. If there is such strong demand for complementary therapies among patients then, arguably, serious consideration should be given to the possibility of providing them on the NHS. A recent survey published in April 1993 conducted by the National Association of Health Authorities and Trusts showed that £1 million is spent annually on alternative therapies by just 38 health authorities and 34 fund-holding practices. This

[24] The Complementary Medical Practitioners Union now represents complementary practitioners working in the NHS. The CMPU is an autonomous section of the MSF, one of the UK's largest trade unions. CMPU membership is open to qualified practitioners on the British Register of Complementary Practitioners (*infra*) or comparable register. It lists as its benefits of membership: legal advice and representation, health and safety advice, pensions advice, and professional representation at a national level.

figure is predicted by NAHAT to run into tens of millions for the NHS as a whole, and NHS managers are now calling for more money to be spent on complementary therapies to cope with the growing popularity.

There are a number of obstacles to the greater introduction of complementary therapies in the NHS. One major problem is the lack of scientific validation of the efficacy of many of these therapies. If the major criteria for the integration of complementary therapies rests on an insistence on proof of efficacy in scientific terms, then many therapies will effectively be barred from ever becoming available. Related to this problem is the issue of establishing cost-efficiency. If a complementary therapy cannot conclusively be shown to *work* its cost-efficiency must also remain in doubt. However, the interest of nurses taking up such therapies as aromatherapy indicates that other factors will be taken into account. Particularly in the areas of care of the terminally ill and pain management, more subjective assessment of the value of these therapies is likely to be sufficient to convince purchasers that such therapies are valuable additions to the range of more orthodox care.

Other difficulties in the way of greater integration include the lack of sufficient highly trained therapists to work with the NHS. Studies have shown that there is already an uneven geographical distribution of therapists which would act as a barrier to providing such services on a national basis. The primary point is that if and when larger numbers of complementary therapists begin to work within the NHS, a number of legal and ethical considerations will have to be worked through, which will inevitably have a bearing on the regulatory debate.

It is reasonable to suppose that the unmet demand is, at least partly, a consequence of the lack of understanding about the legal and ethical dimensions of complementary medicine. Resources are another factor, but cost-efficiency exercises are currently being conducted at Lewisham and elsewhere. If a saving is shown, this may act as a spur to introduce more therapies. If it can definitively be established that complementary therapy can not only work but be cheaper to deliver, then the NHS can be expected to commit itself to a far greater extent to the provision of complementary health care. Should the NHS then introduce complementary therapies on a wider scale, policy decisions will have to be taken on such issues as whether to employ non-medically qualified staff. Here there will be something of a dilemma. One might expect doctors delegating treatment to prefer to do so when a practitioner is registered with a central body. However, ensuring this would necessitate wide-scale regulations which neither the medical profession nor the Government may want. This will increase the argument for greater use of medically qualified personnel and will slow down the rate of integration. Integration however, may conceivably have the effect of speeding up the move towards statutory regulation for some therapies.

It is impossible to escape the impression that the real drive to bring complementary therapies into the NHS has been consumer demand. Some authorities are looking at the cost-saving and efficacy implications of complementary therapies, but despite the more ambitious schemes such as that at Lewisham, most of these initiatives are very small scale. The conclusion would have to be that at present integration is not a critical determining issue in how complementary medicine should be regulated.

C. Traditional Medicine in the United Kingdom

Traditional medicine such as Ayurveda, Unani, Siddha medicine and traditional Chinese herbal medicine continue to be used by the Asian community in addition to the orthodox medicine available through the NHS. Traditional practitioners have established themselves within immigrant communities and cater to the Asian community, many of whom may prefer to see a practitioner from their own ethnic and cultural background. One author estimated ten years ago that there were approximately five hakims in every city in Britain with a significant Asian population: indeed, demand is such that a number of hakims regularly fly over to Britain for temporary consultations.[25]

There are a number of problems relating to the use of traditional medicine in Britain. One well-publicized problem is the uncontrolled availability of unlicensed imported Asian drugs, some of which contain unacceptably high levels of poisonous heavy metals.[26] A further problem, which is potentially very harmful, is that of authenticating plants. Experienced Chinese practitioners of traditional Chinese

---

[25] Bannerman, R., Burton, J., Ch'en, W. C. (edd.), *Traditional Medicine and Health Care Coverage*, p. 242.
[26] Ibid., p. 242. See also: Fulder, S. J., *The Handbook of Complementary Medicine*, p. 164.

herbal medicines in London describe the problems in obtaining, not just plants of a suitably high quality, but the *correct* plants.

   This uncontrolled and unregulated availability of traditional medicines poses a number of difficult political as well as regulatory problems. It is known that many of these remedies are untested and, furthermore, that not all practitioners of traditional Asian medicine are equally well trained and competent. The Government however, seems concerned not to intervene in too heavy-handed a way. It may be assumed that this reluctance is partly based on a respect for cultural diversity in health care matters and for the right of individuals to make their own health care choices. However, this apparent tolerance may also be indicative of a lack of understanding of health care within the more closed ethnic communities. Unless there were strong evidence of abuse, the Government would be unlikely to interfere with what might be viewed as the rights of individuals to choose the traditional health care therapies in which they have confidence.

   The pressure on the Government to take a firmer line may well be precipitated now that traditional ethnic medicines are beginning to be used outside ethnic groups. There are estimated to be more than 600 clinics offering traditional Chinese medicine in the United Kingdom. Part of this increase in public interest in traditional Chinese herbal medicine is the consequence of media coverage of its success in the treatment of disorders such as eczema. However, equal publicity has recently been given to some of its tragedies.[27] Less sensationally, Dr John Harper, a Consultant in paediatric dermatology at Great Ormond Street has written on the dangers of unsupervised prescribing of Chinese herbs for treating eczema.[28]

   The extension of ethnic medicine to communities which have no tradition of these therapies is not without its problems. Many of these difficulties arise as a consequence of translocating the practices of one medical culture into another, very different culture. As the popularity of traditional Asian medicine grows, so do the number of schools purporting to teach these therapies. Some of these schools offer

---

[27] E.g., *The Times* reported a case of 30 women who were prescribed Chinese herbs in a Brussels clinic as part of a slimming treatment and who subsequently suffered severe kidney damage: 'with 30 of them needing dialysis or transplants to keep them alive . . . '. 'Old Chinese cure or killer?' Nigel Hawkes, *The Times*, 1 Feb. 1994. The women had been given the wrong herb, a mistake which apparently arose out of the fact that there are three plants with the same name in Chinese, *fangchi*.

[28] See Harper, J., 'Traditional Chinese medicine for eczema' 308 BMJ 308 (1994).

a reasonable training, but all too many offer inadequate, attenuated courses attracting, for the main part, English-speaking students with no knowledge of the language or culture from which such therapies derive. Such students have no access to the rich heritage of original writings on the subject, neither can they usually read product information relating to the imported herbs and medicinal preparations they prescribe. Equally important, they have almost no access to the long and protracted apprenticeship systems that are considered such a vital part of the training in these therapies in the country of origin.

In short there are significant dangers in the extension of therapies beyond the confines of the ethnic communities that they serve. It cannot be considered desirable that therapies such as Ayurveda and Chinese herbal medicine which require years of serious and arduous training in the country of origin, should be available in Britain from practitioners whose training sometimes amounts to little more than a year or two of part-time study. It is interesting that even in those countries with a long history of traditional medicine, some Governments are introducing regulation as a consequence of the breakdown of the framework of traditional training methods. In Japan, for example, traditional herbal medicine (*kampo*) is only available from a registered medical practitioner or from a properly licensed pharmacy. However, since 1976, *Kampo* medicine, prescribed by a registered medical practitioner, is covered by health insurance. In 1988, the Japanese Oriental Medicine Society was approved as part of the Japan Medical Association: a system was also established for doctors wishing to specialize and qualify in Oriental Medicine. The Japanese Government has also introduced the licensing systems for acupuncture and shiatsu.

In conclusion, it is unlikely that the Government will intervene unless there are compelling reasons for doing so. However, if prohibitive legislation is enacted as a consequence of the misuse of traditional herbal medicine within the 'white' community, this may prejudice the choice of ethnic communities to use their own medicine and will raise some sensitive political issues. The growing interest in Asian traditional medicine in Britain is a reflection of the increasing plurality of health care in Britain, and of the need for policy-makers to take account of the issues which will eventually emerge as a consequence of this diversity.

D. Global Increase

This remarkable and sustained increase in the use of non-orthodox medicine is not confined to Britain but can be observed on a more or less global basis. Statistics on the usage of complementary medicine are broadly reflected throughout many of the developed countries of the West. While this is unlikely to have a direct impact on the direction of regulation within Britain, it will almost certainly add to the political argument for taking complementary therapies seriously. The issues we address throughout this book have their counterpart in many countries throughout the world: some of the solutions discussed and implemented by other countries may also provide potential models of regulation within Britain.

We have already made reference to the developments in Third World nations, many of whom have instituted policies to promote the greater use of traditional medicine at primary care level. To accommodate this policy shift, some developing countries have changed, or are in the process of changing, the monopolistic position of orthodox medicine which has characterized their inherited legal systems. However, most relevant to Britain's experience are parallel developments observable in almost all of the world's industrialized countries to include and make greater use of non-orthodox therapies. Similar increases in the usage of complementary medicine are reported in Europe.[29]

II. PROBLEMS ASSOCIATED WITH GROWTH

With one or two notable exceptions the growth of complementary medicine has not been accompanied by a corresponding growth in negligence claims despite its unregulated state. There may be a number of reasons why this should be so. One of the reasons most commonly given by practitioners of complementary medicine is that the therapies are safe and lacking in toxic side-effects and therefore unlikely to cause harm to patients. Another reason that has been put forward to explain the lack of litigation in this area is that the

---

[29] For an overview, see the article by Fisher, P. and Ward, A.: 'Complementary Medicine in Europe', 309 BMJ 107–8 (1994) and BMA *Complementary Medicine: New Approach to Good Practice*, Ch. 2.

relationship between the patient and therapist which characterizes complementary medicine, with its reliance on shared responsibility, is not likely to result in problems serious enough to warrant litigation. Despite the almost complete absence of legal activity in this area, it is quite common to see warnings of impending legal catastrophe, often curiously unsubstantiated. In a chapter entitled 'Therapeutic responsibility and the law', Robert Summerling writes: 'I have not discovered any recently reported cases of civil negligence against complementary practitioners in the United Kingdom. This suggests that complementary practitioners have only a limited time in which to organise themselves to meet professional negligence claims . . .'.[30]

If, after ten years of sustained and increased usage of complementary therapies, there is still no rush of negligence cases, the most logical conclusion to draw is quite the opposite—that professional negligence claims will be the *least* of the factors influencing complementary practitioners to organize themselves. So, when we talk about legal problems, we need to make it clear that we do not consider negligence as the most pressing legal problem that complementary medicine has to face. Primarily, we are interested in the *potential* problems which may conceivably arise as a consequence of both the increased usage of complementary medicine and as a consequence of its greater integration within a National Health Service which is largely unprepared for the event in any legal sense.

A. Within complementary medicine

Many of the difficulties which beset complementary medicine have their origins in organizational weaknesses of one kind or another. There is a wide divergence between those therapies which are well-established with well-organized infrastructures and those therapies which are fragmented, disunited, and disorganized. While the overall trend to organization is improving, as we shall see, this trend is by no means universal.

This should surprise no one. With one or two very recent exceptions, training in complementary therapies has always been in the hands of private, usually profit-based enterprises. Many such schools are small and run on a strict budget by men and women with little

---

[30] Summerling, R. 'Therapeutic Responsibility and the Law' in Budd, S., and Sharma, U., *The Healing Bond: The patient-practitioner relationship and therapeutic responsibility* (Routledge, 1994) p. 140.

time to spare for the costly and often unrewarding business of trade union and political activity. Equally, until the last decade or so, there was no very strong compulsion to become organized.

Complementary medicine, composed of dozens of small and often disparate therapies, has none of the organizational infrastructures that have been set up to support and organize orthodox medicine. In addition, complementary medicine, which generally eschews pharmaceutical drugs, has never had the financial backing of drug companies for research and publishing purposes that orthodox medicine receives.

There are other factors, however, which explain why complementary medicine remains organizationally weak. An important reason, which still underlies the apparent slowness with which some therapies are able to unite, is that the commercial basis of training schools inhibits the development of unified training standards. Many schools teaching complementary medicine have been set up by individuals who have developed their own particular theoretical approach, often at variance with that offered in other schools. Commercial survival may depend on the maintenance of these philosophical and theoretical distinctions thus making initiatives in the direction of the unification of training standards extremely difficult. The schism within aromatherapy with regard to the prescription of oils for internal ingestion is an example of this problem.

Some therapies, notably those seeking statutory regulation, are now well organized with highly formalized codes of practice and disciplinary procedures. The success with which these therapies have been able to organize themselves is creditable and has done much to impress the Government of their willingness to set their own house in order.

Beyond these well-established therapies the situation is too often a messy and disorganized array of fragmentary legitimizing bodies which must be a cause of considerable bewilderment to even the most determined and conscientious of consumers. This fragmentation has several drawbacks with potential legal consequences. It is difficult to establish the precise nature of the credentials of most complementary therapists. There are often several different legitimizing bodies, all issuing their own diplomas and often with wide variations in standards of training. Thus, notwithstanding the recent formation of the British Acupuncture Council, there are still plenty of courses around which offer inadequate training in acupuncture, often without substantial clinical exposure. One such course offers instruction by way of videos! The existence of three major pan-professional organizations adds to the confusion.

As can be seen, with many therapies, it is quite impossible for responsible consumers to identify easily what a therapist's qualifications actually mean. How do they compare to other qualifications held by therapists practising in the same field? How do consumers know that the qualifications a therapist claims to have are indeed genuine? In reality, at present, with one or two exceptions, most complementary therapists can call themselves whatever they like and get away with it. They can, and some do, give themselves bogus qualifications, or claim allegiance to an association that has no real meaning. In the end, the consumer will usually rely on word of mouth; failing this, she will take pot luck. If she is fortunate and makes her choice well, the lack of preliminary objective information may not matter, but problems do occur if the consumer is unfortunate and finds herself with an incompetent or even negligent practitioner. Then the problems of organization weakness are compounded. As we shall see in Part II, an aggrieved consumer may well find she has no adequate means of redress; there may be no complaints or disciplinary procedures, and her grievances either go unheard or the response is weak and ineffectual.

B. Within orthodox medicine

1. General

A problem which exists quite independently of any difficulties within complementary medicine, is the reluctance of many doctors to recommend a therapy they do not really understand or have any knowledge about. It has to be said that this attitude is sometimes compounded by an intrinsically hostile approach to complementary medicine. Osteopathy and chiropractic have suffered significantly from this problem for years. Their skills are documented as being of significant help in dealing with back pain and yet GPs have often been loath to recommend that a patient consult an osteopath or a chiropractor. Although, as we have suggested, gaining statutory recognition may partially remedy this situation, there is no guarantee that this will be the case. Some doctors will remain implacably hostile to complementary medicine and no amount of reform or regulation will change their attitude. These doctors choose to remain ill-informed, and will frequently mask their hostility with views on the scientific uncertainty, and more recently, the legal uncertainty which blights complementary medicine.

This issue aside, doctors have much the same difficulty as a consumer when it comes to working out who is a properly qualified complementary practitioner. The consequences for a doctor making a faulty decision could be as devastating. As *gatekeepers*, their task is to recommend certain kinds of specialist treatment, and it is critical for patients and practitioners that they may be able to do so with confidence.

However, this is just one of a number of communication problems that have potential legal implications. Many complementary therapists, for example, have only rudimentary or basic training in the biological and physiological sciences. Who is to take responsibility for the fact that much medical terminology would go beyond many complementary therapists' understanding? A variation of this problem operates in reverse: an acupuncturist working with the *classical Chinese meridian model* may be quite unintelligible to an orthodox doctor. How are both sorts of practitioners to communicate, and, very importantly, who is responsible should this communication break down with serious consequences for the patient? How are health care professionals to communicate when they operate with two different notions of disease? Is this likely to cause confusion, and possible distress for the patient? What about the doctor using holistic therapies? Does a patient have a right to know what model of disease a therapist is working with, and, if so, is this likely to result in potential distress and confusion?

Given these problems, it is not surprising that many conventional doctors should express a desire that non-orthodox treatment in a NHS environment be administered by qualified health care professionals. On the face of it, this approach has much to commend it. However, the situation in which health care professionals are able to 'qualify' in therapies such as acupuncture by attending a few weekend sessions, is clearly not an appropriate solution. Why should it be thought that a doctor need spend only a few weekends acquiring the skills which make take a lay practitioner three years of full-time study?

In the recent 1993 BMA *Report on Complementary Medicine*, the guidelines of the General Medical Council were reiterated to the effect that a charge of serious professional misconduct may arise by 'a doctor persisting in unsupervised practice of a branch of medicine without having the appropriate knowledge and skill or having acquired the skill which is necessary . . . '.[31]

The BMA therefore recommended that: 'Medically qualified practitioners wishing to practice any form of non-conventional therapy should undertake recognised training in that field approved by the appropriate regulatory body, and should only practise after registration'.[32]

There is more than a little uncertainty as to the extent of doctors' professional and legal liability in relation to recommending complementary practitioners to patients. As these have been used as a reason for not working with complementary practitioners, it is necessary to spend some time unravelling these issues.

2. Delegation or referral?

In an attempt to make the position on the provision of complementary medicine within the NHS more clear, Stephen Dorrell, the then Parliamentary Secretary of State for Health, issued a statement in December 1991. The statement was to the effect that a doctor may delegate the treatment of patients to complementary therapists providing he remains clinically accountable for the patient. However, it was stressed that:

It is not a 'referral' system, whereby one practitioner refers to a patient for treatment by another. It is a 'delegation' system, whereby the GP asks another professional to provide care for which he remains clinically accountable. It is therefore for the individual GP to decide in the case of each individual patient whether the alternative therapist offers the most appropriate care to treat the patient's condition . . . [33]

This statement is in accordance with guidance found in paragraphs 42 and 43 of the GMC's *Professional Conduct and Discipline: Fitness to Practise* ('the Blue Book').[34] These sections permit doctors to delegate to persons trained to perform specialized treatments or procedures, provided that the doctor retains ultimate clinical accountability for the overall management of the patient. This was not always the case. The GMC's January 1976 guidance read: 'A doctor who improperly delegates to a person who is not a registered medical

---

[31] BMA, *Complementary Medicine—New Approaches to Good Practice*, p. 148.
[32] Ibid.
[33] *Press Release*, Department of Health, 3 Dec. 1991.
[34] GMC (Dec. 1993).

practitioner duties or functions requiring the knowledge and skill of a medical practitioner is liable to disciplinary proceedings'. In May 1977, the Council modified its stance. It changed its guidance so as to read: 'The Council recognizes and welcomes the growing contribution made to health care by nurses and other persons trained to perform specialised functions . . . '. None the less, it still emphasized the doctor's ultimate responsibility: 'But a doctor who delegates treatment or other procedures must be satisfied that the person to whom they are delegated is competent to carry them out. It is also important that the doctor should retain ultimate responsibility for the management of his patients because only the doctor has received the necessary training to undertake this responsibility'.

Notwithstanding the apparent softening of the GMC's stance, there are still formidable obstacles in the notion of retaining *clinical accountability* which make many doctors wary of utilizing the services of complementary therapists, even if they would like to do so. The more hostile element of the medical profession is at present easily able to take refuge behind vague references to the 'legal uncertainty' of the situation and thus keep public demand effectively at bay. It is hard to assess the impact if barriers to the greater use of complementary therapy were effectively removed by a clearer exposition of the legal liabilities of doctors using them.

One of the main areas of difficulty is the legal significance of the distinction between the powers of *referral* and *delegation*. When a doctor *refers* a patient to another health care professional he does so on an understanding that the specialist to whom he has referred the patient will assess and treat the patient, although the general practitioner retains clinical responsibility for the overall care of the patient. None the less, provided the doctor has made a responsible referral, it is the professional to whom the patient has been referred who will assume professional and legal liability for treating the patient.

By contrast, in the *delegation* model, the doctor transfers tasks to another health care professional but remains *clinically accountable* for the patient throughout that treatment. A GP may incur legal liability for inappropriately delegating a task to someone who is not qualified to perform that task. Thus a GP who employs a practice nurse may be vicariously liable if that nurse harms the patient. This does not mean that the nurse must not also exercise professional accountability and that, in the event of being sued, a contribution would not be sought against the nurse's professional indemnity.

Is the delegation model appropriate for doctors wishing to use the services of complementary practitioners? Both the diagnosis and the treatment will often go beyond the range of the doctor's own expertise. It is thus hard to see how this can properly be regarded as delegation, which presupposes that the skills being delegated are skills which could be performed by the doctor. Realistically, even when complementary practitioners are employed within doctors' surgeries, the relationship is that of referral, not delegation. Politically, however, this interpretation may give rise to problems in that complementary health practitioners would then be classed on a par with specialists.

An additional difficulty, previously discussed, is how doctors can determine who is a properly qualified practitioner. Statutory regulation would remove some of these obstacles in that the doctor would be confident that in referring to a statutorily registered practitioner, this would be a proper exercise of professional accountability. As yet, however, there is no indication from the GMC that they would recommend referrals to statutorily registered professionals. Their view would be that each case turns on its facts, and in each situation the GP would have to demonstrate that the referral was a proper one in all the circumstances.

In summary, whether statutory registration or voluntary self-regulation is sought, no system will work effectively unless the present organizational weaknesses are remedied. This much has always been made plain by Government ministers in their few pronouncements on the matter of regulation for complementary medicine. However, the converse of this is that *no amount of formal regulation* will guarantee more effective and safe incorporation of complementary therapies within the NHS unless other difficulties are resolved. If GPs remain ignorant of the differences between, say, osteopathy, chiropractic, and physiotherapy they will continue to be unwilling to refer patients to osteopaths and chiropractors. Regulation cannot be relied on to solve problems which need to be tackled by other means.

C. Outgrowing existing structures?

The recognized problems attendant upon the growth of complementary medicine can largely be traced to problems of organizational weaknesses. However, it has to be said that the adverse consequences of such weaknesses are more political than directly legal. The pace of change has been so fast that it has rapidly outgrown the organizational structures which presently exist to represent it. As a matter of consumer protection, those therapies without efficient, visible, independent, and accountable disciplinary and complaint procedures will be increasingly criticized and pressurized into providing them. For those therapies set on achieving statutory registration of title, the need for reform is particularly pressing.

Lack of organizational competence will also hold back integration as health service purchasers are often hampered by not knowing which body they should properly negotiate with. However, this is not the disaster it is often held to be. Many therapists are entirely uninterested in working within the NHS in its present state, and unless there is serious political conviction in a drive to provide complementary therapy, the prospect is too remote to occupy the energies of many of the bodies representing complementary medicine.

4

Criteria Which May Shape Regulation

The term 'complementary medicine' groups together so many diverse therapies, that it is now generally accepted that no single regulatory solution will be appropriate for all therapies. Thus, we shall begin our examination by looking at some of the features of complementary therapies in an attempt to identify criteria that will act as a determining influence on the shape of regulation. We shall also ask whether there is any correlation between certain features of these therapies and the types of regulatory solutions in which they are interested.

I. TAXONOMY OF COMPLEMENTARY MEDICINE—FOURFOLD

There have been a number of attempts to find a suitable taxonomy with which to categorize the various healing modalities of complementary medicine. One example is that given by Patrick Pietroni, in his interesting book, *The Greening of Medicine*.[1] His taxonomy was also used by the BMA in its 1993 *Report*.

A. Complete systems of healing

Examples of this category are acupuncture or traditional Chinese medicine, herbal medicine, osteopathy, chiropractic, homoeopathy, and naturopathy. These therapies are characterized by a theoretical base which offers an explanation of the causes of disease. Pietroni writes: 'They have a diagnostic, investigative and therapeutic understanding which share some similarities with orthodox medicine'.[2] The BMA points out that a number of these therapies do not claim to be 'whole systems' of medicine in the same way as orthodox medicine, and prefers the term *discrete clinical disciplines*. However, the 'complete system' approach of these therapies is the feature that distinguishes this group

---

[1] Pietroni, P., *The Greening of Medicine*, p. 180–1.
[2] Ibid., p. 180.

most clearly from other complementary therapies, and accordingly, it exercises a critical influence on such issues as organization and education. Furthermore, it is this group that is usually identified as having the greatest potential to cause harm.[3]

B. Diagnostic methods

Examples of this category are iridology, kinesiology, medical dowsing, and aura diagnosis. These therapies are essentially diagnostic and claim to be able to detect the presence of disease using a wide variety of techniques.

C. Therapeutic modalities

Examples of this category are massage, reflexology, aromatherapy, spiritual healing, and shiatsu. Many of the therapies claim that as they are not based on a complete system of medicine, they do not involve the therapist in making overt diagnostic decisions. It is perhaps truer to say that, in general, these practices are focused on the beneficial action of the *therapeutic effect* rather than on any underlying diagnosis.

D. Self-help measures

Examples of this category are relaxation, yoga, qi gong, tai chi, meditation, guided visualization, fasting. This group includes practices and exercises which have as their object the improvement of health and well-being.

This four-fold categorization is a useful framework in which to discuss the *therapeutic* approach of the various practices which comprise complementary medicine. However, in the context of *regulation*, we shall offer a simpler, two-tiered division, arguing here and in Part II that some therapies are more akin to orthodox medicine and are thus more appropriately regulated in the same way.

Furthermore, the politics of regulation are such that it is likely that this similarity between orthodox medicine and the so-called 'complete systems' of medicine will increase over the next few years. This will be accompanied by an intensification of the argument that where a therapeutic method has the potential to cause serious harm it should

---

[3] BMA, *Complementary Medicine—New Approaches to Good Practice*, p. 61.

be subject to the same regulatory rigour that presently controls orthodox medicine. Additionally, the closer these complementary therapies
come to encroaching on the professional territory of orthodox medicine, the more political sense there will be in those therapies acquiring the protection of statutory recognition in order to secure their
own independence.

The criteria discussed below are all considered relevant to the issue
of regulation. Some criteria will be seen to be more obviously
political than others: but the Government is unlikely to introduce
regulation for complementary therapies without the involvement and
broad agreement of the medical profession.

Complementary therapies may be opposed by the medical profession because they are seen as encroaching on medical territory: some
of them are considered with suspicion because they represent a philosophical, as well as a professional challenge. Those therapies that are
a threat on both counts will find themselves particularly at risk in a
regulatory context. In looking at the criteria below therefore, it is
almost impossible to extricate the political from the purely 'therapeutic' arguments. It is unavoidable that the political context will
determine that some criteria will be more important to the regulatory
debate than others. We shall analyse this point further in Part II.

II. COMPLETE SYSTEMS OF HEALING

Those therapies which are complete systems of medicine will claim
to be able to treat a wide range of disorders and health problems.
Traditional Chinese medicine, Ayurveda, herbalism, homoeopathy,
and naturopathy are the clearest examples of complete systems of
medicine. Today, most of the therapies which belong to this category
are cautious in making this claim, recognizing that they are unable to
deal as effectively as orthodox medicine with emergency and acute
situations.

A 'complete system' therapy will be seen as a greater philosophical
and professional threat to the orthodox profession and hence will be
under significant pressure to substantiate its claims. The history of
decades of hostility and protracted political wrangling will persuade
many practitioners within their respective therapeutic organizations
that long-term security can only be safeguarded by obtaining statutory
registration and protection of title.

III. MODE OF INTERVENTION

The mode of therapeutic intervention will also influence the choice of regulation. Where the therapeutic mode of intervention is comparable to orthodox medicine, there is a *prima facie* argument that similarly formal regulatory mechanisms may be required. Some of the most popular therapies use forms of treatment that can be compared at some level with orthodox medicine. Thus, osteopathy and chiropractic use physical manipulation, including some high-velocity techniques. Herbal medicine and homoeopathy, in a similar way to some chemotherapeutic drugs, depend on ingestive remedies for their therapeutic effect. All these examples have obvious parallels in orthodox medicine. Likewise, although acupuncture works within an entirely different paradigm to orthodox medicine, the concept of sticking needles into people would be recognized as a 'medical' activity which should be restricted to suitably trained practitioners.

IV. POTENTIAL FOR CAUSING HARM

In the opinion of the British Medical Association, patients can be caused harm in two ways:

(1) Where a therapy is directly harmful if practised by an untrained or incompetent practitioner.

(2) If the patient is prevented from seeking appropriate orthodox care which could provide a more effective cure. The implication here is that harm may result as a consequence of serious medical problems going undetected or ignored.[4]

The second definition of harm is one that is applied across the board to all complementary therapies. We take the view that this suggestion is prompted more by political considerations, unsupported as it is with any evidence that this is happening on a scale to cause concern. The differentiation of these two sorts of harm has legal implications as well. As we shall go on to see in Part II, whilst it may be possible, theoretically, to base a cause of action on the first sort of harm, it will be almost impossible to do so in the second situation.

A more plausible argument can, in fact, be constructed to support

---

[4] BMA, *Complementary Medicine—New Approaches to Good Practice*, p. 60.

quite the reverse proposition: that people who are prepared to pay for complementary medicine are among those who place a high priority on their own health. Statistics show that those people using complementary medicine are *more* likely to have seen their GP recently.[5] Additionally, as is now known, they are likely to use complementary medicine as a supplement to, and not a substitute for, orthodox treatment.

Complementary practitioners habitually emphasize the preventative nature of their approach. People who make regular use of bodywork therapies such as osteopathy, chiropractic, aromatherapy, and massage, will receive the kind of whole body scrutiny that a doctor very rarely provides. Furthermore, most therapists are well aware of their ethical obligation to recommend medical attention. It is thus logical to suggest that users of complementary medicine are *more* likely to have their serious health problems detected at an early stage.

The only situation in which taking the advice of a complementary health practitioner might conceivably be harmful is where the therapist takes advantage of a vulnerable patient and persuades him not to seek medical advice. The possibility of the therapist exercising undue influence on the ability of a patient to make a rational choice about treatment is an ethical issue and will be discussed in Part III. But this problem cannot be considered exclusive to complementary medicine. One feels obliged to ask just how many patients have endured years of needless back pain largely because their doctors have forcefully discouraged them from even investigating the possibility of osteopathic treatment.

Therefore, for the above reasons, we confine our discussion to the significance of the potential to cause harm to that of the first type, that is, direct physical harm being caused by an incompetent or unskilled practitioner. Despite the assertions that herbal and homoeopathic remedies are relatively non-toxic and lacking in side-effects, the argument linking mode of therapeutic intervention to the potential to cause harm is inescapable and rightly given considerable attention. The degree of skill and training required in these therapies must therefore be of a significantly higher standard than that which is accepted as being adequate in other therapies.

The difficulty in determining what is a high standard of training in any healing therapy is that the standard is now heavily influenced by that of the medical profession. Thus, it will be impossible to sustain any

[5] Ibid., pp. 30–1.

claim to a high standard of training unless the curriculum includes substantial training in the biomedical sciences, anatomy and physiology and, in some cases, pharmacology. In order for these therapies to support their claim to a safe and high standard of training, they will be forced into adopting a standard largely determined and defined by the practice of scientific medicine. This may, of necessity, result in profound changes in the nature of those therapies which decide to opt for this approach.

IV. DEGREE OF SKILL REQUIRED

Some therapeutic skills within complementary medicine may be seen as a gift or as being dependent on intuitive abilities as well as rational knowledge. However, for those therapies called upon to justify their standards of practice and training, there will be a considerable pull towards an increasingly knowledge-based approach. This will partly be a consequence of the need to teach subjects which previously had not been given much prominence. It will also be the consequence of having to establish more rigorous examination procedures. Factual, and especially, scientific knowledge is more easily measurable and examinable.

VI. SCIENTIFIC VALIDATION

This issue is linked to the interminable argument of whether the law should be used to legitimize therapies which have no proven scientific validity. Certainly, the argument that therapies should be able to provide scientific validation of their efficacy before winning the right to statutory protection is very prominent within the medical establishment.

Governments do not necessarily give this argument the weight that some in the medical profession would like to see. The Commission for Alternative Systems of Medicine established by the Dutch Government produced a Report in which it was stated:

The Commission believes that the division between alternative and orthodox medicine is not—or is not principally—of a scientific nature, but owes its origins and its continued existence to both politico-social and scientific factors. This implies that the gap cannot be closed simply by making scientific recommendations. The demand that alternative practitioners must demonstrate the effectiveness of their treatment before they can be granted any form of recognition thus seems to the Commission to be indefensible.[6]

It is being increasingly accepted that when usage levels of complementary therapies are reaching 25 per cent of the population, an insistence on scientific validation is at worst a 'red herring' and at best a detraction from the need to focus on higher priorities such as establishing higher training standards,

Nevertheless, the argument for scientific validation is likely to remain very strong, especially for the discrete clinical disciplines. Unless such therapies can eventually substantiate their claims through scientific research *in some form or other*, they are likely to lose some of their therapeutic and political credibility. It is yet another factor that will draw these therapies towards standards of training and therapeutic practices that will increasingly have more in common with scientific medicine.

VII. QUANTIFIABLE RESULTS

The more a therapy is centred on the administration of an ingestive remedy or an invasive technique, the more the nature of the therapeutic intervention can be determined with precision, and thus the more amenable to measurement. The more that skill in a therapy is determined by the acquisition of scientific knowledge, the greater will be the need for systems of assessment to test that knowledge. Hence the likelihood of a greater prominence given to examinable, quantifiable, measurable skills, possibly at the expense of more *'humanistic'* skills. Thus it is arguable that some therapies, most notably the discrete clinical disciplines, will gravitate to a greater bias towards the quantifiable and measurable, for much the same reasons as orthodox medicine.

VIII. HOW LONG ESTABLISHED?

Some therapies, such as herbalism have been practised in England for centuries. Others, such as acupuncture, have been practised in their

[6] *Alternative Medicine in the Netherlands*. Summary of the *Report of the Commission for Alternative Systems of Medicine* (The Hague, 1981).

culture of origin for thousands of years, but are relatively new to England. There are a large number of the smaller therapies which have their origins within the past sixty years, many having emerged with the New Age movement. More important than the length of establishment is the degree of organization of the therapy. A credible system of voluntary regulation will be a vital pre-requisite of statutory regulation. The osteopaths and chiropractors were well established and well organized as professional groups for decades before achieving statutory recognition.

IX. DEGREE OF MEDICAL INTEREST

It might be thought that those therapies which most obviously fall foul of scientific theory would be the therapies less likely to win medical support. The success of homoeopathy proves that this is not necessarily the case. Medical interest in both acupuncture and homoeopathy suggests that incompatibility is less of a barrier than lay practice. In general, the greater the degree of congruence between the complementary therapy and orthodox medical practice, the greater the interest is likely to be within the medical profession. Arguments about the need for these therapies to be regulated or administered by trained medical personnel will surface with more vigour. It is, for example, unlikely that doctors will take an abiding interest in practising aromatherapy, and therefore will not be overly active in issues related to its regulation. The situation concerning homoeopathy is, however, quite different. It is the *lay* practice of unorthodox therapy to which doctors seem particularly hostile, particularly where there is a strong practising medical wing.

A further relevant factor is the extent to which these therapies can be explained in more relevant mechanistic terms and thus isolated from their alien philosophical underpinnings. This is most obvious in the medical application of acupuncture which is often stripped of its underlying traditional philosophy and used mainly for pain relief.

X. CREDIBILITY

As a matter of common sense, it can be expected that the more cranky the therapy, the less likely it is that it will achieve statutory recognition. However, credibility is determined by many factors—a high profile patronage may confer credibility, so also does scientific validation. It also depends on who is defining credibility. The medical profession tend to consider credibility as being wholly dependent on scientific validation. However, the degree to which aromatherapy and reflexology are being taken up by the nursing profession suggests that credibility even among orthodox health care professionals can be differently defined.

XI. SUMMARY

Most of the therapies which can be described as complete systems of medicine are also those that have the greatest potential to harm the patient. Consequently, these are the therapies that will be under the greatest pressure to ensure safe standards of practice. Herbal medicine, traditional Chinese medicine (including acupuncture), homoeopathy and naturopathy are the therapies most clearly identified. If they have not already done so, most of them are likely to recognize that statutory regulation will be the most effective way of securing high standards within their profession and of simultaneously protecting their future existence. However, in order to win autonomous regulation, they will have to satisfy certain requirements, most of which will be strongly influenced by the medical profession.

In order to maintain their therapeutic and political credibility, such therapies will increasingly be drawn into recognizing the necessity of demonstrating the efficacy of their therapies in scientific terms. Additionally, they will also be under intense pressure to demonstrate the *safety* of their therapeutic practices. They will find it increasingly difficult to rely on the argument that their therapy has been used safely for hundreds of years. Thus, alongside establishing clinical validity, they will be drawn into incorporating ever more biomedical science into their training courses to strengthen the scientific basis of their educational programmes. Their training will stress factual, scientifically based knowledge which is measurable, accessible, and examinable. As we shall explore in Part II, the more quantifiable and measurable the therapy becomes in terms of its theoretical knowledge base, the more amenable it will become to the processes of law.

Many practitioners within these therapies will dislike the nature of the compromise and feel that their therapy is losing contact with its traditional, holistic origins. Others will point to political realities and, with the prospect of European harmonization ever present on the horizon, will argue strongly for the need to change in order to survive and prosper.

However, the compromise may be quite willingly made. The growing professionalism which has been a marked trend in most of the discrete clinical disciplines will foster a desire for security on the part of those who have studied so hard to gain their qualifications. The abandonment of the more esoteric side of some of these therapies may be considered a small price to pay for respectability, security, and arguably, a more responsible profession.

Our suggestion in the foregoing paragraphs is the starting point of a much more complex argument: that some therapies are so close to orthodox medicine that they are very likely to be regulated along the same lines, that is, by State-sanctioned self-regulation. What about all the other therapies which belong within complementary medicine?

Next we shall ask whether there are any criteria which have been left out of the analysis, and if so should they be considered relevant to the issue of regulation? We argue that the notion of regulating *holistic* medicine has never been seriously considered, and therefore a very important dimension has been entirely omitted from the debate.

As most complementary practitioners regard their therapy as being essentially holistic, their therapeutic approach needs to take into account the emotional, and possibly the spiritual aspects of the patient in addition to the physical. The notion of *harm* as discussed by the BMA and most other writers on regulation for complementary medicine, has been entirely too focused on the notion of *physical* harm. The holistic approach has suffered from being discussed almost exclusively within a framework pre-determined by the biomedical model. The persistence with which the medical profession has focused its criticisms of complementary medicine on the threat of *physical* harm has misdirected the debate for the many therapies which lie outside the 'big five' therapies, namely, osteopathy, chiropractic, acupuncture, homoeopathy, and herbalism.

Given the psychosomatic and stress-related origins of so many disorders, the therapist may often be in the position of treating a patient with varying degrees of mental and emotional imbalance. Are therapists adequately trained to cope with this eventuality? In the vast majority of cases, the answer must be 'no'. What about those practitioners holding strong esoteric convictions concerning the origin of disease? Might not they cause significant psychological damage to a vulnerable patient? The point here is that notions of harm have been heavily influenced by the medical and legal professions, both of whom have problems wrestling with any other notion of harm beyond the quantifiable, measurable notion of physical harm. Holistic practitioners need to do better than this. In Part II we shall look at the difficulties which the law has in responding to emotional harm and develop an argument as to why ethical safeguards will be required to protect patients from non-physical harm.

5

Political Factors Impacting on Regulation

I. DOMESTIC POLITICS

The outcome of the debate on regulation will be a political compromise in which the Government will have to balance the competing interests of a number of different groups. As Breyer has remarked: 'There is no scientific discipline of regulation'.[1] Regulators are often recruited from political backgrounds and rarely have specialized regulation expertise. Regulatory mechanisms are therefore infrequently subject to radical innovation or redesign and consequently historical practice along with political and administrative factors will strongly influence regulatory decision-making.

'Benevolent neutrality', the term frequently used by the Government to describe its stance on complementary medicine is an expression with a long history. It seems to express well the attitude of successive Governments towards non-orthodox medicine. It is taken to mean that whilst the Government may not overtly support complementary medicine, neither will it initiate proscriptive legislation restricting its use. It may also convey the fact that the Government is waiting to see what transpires before committing itself to one policy in preference to another. More cynically, perhaps, the phrase 'benevolent neutrality' masks the Government's reluctance to act in this area.

The Government is undoubtedly influenced by public opinion. The cause of complementary medicine has also been furthered by friends in high places. Members of the royal family are prominent among the users and enthusiastic supporters of complementary medicine. It is widely thought that Prince Charles' remarks during his valedictory address to the BMA as chairman was the incident that sparked off the BMA's ill-timed and misjudged Report on complementary medicine published in 1986. The fact that members of the royal family and the

---

[1] Breyer, S., *Regulation and its Reform* (Harvard University Press, Cambridge, Mass., 1986) p. 3.

House of Lords have been prepared to lend complementary medicine such active and public support has certainly helped. It is difficult to imagine that this support has a major impact on the current regulatory debate, although it probably was quite influential ten years ago. An all-party Parliamentary Group on Complementary Medicine ensures that the subject is kept on the political agenda.

The period of the greatest growth for complementary medicine has occurred almost entirely during a period in which there has been a Conservative Government. Successive Conservative Governments have been concerned to encourage private initiatives, in health care as much as in other areas of economic life. It is probably for these reasons that the preventative, self-help thrust of complementary health movement has political appeal for the Conservative Government.

In contrast to the Government's non-interventionist stance, the Labour Party has been considerably more active in its pronouncements on complementary medicine. In June 1994, after an extensive consultation exercise, it launched a document *Facilitation not Prescription*. Taking into view that 'health is too important to be left to Private Member's Bills to introduce piecemeal legislation', the Labour Party expressed a wish to facilitate the developmental process taking place within complementary medicine on the basis that complementary therapies have value in health care and should be available to NHS patients as part of an effective and comprehensive National Health Service.

The paper said that the Labour Party would establish, through the Department of Health, an Office of Complementary Medicine to co-ordinate implementation of policy regarding complementary medicine and to administer a ring-fenced fund to finance research-based innovative practice. A Labour-run Department of Health would also introduce autonomous legislation for acupuncture, herbalism, and homoeopathy. General practitioners would remain gatekeepers to complementary therapists within the NHS, but the paper recognized that successful GP referral would depend on familiarization courses being made more widely available for existing GPs and the inclusion of such courses as part of the undergraduate curriculum. Responses to this document from the medical profession reiterated the need for therapies to be able to demonstrate clinical efficacy.

The current crisis situation within the NHS is another important factor which will impact on the regulation of complementary medicine. Britain already spends a much lower percentage of her national income on health care provisions than many other industrialized countries. There are serious restraints on resources which will increase in severity as the impact of an increasingly ageing population becomes more evident. Unless the Government is willing to re-allocate resources on a macro level and spend an increased amount on health care, significant changes will have to be made in health care provision and financing.

Promoters of complementary medicine have not been slow to stress the benefits of an approach to health care that emphasizes self-help, self-responsibility, and reliance. The approach of complementary medicine is heavily preventative and addresses in particular chronic degenerative disease and stress-related conditions that are life-style-related. It has been suggested that many complementary therapies might be cheaper and more efficient than expensive drug alternatives. Certainly, there is increasing interest among purchasers.

Whilst this appeal to resources has superficial attraction, it is not without difficulties. Were complementary medicine shown to be significantly more cost-effective in the long term, the Government would have to invest a huge amount of money in making it widely available. It would have to invest in training practitioners, as the number of therapists who are adequately trained would not fulfil national demand. The reluctance of the Government to commit significant sums of money towards determining cost-effectiveness may well spring from the fact that if results were favourable to complementary medicine, it would have to retreat from the shelter of 'benevolent neutrality' and come up with some hard cash.[2] No change can be expected overnight. Practices and therapies will be introduced piecemeal in the usual pragmatic British style, and a drastic overturn in policy is unlikely.

We should not overlook the political influence of the pharmaceutical industry on the debate. The pharmaceutical drug industry is a high export earner throughout Europe, and especially in the United Kingdom. It funds a great deal of important research and its financial

[2] The Department of Health has, however, commissioned the University of Sheffield's Medical Care Research Unit to carry out a 2-year research project surveying GPs in order to describe the nature and availability of complementary health care obtained via general practice: Thomas, K. J., Fall, M. and Nicholl, J., *National Survey of Access to Complementary Therapies via General Practice* (Report to Department of Health. Medical Care Research Unit, SCHARR, Regent Court, 30 Regent Street, Sheffield, S1 4DA.)

power, and consequent influence within the medical profession, has been the subject of much public debate and media interest of late. An issue which received rather more concern some years ago than it does today, is the extent to which the pharmaceutical industry and the medical profession will collude to prevent the complementary health movement from winning popular and government support. Such conspiracy theories abounded ten or fifteen years ago. If there is to be a conspiracy, it would have to be judged to be extremely unsuccessful given the phenomenal growth of complementary medicine over the last fifteen years.

II. EUROPEAN POLITICS

Complementary practitioners express great concern about the extent to which harmonization might affect the regulation of complementary medicine. They fear that lay practice may, effectively, be wiped out. This fear has led to much scaremongering and has no doubt been a significant factor in the impetus towards greater professional organization amongst therapies.

Concern focuses on the more restrictive statutory regimes in many European countries, including Belgium, France, Spain, Italy and Greece, where only registered medical practitioners may practise any form of medicine (even though these laws are regularly flouted on a wide scale, and such prosecutions as there are often result in acquittals).[3] Reforms of the law are being enacted in the Netherlands which is establishing a series of legally protected titles for complementary therapists. Germany has, since 1939, had a *heilpraktiker* system, which allows non-medically qualified practitioners to practise certain forms of medicine provided they have passed an examination in basic medical knowledge and are registered. However, the system is not centrally administered and regional standards are thought to vary considerably.

Interest in greater harmonization arises primarily out of awareness of the principle of free movement of labour within the European Union, as enshrined in the Treaty of Rome. Currently, such movement would be impossible for complementary health practitioners,

---

[3] For a helpful overview of the European scene, see Fisher, P. and Ward, A., 'Complementary medicine in Europe' 309 BMJ 107–11 (1994).

given the diversity in training standards and the widely differing legal requirements operating in different European countries.

In 1993, the Committee on the Environment, Public Health and Consumer Protection of the European Parliament proposed a motion for a resolution on alternative medicine and appointed Belgian MEP, Mr Paul Lannoye, to act as *rapporteur*. In May 1994, the *Lannoye Report*, as it has subsequently become known, failed to get through a plenary session of the Parliament in its existing form but an amended version is likely to be resubmitted in the future. The ultimate outcome of this exercise will have significant consequences for complementary practitioners, particularly in relation to training and qualifications and the provision of alternative medicine within social security systems. Whilst European initiatives are unlikely to affect domestic policy in the short term, the prospect of European harmonization is likely to act as a spur to those interested in promoting higher, uniform standards of training.

statutory regulation is now a feasible goal for those therapies who wish to pursue this end. In previous decades, the possibility of statutory recognition was not thought to be a politically viable option. All this has recently changed, and has been given increased impetus with the passing of the Osteopaths Act 1993 and the Chiropractors Act 1994. The response of complementary medicine to the challenge posed by the prospect of regulation has been impressive considering the comparatively unorganized state of most therapies a decade ago.

Statutory registration and protection of title is favoured by many therapies for a number of reasons, some of which are positive while others are essentially defensive. Primarily, it affords the therapy the chance to determine its own affairs with a much greater degree of control. Statutory protection of title ensures that practitioners using such a title are required by law to have passed the approved training course and to be registered with the body legally empowered to regulate the profession. Entry to the profession is thus far more easily controlled, and, it is argued, standards can be maintained at a uniformly high level. Controlling entry of numbers to the profession helps to maintain fees at a respectable level, and statutory registration is also seen as improving the chances of that profession being brought into the National Health Service arrangements in the near future. Sanctions via disciplinary proceedings against incompetent and inadequate practitioners can be far more effectively enforced.

State-supported self-regulation is widely believed to help safeguard the independence of the profession from encroachment by the medical profession. In the same way it is also seen as conferring protection against any threat as a consequence of European 'harmonization' measures. In Part II we shall critically evaluate how correct some of these widely held views on statutory regulation actually are.

Some therapies are organizing themselves with a view to statutory registration; others, however, realize that statutory self-regulation is not a feasible proposition for them at the present time, and have their sights set on more realistic goals such as raising standards and setting levels of competence. Those therapies which offer complete systems of healing can be contrasted with the larger number of diagnostic or therapeutic modalities whose therapeutic methods are quite far removed from those of scientific medicine. These less well-organized therapies are politically fragmented and often have no clear aims with respect to regulation. Their energies are more taken up with uniting as a therapy and forming umbrella organizations. Discussion of statutory regulation seems premature for these therapies, and yet a number of them appear to be interested in this solution for the future.

II. PAN-PROFESSIONAL BODIES

The acceleration of complementary therapies towards greater organizational convergence has been accompanied by the development of bodies which attempt to represent the interests of complementary medicine on a broader front. There are three main pan-professional organizations, all of which were established between 1982 and 1990. There has been more than a little rivalry and hostility between these three groups, a consequence of the fact that their aims and political styles are quite different. These pan-professional bodies are involved in a wide range of activities that impact on complementary medicine. Here, we intend to confine ourselves to discussing those which impinge most directly on regulation.

The Institute of Complementary Medicine (ICM) was established as an independent charity in 1982 with the primary task of providing information about complementary medicine to the public. It currently handles some 30,000 enquiries annually. In 1989 it set up the British Register of Complementary Practitioners, the first attempt by any organization to produce a national listing of qualified practitioners. In its own words: '[T]hose admitted to the Register are fully qualified to carry out treatments, are insured for both professional indemnity and public liability and work to a code of conduct and practice . . . '.

At the time of writing, there are 366 organizations affiliated to the ICM. The British Council for Complementary Medicine which the ICM also set up in 1989 is planned to function as a self-governing professional body, taking control of the British Register within three years. The officers of the ICM are not elected; they see themselves as functioning in an advisory capacity. In particular, they stress that, as they are not involved in what might be called trade union activities, they can substantiate their claim to greater independence than the other bodies.

The British Complementary Medicine Association (BCMA) was established in 1990 to provide a consultative body for complementary medicine. In many ways it duplicates the activities and functions of the ICM, which is the cause of much of the tension between them. Their officers are elected and thus they can lay claim to being far more representative than the ICM, often portrayed by them as being undemocratic. The BCMA represents 40 organizations in 30 therapies, and was the first pan-professional body to produce a code of conduct, common to all member organizations. A Public Register, on identical lines to that of the ICM is planned shortly.

The Council for Complementary and Alternative Medicine (CCAM) provides 'a forum for communication and cooperation between professional bodies representing acupuncture, herbal medicine, homoeopathy and osteopathy . . . ' The CCAM makes no claim to be an umbrella organization. Its main area of activity is in representing the interests of the major therapies of acupuncture, herbalism, homoeopathy, and one osteopathic organization not part of the General Register and Council of Osteopaths. It is essentially constituted as a council of professional bodies set up to provide a forum to work on matters such as education, ethics, and discipline.

III. THE MEDICAL ESTABLISHMENT

In as far as the medical establishment can be said to have an official position, it has to be taken that the reports of the BMA on complementary medicine constitute that view. It should be noted however, that while the BMA is a very influential body, it is not representative of the medical profession as a whole. There are a number of organizations such as the British Holistic Medical Association and the British Medical Acupuncture Society, membership of which is restricted to doctors, but which aim to promote a more holistic approach within orthodox medicine. Furthermore, surveys reveal that general practitioners and young doctors are showing significantly more interest in complementary medicine than the more senior hospital doctors.[1] Many doctors do not concur with the opinions of the BMA, and the possibility of a discrepancy between the 'official' position and the views of many doctors must be kept in mind.

The resolutely hostile attitude that once characterized the official position of orthodox medicine to non-conventional therapies has noticeably diminished over the past two decades. There are encouraging signs of a greater spirit of tolerance and co-operation, fostered no doubt by a recognition of the political realities as well as by a

[1] Reilly, D., 'Young doctors views on alternative medicine' 287 BMJ 337–9 (1993).

genuine change of attitude. This change is reflected in the rather different tenor of the two major reports published by the BMA in the past decade.

In 1986, the BMA published a highly critical report on alternative therapy.[2] The working party included not one single doctor with any practising knowledge of complementary medicine. Consequently, the report was flawed by fundamental inaccuracies which tended to diminish its overall impact. Cult practices were discussed alongside the more serious therapies; all were dismissed as being primitive, untested, ineffective, and potentially harmful.

In noting the need to first identify and then redress the underlying causes of the criticism, we have to recognize that a consequence of ignoring these factors is a reversion to primitive beliefs and outmoded practices, almost all without basis. Some are not without danger, others appear to be promoted for less than laudable purposes ... '[3]

The report concluded that the popularity of complementary medicine could be attributed both to the irrationality of the consumer and to the failure of orthodox doctors to address the wider needs of their patients.

It was a misjudged and mistimed exercise, and in the words of Stephen Fulder, 'scored a much publicised own goal'.[4] An Early Day Motion deploring the report was signed by almost 25 per cent of the members of the House of Commons. Even the Department of Health and Social Security was drawn into remarking unofficially that the report was: 'premature, unhelpful and biased'.[5] Arguably, the lack of judgement shown by the decision to publish such a transparently biased document could be considered a reflection of the more general lack of contact with public sentiment over health issues.

That there was some disagreement about the report even within the medical profession was indicated by the appearance of a new report published in 1993, entitled *Complementary Medicine: New Approaches to Good Practice*.[6] A noticeably more balanced approach is evident from the scope of the book which restricted itself to

[2] Board of Education and Science, BMA, *Alternative therapies* (BMA, London, 1986).
[3] Ibid., p. 64.
[4] Fulder, S. J., *The Handbook of Contemporary Medicine*, p. 17.
[5] 'Pressure grows in Parliament', *Journal of Alternative Medicine* (editorial, 1986) 4, 7, p. 1.
[6] BMA (OUP, 1993).

considering, 'as a *public health* issue, the principles of good practice in non-conventional therapies which would safeguard the individuals against possible harm to health and maximise the potential benefits of particular methods . . . '. In its second report, the BMA recommends that a *single* regulating body be established for each therapy. In addition, the BMA expresses the view that in order to protect patients, some therapies should be regulated by statute. The report says: 'Those therapies posing greater potential risks to patients require *legal regulation by statute* to protect consumers from unskilled or incompetent practitioners'.[7]

Relying on Pietroni's classification, the BMA finds the discrete clinical disciplines of osteopathy, chiropractic, acupuncture, homoeopathy, and herbalism to be the therapies which probably have the greatest potential to do harm to the patient, whilst conceding: '[W]ithin defined parameters, these therapies perhaps have the greatest potential for use in conjunction with orthodox structures of health care'.[8] The BMA appears to support the conditions laid down by the government for any therapy seeking regulation, namely:

(1) that the therapy has been long established and has an established and credible system of voluntary regulation;
(2) that there should be recognized courses of training, including a structured system of assessment with external examiners;
(3) that there is consensus upon the way forward amongst all the different organizations within that therapy;
(4) that the medial profession is broadly supportive of the move towards statutory regulation.[9]

Three main currents of opinion can be discerned within orthodox medicine on the issue of complementary medicine. A minority of doctors will always remain implacably opposed to non-conventional therapies. A second, more open-minded approach, allows that complementary medicine may have some value but argues that it should only be administered by medically qualified personnel. Proponents of this argument can point to the practice within a number of the European States where this is the current legal position. This view depends heavily on the assertion that there is the risk of serious health problems going undetected where a patient consults a non-medically

---

[7] BMA (OUP, 1993) at para. 5.3.　　　[8] Ibid., at 5.2.
[9] *Hansard* vol. 489, col. 1379–416 (HMSO, London, 1987).

trained practitioner. A more cogent argument stresses the problems of integrating complementary therapies within the NHS and the difficulties of using non-medically trained personnel. Certainly there are concerns as to the feasibility of trying to bring together using two conflicting models of disease theory and mutually unintelligible terminology.[10]

A third view which is noticeably gaining ground within the medical profession is the opinion that all complementary health practitioners should have some training in anatomy and physiology. This opinion reflects the direction of thinking within complementary medicine itself, as more training schools are stressing the importance of courses in anatomy, physiology and basic biological sciences. The emphasis here is on raising educational standards and establishing uniform competence levels in training. Almost universal to all views is an insistence on the need to establish efficacy and the value of clinical research, although even this is sometimes now tempered with an understanding of the difficulties of conducting clinical research in many complementary therapies.

With regard to regulation for complementary medicine, the more hostile members of the medical profession are now in an interesting dilemma. In the early 1980s when there was not the slightest prospect of regulation of complementary practitioners, many hostile doctors were among those at the forefront of the demand for tighter regulation. Now that complementary therapists are actively pursuing and obtaining regulation for themselves, there has been something of a reversal of the argument to the view that the law should not be used to legitimize scientifically invalidated therapies.

IV. CONSUMER ORGANIZATIONS

As we have seen, the growth in complementary medicine, particularly within the NHS, has been consumer driven. An important factor has been the dissatisfaction patients have expressed towards the limitations of orthodox health care, particularly in relation to the treatment of chronic, degenerative diseases and stress-related disorders. Patients are becoming increasingly aware of the disparity between what modern

---

[10] In this regard, it is reasonable to expect that were complementary medicine to be practised within the NHS, a hybrid, 'medicalized' version would emerge, adapted to the clinical and financial constraints of modern NHS conditions.

medicine claims it can do and what it can actually deliver. NHS constraints have meant that few doctors have sufficient time to give their patients the time and space they would like. All of these factors have precipitated a greater willingness for people to pay for their own health care, both within orthodox and complementary medicine. In this sense, patients, no less than health authorities and NHS Trusts, must be seen as purchasers.

As a general rule, consumer associations are supportive of complementary medicine because of the extra choice it makes available to the patient. However, this welcoming of consumer choice in health care is tempered by warnings about the dangerous lack of training and uniform standards and the lack of protection from charlatanism.[11] A 1985 *Which?* survey testified to consumer satisfaction with complementary medicine, citing the fact that 82 per cent of those who had used complementary therapies claimed that they had been cured or had their condition improved. The same report recommended the following measures:

(1) The need for better communications between complementary and conventional medicine. It would be in patients' interests to be able to discuss their desire to see a complementary therapist with their doctor.
(2) There should be agreed national standards for the training of practitioners in each form of complementary medicine.
(3) A registration system would further reassure patients that they were being treated by a properly qualified practitioner.
(4) The establishment of a single independent council of practitioners of all types of complementary medicine which would monitor standards and maintain a register. The General Medical Council was recommended as a model for this type of independent regulatory body.

The recognition of the individual right to choice in health care is a view that has also been gaining ground throughout Europe. The *Report of the Commission for Alternative Systems of Medicine* in the Netherlands represented this view:

A number of reasons have prompted the State Secretary to seek advice on alternative medicine. One was the frequency with which the Medical

---

[11] See, e.g., *Association of Community Health Councils for England and Wales: The State of Non-Conventional Medicine—The Consumer View* (ACHCEW, 1988).

Practice Act 1865 was being broken. . . . The consensus of public opinion is no longer behind the (medical) monopoly, and the law is broken a thousand times a day as sick and disabled people seek the help of people who are not legally authorised to provide it . . . [12]

It can reasonably be expected that consumer associations will continue to support the independent existence of complementary medicine, provided certain safeguards regarding qualifications and training standards can be assured.

In Part II we shall look at the current regulatory controls over complementary medicine.

[12] *Alternative Medicine in the Netherlands* (Summary of the Report of the Commission for Alternative Systems of Medicine, The Hague, 1981).

PART II

Legal and Ethical Controls

7

An Overview of Existing Controls

In Part I we have attempted to contextualize the regulation debate and to discuss various considerations which we believe will determine regulation. As we have seen, although consumer protection is usually presented as the primary motivation, other interests are at stake, and therapeutic efficacy, whilst important, is not the sole determining factor. We have looked at some of the problems which have already emerged because of the lack of formal regulation, and considered some of the problems which may occur in the future.

In the last ten to fifteen years, controversial medical issues have dominated headlines. Often focusing on life and death issues, ethical dilemmas in medicine have become a staple focus of media discussion. Not infrequently, a particularly controversial case may prompt calls for the regulation or the banning of a practice altogether. Increasingly, papers carry reports of large settlements for medical negligence actions, and most practitioners are becoming aware of risk avoidance practices.[1]

But how much relevance do these issues have to the practice of complementary medicine? For, as we have observed, despite a significant increase in litigation against orthodox practitioners, this has not been matched by a corresponding increase in formal complaints against complementary health practitioners. We can speculate as to why this is the case. A preliminary observation might be that because most holistic therapies are gentler, there is less risk of harm. Certainly, many therapies trade on the notion that complementary therapies are, by and large, natural, and therefore, safe; no patient has died for want of a health authority employing a spiritual healer, nor will an aromatherapist cause significant harm by using lavender oil rather than rose geranium. Superficially attractive as this argument might be, complementary therapies patently are not universally safe. Product-based therapies carry risk of toxicity; acupuncture can, at worst, cause

[1] The newly created Clinical Negligence Scheme for Trusts, a mutual fund for NHS Trusts facing medical negligence claims, offers reduced contributions if risk management practices are in place.

injuries such as pneumothorax and induce blood-borne disease; the wrong potency of homoeopathy can provoke an extremely violent reaction. These harms should not be dismissed, although media irresponsibility could mislead potential patients into believing that these are frequent occurrences, rather than being extremely rare.[2]

Whilst some therapies carry greater inherent risks of harm than others, every healing encounter raises potential legal and ethical concerns. The complementary practitioner/patient relationship confers legal duties upon therapists and breaches of that duty may give rise to actions in law. More importantly however, the offer to treat carries ethical responsibilities. As soon as a therapist makes therapeutic claims, this raises expectations in the patient, creating a sense of optimism, and quite possibly, inducing a sense of reliance on that therapist. It is these responsibilities, integral to the way in which the therapeutic interchange takes place, which mark healing professions out from other occupational groups.

Given the strong cultural bias in favour of the allopathic, bio-medical model, we should not be too surprised that in both the United Kingdom and the United States, discussion of law and ethics in the healing professions has been dominated by medical ethics and medico-legal issues, focusing almost entirely on the doctor/patient relationship. For example, the ethical dilemmas seized upon by the media reflect the highly technological, invasive nature that characterizes much of modern medicine—whether to treat very low birthweight babies, whether to remove artificial life support from dying patients—whether to carry out pre-natal screening for genetically inherited disease. So much of the ethical debate concerns the use and potential abuse of modern medical technology.

So all-pervasive is the medical model that it is sometimes overlooked that other health professionals may have quite different dilemmas. Thus, it is only very recently that nursing law and ethics has emerged as a discipline in its own right, raising issues distinct from medical ethics. The degree of usage of complementary medicine, and the extent to which it forms a significant part of contemporary health care, means that it is no longer plausible to exclude complementary practitioners from discussions of law and ethics. The purpose of this section of the book is to determine, by means of

---

[2] Whilst there is scant evidence of adverse outcomes, the absence of formal monitoring mechanisms such as the yellow card system for allopathic drugs is a legitimate concern.

looking at how existing regulatory controls are applied, whether the distinct issues raised by complementary medicine can be conflated within the existing framework of health care law and ethics, or whether an entirely new paradigm is required.

It will emerge that the very discourse of law and ethics has been shaped with reference to the prevailing doctor/patient relationship as the dominant model. In legal terms, the law of negligence presupposes the power imbalance which has previously characterized the doctor/patient relationship in orthodox settings. In this model, the doctor, with his professional status, superior knowledge, and technical skills, has a legal duty of care towards patients upon whom care is bestowed. Conversely, the patient, who is often viewed as the passive recipient of medical treatment, bears no responsibility in law. As the law of consent demonstrates, there is a reluctance to take patients' rights to make their own decisions fully into account. Thus, the amount of information that a practitioner has to disclose about an intended procedure is determined not by the amount of information that the individual patient wants, but primarily on the basis of the amount of information that a reasonable doctor would give.[3]

When we examine how law has been applied to conventional medicine, we shall see repeatedly that the legal standard is determined by objective reasonableness. The law asks: did the doctor act in accordance with a reasonable body of medical opinion?[4] How would the law be applied to complementary medicine? Is it realistic to attempt to apply this standard to therapeutic relationships which are highly subjective and individualized? When diagnosis may depend more on the practitioner's intuition and less on the outcome of technological diagnostic measures, how possible or relevant is it to ask retrospectively what a responsible body of practitioners would have done in the circumstances?

Again, in statutory and voluntary codes of practice, the language reinforces professional responsibilities towards the patients, borne out of duties towards them, rather than arising out of the patients' rights. Codes of practice, to the extent that they represent what it means to act ethically, also emphasize professionals' responsibilities towards the patient. Like the law, they concentrate more on the

[3] *Sidaway* v. *Board of Governors of the Bethlem Royal Hospital and the Maudsley Hospital* [1985] AC 871, [1985] 1 All ER 643, HL.
[4] *Bolam* v. *Friern Hospital Management Committee* [1957] 2 All ER 118, [1957] 1 WLR 582.

practitioner's duty not to harm the patient than explicitly recognizing the need to respect the patient's autonomy. Some therapies have actually modelled their code of conduct on the GMC's *Professional Conduct and Discipline: Fitness to Practice*. Here, as elsewhere, the medical way of doing things is held up as the 'gold standard', not-withstanding the political and philosophical gulf between orthodox and alternative medicine.

Part II will address three interrelated areas. Given that our ultimate objective is to make suggestions for the most appropriate regulatory framework for complementary medicine, the first task will be to identify what regulation should be seeking to achieve. We must look beyond the standard cliches of 'protecting the public', and 'promoting high standards', and explore what each of these really mean in prac-tice. We must go behind the rhetoric of interested parties all of whom have their own private agenda as to the way in which complementary medicine should be regulated.

Next, we shall look at the mechanisms which currently regulate complementary medicine. Adopting a wide interpretation of the term regulation, we shall look at the variety of regulatory mechanisms currently controlling complementary medicine. We shall concentrate primarily on statutory provisions, the common law and the various forms of voluntary self-regulation. Because these different regulatory schemes operate concurrently, we must look at how these schemes overlap and interrelate.

Finally, we need to question how successful each mechanism is in meeting the aims of regulation which we have identified. In look-ing at the various regulatory controls, we must focus on the features of the complementary medical relationship which differentiate it from the conventional doctor/patient relationship. We may find that rather than trying to squeeze complementary medicine into an inap-propriate regulatory framework, we might, instead, need to formulate an entirely new approach to regulation.

8

Regulation: Aims and Sources

In Part I we looked at who wants regulation and why. There, we saw that a variety of reasons account for why practitioners are now seeking formal regulation more vigorously. Whilst all cite protection of the public as their primary motivation, we have seen that many therapies view formal regulation as the only way to protect themselves from medical colonization or even annihilation. At this stage, however, we are less concerned with political and other aspirations of regulation, and more concerned with teasing out how patients' interests are best served in practice. Much lip-service is paid to protecting the needs of the public, although there is little focused debate as to how this is best achieved in the sphere of complementary medicine.

Before we delve deeper, let us remind ourselves once again that our use of language shapes the debate. The goal of 'consumer protection' is repeated so often and so glibly that it is taken as something of a truisim. Whilst we do not underestimate the need for safeguards in complementary medicine, the term 'consumer protection' automatically invokes negative connotations of patients who need protecting. If, as we have argued, a major difference between alternative approaches and conventional medicine is the former's genuine desire to share knowledge and empower patients to heal themselves, then even the language used to describe aims of regulation should reflect that more positive ideal, rather than prejudicing the agenda with disempowering, protectionist language. This is not merely pedantry. As we pointed out in the Introduction to this book, nomenclature has political implications. Thus, to the extent that we use the term 'consumer protection' for convenience, we should keep in mind the fact that users of health care have rights and they have choices. To the extent that further or better regulation is required, it should be directed at promoting informed choices about health care.

Critically, at this stage, we are concerned with identifying the aims of regulation in their broadest terms. We must start our enquiry by being open-minded as to the most effective means of achieving these goals. As always, we must not make the assumption that, because certain models have been relied upon in the past, these will necessarily be effective in relation to complementary medicine.

What, then, are the central aims of regulating complementary medicine?

A. High, uniform standards of practice

Consumers are best served by ensuring that all practitioners are able to practice the skills of their particular therapy or therapies in a safe and competent manner. To this end, ensuring high standards of training is of critical importance. Usually, it is assumed that the best way to achieve this is through some system of licensing or registration so that all therapists who use a particular title have received appropriate education and have demonstrated an ability to apply their therapeutic skills in practice. Whilst some therapies have the sort of knowledge base which can be tested by means of formal written examinations, others may equally rely on the demonstration of various practical skills. Others depend almost entirely on non-measurable, intuitive skills. Certainly, the starting point for any therapy is to define what its required competencies are, and to proceed to develop methods of imparting those skills and measuring them. Within the concept of competent practice, we would stress the need for practitioners to act ethically, reconciling duties to the patient, particularly the need to respect the patient's autonomy, duties to professional colleagues, and wider duties to society.

B. Identification of competent practitioners

Having ensured that patients are suitably 'qualified', patients must then be able to identify an appropriate practitioner for their needs. Also, to the extent that doctors wish to recommend, employ, or refer to complementary therapists, they will need assurance that therapists are competent. Most therapies have a register of competent practitioners to enable the public to choose from appropriately qualified practitioners. Many therapies, as we have seen, are still fragmented and may have several registering bodies. Obviously, the more united a therapy becomes, and the fewer registers a patient has to consult, the better. Most patients will assume, quite legitimately, that provided practitioners are registered, their *bona fides* is guaranteed. Unfortunately, this may not be the case, given that each registering body will claim to ensure high standards.

C. Accountability

The concomitant of high standards of practice is having mechanisms to ensure that professional standards are enforced. Whilst one might hope that education alone will protect patients from harm, this cannot be guaranteed. No practitioner is perfect and mistakes will occur in any occupation. Whilst some mistakes may be excusable, others may require action to be taken against the practitioner. Disciplinary procedures must be sufficiently flexible to take account of the seriousness of the complaint, and must be able to respond appropriately. In order to protect the public, disciplinary mechanisms must be both accessible and visible and must be capable of responding to complainants in a meaningful way.

II. SOURCES OF REGULATION

People often assume that the term 'regulation' is synonymous with formal statutory regulation. No doubt this is because, historically, medicine has been regulated in this way. Since 1858, a succession of Medical Acts has set down who may practise medicine, the qualifications required, and the limits upon persons practising. Alongside the regulation of practitioners, statutory provisions regulate the manufacture and supply of medicinal products and devices.[1]

We must recognize, however, that regulation may take many different forms, and that a diverse range of regulatory controls operate simultaneously. In considering the regulation therefore, we shall not simply be looking at statutory regulation, but will be referring to regulation in its broadest sense. We shall consider the various regulatory factors which control health practitioners. Principally, we shall concentrate on three main types of regulatory control. These are:

(1) Statute law.
(2) Common law.
(3) Voluntary self-regulating mechanisms.

[1] See Medicines Act 1968.

Brief mention is required of two further possible regulatory bases which we do not intend to deal with at any great length. The first is the NHS complaints machinery. It is unlikely that the hospital complaints procedures will have any significant impact on complementary medicine in the immediate future. Whilst an increasing number of existing health professionals are beginning to provide complementary therapies within the NHS, this still represents such a small proportion of working practitioners that we feel an in-depth consideration is inappropriate. If, at some point in the future, there were to be greater integration into the NHS, these mechanisms would constitute an additional regulatory control which would need to be considered further. We recognize however, that the spectrum of NHS complaints mechanisms do have a bearing on existing NHS health care workers using complementary therapies, who are already subject to NHS regulatory mechanisms by virtue of their current employment. To the extent that these workers are starting to introduce complementary health care techniques into their regular working practices, they will be subject to this additional regulatory control.

The Hospital Complaints Procedures Act 1985 directs that health authorities must ensure that arrangements are made within each hospital to deal with patient complaints. Both the hospital complaints procedures and the general practice complaints procedures are widely perceived to be flawed and inadequate. One of the reasons that these mechanisms have not been seen as particularly effective is that the Health Service Commissioner (the Ombudsman) who is responsible for administering the hospital complaints system has had a fairly limited jurisdiction. Significantly, this remit has not extended to matters of clinical judgement, nor to complaints about family health services (including the services of general practitioners, dentists, opticians, and pharmacists).

As a result of major dissatisfactions with the hospital complaints system, the Department of Health set up a committee under the chairmanship of Professor Alan Wilson. Its report, *Being Heard—The Report of a Review Committee on NHS Complaints Procedures*, has recommended widespread changes aimed at making complaints speedier and more accessible, with complaints, wherever possible, being dealt with at a local level.

Both before and after the 1985 Act, one major problem has been one of obtaining the information necessary to forming an objective judgement of a complaint. Doctors are particularly reluctant to provide any statement which may be taken as an admission of civil liability. The Wilson Report admits that there is evidence that fear of litigation can hamper the handling of complaints, and that some hospitals have attempted to persuade complainants to waive their legal rights before a complaint will be investigated (notwithstanding the fact that such a waiver has no legal status).[2] The report continues:

it is important to acknowledge the moral principle here: where complainants suffer compensatable harm as a result of NHS treatment, the NHS should not try to avoid its responsibilities towards them or to withhold information ... Indeed, there is anecdotal evidence to suggest that a defensive response to complaints of this nature is more likely to prompt recourse to litigation than to prevent it.[3]

Brazier is highly critical of the 'whole maze' of the complaints procedures. Not only are the complaints procedures ineffective at doing the job they are meant to do, they are subverted to deal with inappropriate matters such as disputes between medical colleagues. She says: 'Speaking out against inadequate and unsafe conditions in our hospitals, failure to conform to the majority view of your specialty, seems more likely to result in disciplinary proceedings against a hospital doctor than failing to meet patients' needs ... '.[4]

It is too early to say whether the reforms, when implemented, will achieve their desired effect. Certainly, up until now, hospital complaints mechanisms have not been a particularly effective means of ensuring accountability.[5]

The second quasi-regulatory source which we need to touch upon is that of market forces. It could certainly be argued that in a free market environment, a therapist's clientele would surely dry up if the quality of services provided were less attractive than those provided by other practitioners, and that this factor would serve to raise standards generally. Differences in service may well explain why some practitioners' practices are more successful than others. However, we reject the notion that contracting for health services is equivalent to the purchase of other goods and services and do not believe that

[2] Medicines Act 1968 at para. 34.   [3] Ibid., at para. 38.
[4] Ibid., p. 211.
[5] For further reading on hospital complaints procedures see chapters by Arthur C. Taylor in *Medical Negligence*, Powers, M. and Harris, N. (ed.) (Butterworths, London, 1994, 2nd edn), and Arnold Simanowitz, 'Patient Complaints in Health Care Provisions in *Nursing Law and Ethics*, Tingle, J. and Cribb, A. (edd) (Blackwell, Oxford, 1995).

market forces provide anything like sufficient safeguards for the public.[6] In an otherwise unregulated arena, a patient could suffer considerable harm before breaking off the therapy. An unscrupulous practitioner could even try to persuade a patient that unexpected side-effects, or even worsening of existing symptoms, were an acceptable part of the therapeutic process, rather than evidence of the practitioner's incompetence. There is even a recognized term of art in complementary medicine, known as the 'healing crisis', which explicitly recognizes the not uncommon phenomenon of the patient's symptoms worsening before they improve. Initially, however, there is little to distinguish a healing crisis from the adverse consequences of inappropriate treatment.

A. Statute law

Unlike orthodox medicine, which is the subject of formal statutory regulation, complementary medicine has not, until recently, been regulated by any specific formal means. In the absence of a high-profile overarching professional body such as the General Medical Council, or a body such as the British Medical Association, it has been widely assumed that complementary medicine is entirely unregulated. We have already seen that this is far from the case and that voluntary self-regulation, exercised in varying degrees, has controlled the practice of complementary therapies since its inception.

Few people, either inside or outside complementary medicine regarded statutory self-regulation as a viable option for complementary therapies prior to the passing of the Osteopaths Act in 1993, and the Chiropractors Act in 1994. The willingness of the Government to pass these two Acts, which create the first two autonomous statutorily protected complementary health professions, has been interpreted as a highly significant development in complementary medicine. Not surprisingly, various other therapies are now vigorously pursuing the same level of recognition. Acupuncturists, homoeopaths, and herbalists, and possibly other therapies are now actively considering statutory regulation.[7]

Whilst this book is concerned primarily with how complementary

[6] We also reject market forces as an equitable basis for ensuring access to necessary health care. See discussion *infra* on distributive justice.

[7] See, e.g., an address on behalf of the National Institute of Herbal Medicine; McIntyre, M. 'European Herbal Remedies', *European Journal of Herbal Medicine*, Vol. 1. No. 2, Summer 1994.

medicine should best be regulated, it would be foolish, at this stage in the debate, to try to predict how responsive this Government, or subsequent Governments, will be towards attempts by other major therapies to gain statutory recognition. Nor can we second guess the eventual outcome of the *Lannoye Report*. It may be worthwhile to consider this Government's stance on regulation and the likelihood of further statutory intervention in the short term. Statutory regulation for osteopaths and chiropractors has been received enthusiastically within complementary medicine as a sign that the Government is now taking complementary medicine seriously, but therapists would be foolhardy to suppose that the Government is now about to grant statutory status to every therapist seeking it, especially before the Osteopaths Act 1993 and Chiropractors Act 1994 have been implemented and evaluated. Moreover, statutory recognition to date has come at an extremely high price—namely acceptance by the medical profession which almost certainly necessitates a distancing from the more intuitive and esoteric underpinnings of holistic medicine.

We shall return to this point frequently, as it is the major reason that statutory regulation, at the present time, is an unrealistic and unworkable goal for many complementary therapies, whose interests are far better served by voluntary self-regulation. This is not to say that no other therapies are likely to achieve statutory self-regulation, or that this is inappropriate, particularly for therapies which exhibit various 'medicalized' characteristics. Having looked at the various statutory controls that there are, we shall go on to examine the limited conditions in which statutory, as opposed to voluntary, self-regulation is likely to be appropriate, and we shall look carefully at why this form of regulation is unlikely to be the appropriate mode of regulation for all but a handful of highly developed, highly medicalized therapies.

Currently, few therapists work under any statutory regulation unless in addition to their complementary skills they are already health care professionals, such as doctors, nurses, or physiotherapists, who will already be regulated by statute and working within their own professional codes of practice. However, in terms of indirect statutory provisions, a wealth of provisions affect what complementary therapists may or may not do. As well as specific health legislation, the full panoply of criminal statutes apply as rigorously to health practitioners as to anyone else.

In the United Kingdom, there is a marked preference for professions to be regulated by statutory self-regulation. This means that the profession is recognized, and protected, by statute, with only people registered within a statutory registration scheme enjoying professional privileges. Statutes of this kind operate by creating a primary statute, such as the Medical Act 1983 or the Nurses, Midwives and Health Visitors Act 1992, which then delegates the bulk of the rule-making to the statutory council created by the Act, constituted primarily by the professions themselves. In this sense, such professions can properly be regarded as statutorily self-regulating, since the professionals themselves supply the content and detail of the regulations.

In recent years, professional self-regulation has been the focus of harsh criticism. Professional bodies have repeatedly been accused of being unduly lenient towards errant members, and complaints mechanisms have been pilloried for being inaccessible to would-be complainants, and insufficient in terms of accountability. Despite the Government's attempts to roll back some of the unnecessary regulation which has hampered (primarily economic) activity, unless self-regulated professions can meet their critics head on, more direct Government intervention may be inevitable. Although the medical profession has been the subject of overt and public criticism, in recent years, every major profession has come under attack.[8]

Meanwhile, the professions, as we have seen, have a strong preference for this type of regulation. Professional status has customarily wielded social status and may confer considerable economic advantages. Historically, professionals, as we have seen, have enjoyed a high degree of autonomy over how they perform their tasks and have the advantage of dictating their own standards. The rules governing conduct will develop out of custom and convention within the profession, so that professionals effectively determine their own standards, taking into account the nature and demands of their specialized field. Indeed the right of professionals to create their own standards sets them apart from other workers, for example, manual labourers, who have less control over their sphere of activity, and have to work within prescriptive regimes. Usually a specialized and highly technical knowledge base, acquired over a period of time, affords a professional group this privilege.

As a prerequisite to deciding whether this form of regulation is appropriate for complementary therapists, we need to consider whether therapists should properly be regarded as 'professionals', and

---

[8] Other professions whose self-regulation has been investigated include accountancy, architecture, and law.

consider what it means to any given group to try to achieve 'professional status'. Is the enhanced sense of power which inevitably accompanies professionalism helpful or injurious to the therapeutic relationship? Are we reassured that consumer protection, as opposed to self-interest is the primary motivation?

By way of introduction, let us consider some of the characteristics which define statutory self-regulation. Health statutes create a framework in which a governing council is empowered to maintain a statutory register of people entitled to practise under the statute. Statutes create a protected title, so that only those registered under the statutory scheme may use that title. Unlawful use of a protected title constitutes a criminal offence. The activities of the governing council will be overseen, and various appointments will be made onto it, by the Privy Council. The governing council may well have a lay membership presence to represent the consumer's view. Statutory committees include an education committee, which determines standards of education and licenses training establishments, and a disciplinary committee, charged with investigating allegations of misconduct. The disciplinary committee will also develop a code of practice, designed to ensure high standards of professional conduct.

Although later on in this section we shall be looking at specific points relating to the Osteopaths Act 1993 and Chiropractors Act 1994, at this stage it is important to note the degree of state intervention in statutorily regulated professions. All appointments to statutory committees are made with the approval of the Privy Council. Although, in practice, the executive never intervenes in the way professions organize themselves, statutory powers granted under these Acts are generally subject to review by the Privy Council. Additionally, there will often be several appointments specifically made by the relevant Secretary of State.

In relation to statutes regulating health professions, we shall see that there has always been a degree of medical representation on various statutory committees. In this way, the medical profession has been able to exert a significant degree of control over the manner in which these professions operate. Note that this presence has not been matched by a corresponding representation of other health care professionals on the General Medical Council.

Most of these statutes require certain statutory committees to have a lay component. The presence of lay membership is an anomaly within a self-regulating system, the basis of which is that professional groups are best placed to regulate their own conduct, because of the specialist knowledge and special circumstances which affect their work. None the less, the incursion of lay representation is seen as an essential safeguard for the public, and may be seen as a trade-off for the right to self-govern.[9] If the Government or the public is given reason to believe that any professional self-regulatory body is unable or unwilling to police its own members or is being unduly lenient, then this is likely to lead to calls to increase the proportion of lay membership.[10]

Inevitably, statutorily regulated professions tend to be more bureaucratic than their voluntary counterparts (although the voluntary self-regulating bodies of some of the more organized complementary theories do operate within extremely formalistic boundaries), and the additional infrastructure makes statutory schemes expensive to operate. The costs of administering such schemes are recouped through membership subscriptions. Thus a member of a statutorily regulated profession can expect to pay considerably more by way of membership subscriptions than a member of a voluntary self-regulating organization. This is a significant factor for practitioners working in the private sector whose outgoings are reflected in their charges to patients.

B. Common law

The operation of the common law also serves as a regulatory mechanism. By common law, we mean law made by judges in court, rather than statute law. Common law encompasses both civil and criminal law. Whereas criminal law is concerned with regulating conduct between individuals and the State, civil law regulates activities between individuals. Law involves the application of legal principles to a set of facts, usually where one party is alleging some wrongdoing, in its broadest sense, against another. The common law is 'precedent-based'. This means that a previous case, already decided, will serve as an authority for future cases which have broadly similar facts. This is because the law aims to deal with like cases alike. In order for that principle not to apply, it has to be shown, in effect, that there are

[9] As we shall see in Part III, the mere presence of lay members does not, of itself, ensure greater accountability if they are not sufficiently empowered to be able to challenge medical judgement.

[10] This has been seen, e.g., with the GMC, whose recent consultation paper proposes an increase in lay membership to account for 25% of the composition of the Council.

features which distinguish the facts of the case in question from earlier cases which seem superficially similar, and that these distinguishing features require the court to arrive at a different decision.

One of the difficulties in establishing what the legal position surrounding complementary medicine is, is that there is a complete dearth of decided cases. Accordingly, no one is in a position to give a definitive legal opinion as to how a court would decide a case against a complementary therapist. Where there is no case law, the best that lawyers can do is to try to predict how they think a court would be likely to decide a case. This is done by looking at related case law, and working by analogy to assess whether a court would be likely to apply the same principles in any given situation. Accordingly, our starting point for analysis must be to look at cases which have been brought against doctors and other health practitioners, and begin by applying those same principles to complementary practitioners.

A civil lawsuit is initiated by an aggrieved party employing formal legal procedures to bring a complaint to court. In criminal cases, it is almost always the Crown Prosecution Service who initiates proceedings, on behalf of the State. Even though criminal law is found in criminal statutes, this still forms part of the common law, because criminal cases involve judges applying statutory provisions to factual situations. Sometimes this may involve an interpretation of what various provisions in a statute actually mean. This builds up a body of case law so that in subsequent cases, a statute will be interpreted consistently.

Unlike ethical rules and statutory rules, which set out permissible standards of conduct and operate prospectively, the common law, as a means of regulatory control, operates retrospectively, by applying legal definitions of acceptable behaviour after the event. To this extent, litigation regulates more by default, its success relying largely on the deterrent effect. This presupposes that others who see that a particular course of action will be harshly penalized (usually by way of financial damages) will desist from behaving in the offending manner. Whilst deterrents may well have an effect on the individual who has had the miserable experience of being taken to court, any wider effect is a matter for conjecture.

C. Voluntary self-regulation

Over the last ten to fifteen years, complementary therapies have been undergoing a process of professionalization, with numerous professional and pan-professional bodies coming in to being. Most voluntary bodies maintain a register of either individual practitioners or member organizations. Functions include setting educational standards and instituting accreditation systems, promulgating ethical advice, usually in the form of codes of conduct, and exercising some level of disciplinary function over members.

Professional bodies vary hugely in their membership requirements. In some well established therapies, successful voluntary self-regulating controls have been in force for decades. Such bodies have careful selection criteria and only admit practitioners onto their register upon successful completion of several years' training, a period of supervised practice, and an agreement to be bound by a comprehensive code of ethics. In other situations, therapists may become members, or affiliated members of professional organizations on the basis of far less rigorous criteria, but invariably upon the payment of a fee.

In terms of educational requirements, there is a considerable variation amongst therapeutic organizations. Some professional bodies define competencies, approve syllabuses and licence, monitor, and advise training establishments, whilst other therapeutic organizations are only at the very beginning of this process. Needless to say, within each therapy there is also a huge variation as to the training standards required by various organizations, and thus as to the value of qualifications gained as a result. Whilst many qualifications are obtained after several hundred hours of training, other certificates and diplomas are awarded after several weekend courses.

Most voluntary self-regulating bodies produce a code of conduct of some form or another. Such codes will consider professionals' relationships with clients, with other professionals, and, possibly, professionals' wider duties to society. These set out professional responsibilities which correlate to the expectation and rights of those whom professionals serve. Beauchamp and Childress describe professional codes as an articulated statement of the morality of the members of the profession. In this way, they say, professional standards are distinguished from standards imposed by external bodies such as Governments.[11] The standard of these codes varies hugely. Some provide detailed guidance whilst others might be no more than a couple of pages. Because it would be impossible to envisage every

[11] Beauchamp, T. and Childress, J., *Principles of Biomedical Ethics* (4th edn., OUP, 1994).

situation in which ethical guidance might be required, most codes of ethics are drafted in fairly generalized terms only, and are usually couched in negative terms, which concentrate on prohibition on practitioners.

The extent to which professional bodies either have disciplinary mechanisms, or exercise their disciplinary functions also varies significantly. On the whole, procedures are not well defined and most professional bodies profess to have no more than a few complaints a year, most of those being of a relatively minor nature. As with statutory self-regulating bodies, there is usually a range of disciplinary options, from warnings at one end, to expulsion at the other. Organizations may have informal compensation procedures, requiring, on occasion, members to refund fees paid by patients.

In general, the present scheme of voluntary self-regulation, backed up by the common law has, on the face of it at least, operated fairly successfully. As with litigation, so there appear to be remarkably few complaints of a serious nature made against complementary therapists. Most of the major therapies have well-established professional structures, and many other therapies are gradually becoming better organized. Strong professional organization does not seem to be particularly visible amongst the more esoteric range of therapies, although, as we shall explore, this may be because such therapies, particularly those which focus on the emotional and spiritual realm, are the least amenable to formal regulation of any kind.

III. REGULATION, LAW, AND ETHICS

Law and ethics are both instruments of regulation, prescribing how people ought to act in response to one another. More specifically, in the health care context, both are instruments capable of determining good practice, shaping how practitioners should behave. We shall see that law and ethics interrelate, with both representing acceptable current *mores*. It goes without saying that laws should not be unethical and that whether there is a requirement to obey 'unjust laws' is a matter for debate.

As with ethics, laws can be justified on the basis of one or more overarching theories. Many of our criminal laws are derived from Judaeo–Christian notions of duties towards each other, and respect for the sanctity of life. Other laws may be justified on the basis of consequentalist arguments, which would include utilitarian notions that the good of society is best served by laws which maximize happiness for the greatest number of people. We shall look at some of these theories in greater detail in Part III.

Whereas the function of ethics, promulgated in the form of codes of practice, has been seen as encouraging optimum standards of behaviour, the law is more concerned with enforcing minimum standards. When we talk about *ethical* decisions, we think in terms of the best possible decisions that can be taken in all of the circumstances. We may even connote by this fair decisions, which do justice to the competing interests of all involved. To behave ethically is to behave rightly, to be morally conscionable, and to arrive at decisions after a careful weighing up of all the relevant facts, having considered respective rights and responsibilities, rather than as a result of thoughtless, arbitrary decision-making with no regard for the consequences. When we talk about *legal* decisions, we ask questions such as: 'What can we get away with?'; or 'Will we be punished if we pursue this course of action?'

Usually what is ethical will be legal and vice versa. This is not always the case though, and we can see that particularly in a health care context, where the law has always tended to protect professional, rather than patients' interests, ethical requirements may be noticeably more stringent than legal requirements. Thus, the principle of respect for confidentiality is seen as one of the cardinal principles of the practitioner/patient relationship, even though the law of confidentiality is poorly developed and rarely protects people once their confidences have been breached.[12] Likewise, in relation to consent to medical treatment, even though the amount of information that a practitioner has to give to a patient about a procedure as a matter of strict law is determined by how much information responsible doctors would give, rather than the amount of information that a responsible patient would wish to know, ethically, there would be strong grounds for disclosing as much information as the individual patient wished to have, such standard being maximally respectful of the principle of respect for the patient's autonomy.

Given, however, that no one can be forced to do anything that they do not wish to do, what is it about *legal* duties that makes those subject to them take them more seriously than other sorts of normative rules?

---

[12] Although, in certain circumstances, the law will grant an injunction to prevent potential or further breaches of confidential information.

The key seems to be the issue of penalties for non-compliance. Customarily legal sanctions are taken more seriously than other forms of sanctions. Only legal sanctions have the backing of the criminal law, and thus, the possibility of depriving people of their liberty for unacceptable conduct by imprisoning them for particularly unacceptable conduct.

This is not to say that breaching ethical codes of conduct may not also have deleterious consequences. Indeed serious transgressions of professional rules may lead to the removal of the practitioner's right to practise and hence his or her livelihood. As with all rules prescribing how people ought to behave, there is a spectrum of unacceptable conduct, and not all transgressions will be dealt with equally rigorously. Where, however, one has acted unethically, often the adverse consequence will be that the decision will sit uneasily with that person's conscience, and that person will have to live with the consequences of his or her decision. Equally, one may attract moral opprobrium from colleagues, which may have unfortunate social effects and may affect future employment opportunities. Although this might be unpleasant, it is, none the less, an essentially private matter.

Where one breaks the law, however, it is no longer a private matter. Particularly when the criminal law is invoked, the police will be called in, family and friends will be affected, employers will inevitably have to know, and a variety of Government agencies will have records on an individual. Even if one is eventually acquitted, the stigma attached will be significant, and the media often have a field day with errant professionals.

To the extent that sanctions impose undesirable consequences on would-be transgressors, their effectiveness as a means of regulating conduct depends critically on their deterrent effect, that is, a belief that people will modify their conduct so as to avoid being penalized. The deterrent effect depends on a number of factors. Clearly, for people to be aware that they face a penalty for certain sorts of action, rules have to be visible and accessible. New rules may have to be given publicity until people are aware of their effect. More significantly though, the deterrent effect will be limited by the extent to which people believe that sanctions will be enforced. If severe penalties exist but are never imposed, their effectiveness will be much reduced. To the extent, for example, that laws prohibiting the possession of cannabis are increasingly overlooked by the police, the deterrent effect of the Misuse of Drugs Act 1971 is lessened. So too, if a voluntary self-regulating profession prohibits certain practices, but practitioners are never punished, the value of that disciplinary mechanism and its deterrent effect will be of limited value.

As well as looking at the extent to which laws are enforced in fact, it is also worth considering the extent to which laws are capable of being enforced. If, for example, there was a law that practitioners shouldn't instil false hopes into patients, this would be impossible to apply in practice. In the first place, who would decide what constituted false hope? For a law to be enforceable elements of any offence must be clear—people must know precisely what it is that they are not allowed to do. Secondly, what if the practitioner genuinely believed that there was some hope and that the patient would benefit from a boosted mental outlook? Moreover, how could one prove that a practitioner spoke or acted in such a way as to instil false hope? Clearly, whilst it may well be appropriate to stop bogus practitioners from peddling hopeless cures to vulnerable patients, the law may not be the best mechanism to achieve this.

Thus, even where normative statements are contained in prescriptive laws or statutes, practitioners cannot be compelled to obey them. Laws could be introduced here, as they have been in certain parts of the United States prohibiting therapists from having sex with their clients. Although this would hopefully make therapists more circumspect about breaching the fundamental trust inherent in the relationship, the mere existence of a law is not going to protect all patients. This seemingly obvious point has important ramifications for our discussion on how complementary medicine should best be regulated. It means that the mere existence of statutory regulation, rather than less formal means of regulation, cannot ensure that practitioners will be 'good' practitioners. Practitioners must choose to behave ethically. Laws cannot make them do so.

Finally, we need to examine the way in which ethics and the law interrelate in the context of professional standards. Essentially, both have the same aspiration, namely, the promotion of high standards. Legal and ethical requirements should be almost parallel. At this point, however, what needs to be appreciated is that ethical standards determine the legal standards. We shall go on to see, for example, how the test of negligence is the test of acceptable professional standards. Put another way, a practitioner will not be negligent provided he or she acts in accordance with an acceptable body of professional opinion. Thus, in determining what constitutes an acceptable standard of behaviour, judges do not pluck legal standards out of the air, rather, they are guided by expert evidence as to what constitute the prevailing ethical standards of that particular profession.

There is an unhelpful misconception that the law is hostile to professionals and imposes an unreasonably high standard on practitioners. In fact, the opposite true. The only standard imposed by the law is that a practitioner acts reasonably. No one is perfect and the law is not interested in penalizing every mistake a professional may make, only those mistakes which are unreasonable, with reasonableness being determined in accordance with prevailing ethical standards. If anything, this may perpetuate lower standards than are ideal, in that if accepted levels of practice are substandard, or in some way unethical, that will set the standard for the profession. It is in this sense that the law enforces minimum standards rather than promotes best practice.

A similar interplay exists as between professional conduct jurisdiction of self-regulating bodies and ethics. As with legal cases, the standard which will be invoked in disciplinary cases to decide whether a practitioner was in breach of his or her professional responsibilities is set by current standards of good practice. Although peer assessment characterizes self-regulation disciplinary committees, as well as the courts, will enlist expert evidence to ascertain what constitutes prevailing professional practice.

It should also be borne in mind that ethics are central to both voluntary and statutory self-regulation, and that in organizational terms there may be very little real difference between voluntary self-regulation and statutory self-regulation. Both may be presided over by ruling professional bodies with similar registration, educational, and disciplinary functions, and both may have a comprehensive code of ethics. Certainly, the level of self-imposed regulation demonstrated by the osteopaths is not radically different in substance from the envisaged statutory scheme. Before assuming that statutory regulation is the preferred route, we must not rule out the fact that effective voluntary self-regulation may do a very good job of fulfilling all the regulatory requirements we have identified.

9
Legal Controls

As we have seen, the general understanding is that complementary medicine is virtually unregulated, the implicit assumption being that this is a dangerous state of affairs. Certainly, with the exception of the Osteopaths Act 1993 and the Chiropractors Act 1994, there is no specific statutory control similar to that regulating other areas of health care, but this does not mean that practitioners operate in a legal or ethical vacuum. We must not overlook the fact that many therapies have a high level of voluntary self-regulation, and have extremely active professional associations with ethical codes and disciplinary mechanisms which have been in place for very many years (although this is not to say that all therapists belong to a professional organization, or that all professional organizations have the necessary infrastructures or power to control members effectively).

We should not fall into the trap of equating voluntary self-regulation with no regulation. Voluntary self-regulation, when it is well designed, can operate extremely effectively as the General Council and Register of Osteopaths demonstrates. Moreover, although most health professions are statutorily regulated, not all service industries are regulated on this basis. Outside the caring professions, other industries, such as advertising and the travel industry, operate more or less successfully within voluntary codes of practice. Other service industries, such as social work, are currently controlled by voluntary codes of practice. Areas such as beauty therapy also depend on voluntary regulation, notwithstanding the potential for harm inherent in many procedures, particularly those using invasive methods like electrolysis.

The point to note is that often, voluntary self-regulation is viewed as being an acceptable way of maintaining standards across a wide field of activity. Where Governments are content that self-regulating industries are not injurious to the public they are unlikely to impose statutory regulation. In other sectors, such as financial services, Governments may decide that the public is not capable of being adequately protected by voluntary regulation and will impose statutory constraints.

As we have already pointed out we should not assume that because other health care professions are statutorily regulated, the broad spectrum of complementary therapies should automatically be regulated in the same way. We should be particularly wary of assumptions that failure to grant statutory status means that complementary therapies are in some way inferior to existing health care professions. Much of the success of complementary therapy is precisely because of the ways in which it differs from orthodox medicine, not least of all because of its less rigid, power-based attitude towards clients. A regulatory scheme is required which will preserve and enhance those differences rather than stifle them. However, as we have seen, much of the impetus for statutory regulation is coming from within complementary medicine itself. We shall discuss at greater length what therapists feel they have to gain by statutory, as opposed to other forms of regulation.

Whether further regulation, or simply different types of regulation, may be required will depend on how successfully the current forms of voluntary self-regulation are operating and whether they do, indeed, provide adequate safeguards for the public. We shall now go on to look at how these self-regulating mechanisms operate, as well as the numerous statutory provisions which affect complementary medicine in a variety of ways. In the coming sections, we shall look at the forms of regulation which are currently in place, and which exert regulatory control over the practice of complementary medicine.

I. STATUTORY REGULATION

In Part I we explored some of the political and historical dimensions of the regulatory debate, and how these shape the creation of legislation in this area. We also looked at how other health care professionals have been statutorily regulated, with a view to seeing whether these might provide us with a useful model for complementary medicine. We must remember, however, that simply because health care professions have tended to be regulated by statute, this does not mean that this model is at all appropriate for the diverse range of therapies that make up complementary medicine. We may conclude that there are characteristics about the relationship that complementary health practitioners have with patients that are so radically different from other therapeutic relationships that statutory regulation is not appropriate, and that more creative options will need to be considered.

Primarily, we shall consider how the Medical Act 1983 has been adapted by the osteopaths and the chiropractors. We shall ask whether the criticisms raised against existing statutory health professionals have been remedied in the new legislation, and we shall be looking at whether this statutory model represents the way ahead for many other therapies.

Before we do so, we need to look briefly at the variety of other statutory provisions which impact on how complementary practitioners may practise. Although it is beyond our remit to consider these provisions in any great depth, we shall start by mentioning some of the miscellaneous statutory provisions which affect the provision of goods and services. Rather than attempting to set these requirements out in any systematic way, we shall merely highlight some of the provisions which seem to us to be critical to practitioners. We would stress that many of these provisions are extremely important to therapists in practice. All complementary therapists who are considering setting up in practice must have a basic understanding of employment law, insurance law, partnership law, occupiers' liability, and such other legal provisions as may be appropriate to their practice. These matters fall outside the scope of this book, although they are matters about which practitioners should seek advice on from lawyers familiar with health care law or from their professional associations

A. Statutes affecting provision of goods and services

1. Medicines Act 1968

Although we do not intend to concentrate on product licensing provisions to any great extent, it is important to realise that, at least in relation to homoeopaths and herbalists, the therapeutic products supplied by therapists as an integral part of the therapy are subject to a strict licensing system, even though, at present, practitioners are not. This will inevitably be an important factor in relation to future regulation.

We have identified throughout the centrality of consumer protection to the regulation debate. If we are attempting to formulate regulatory solutions which promote client safety, we shall need some framework for analysis which takes into account how injurious particular therapies actually are. To this end, it is helpful to look at certain determining characteristics which mark out some therapies from others. As we have seen, homoeopathy, and herbalism share the characteristic of being largely product-based therapies—that is, on the basis of an in-depth history, the complementary practitioner will 'prescribe' a remedy, in the same way that a doctor would. In law, there is a presumption in favour of treating like cases alike, so that if conventional medicines are subject to a strict licensing system, cogent reasons will have to be adduced as to why other remedy-based therapies should not be controlled in a similar manner.

This is not to suggest that homoeopathic or herbal remedies are inherently dangerous, or pose the same risks as allopathic medicines. However, in terms of determining characteristics of any therapy, the giving of potentially harmful substances requires the strictest of controls. Although homoeopathic preparations, in particular, are generally thought of as being harmless because of their extremely diluted nature, none the less, there are certain preparations which may have contra-indications if used inappropriately. Likewise, certain herbal medicines are not as innocuous as their 'natural' image would imply, albeit the risks they pose may be smaller than allopathic pharmaceuticals.

Both herbal and homoeopathic preparations are subject to the Medicines Act 1968 which deals with all medicinal products. Currently, herbal remedies are exempt from the licensing requirements of the Medicines Act 1968.[1] The fact that these licensing requirements are already in place undoubtedly affects the impetus to regulate the therapists as well. However, the existing product licensing laws are not comprehensive omitting, for example, Chinese herbal medicines, Unani and Ayurvedic remedies currently being sold as nutritional supplements. This is a considerable source of concern to both the medical profession and consumer groups. As the recent controversy over the licensing of herbal preparations demonstrated, this is a highly sensitive matter, and one which will undoubtedly be influenced by developments in Europe over the next couple of years.

---

[1] Medicines Act 1968, s. 12 and s. 56. Herbal remedies which did not have a licence prior to 1968 are effectively exempted from licensing procedures. This exemption came under serious threat last year as a result of Directive 65/65 EEC, which requires 'industrially produced medicinal products' to have a licence. After vociferous lobbying by the natural medicines movement, the Government introduced the Medicines for Human Use (Marketing Authorisations etc.) Regs. 1994, SI 1994 No. 3144, which specifically excluded herbal remedies falling within the remit of s. 12 and s. 56 from the term 'industrially produced medicinal products'.

Whilst harmonization of qualifications for therapists is likely to remain elusive, standardization of licensing requirements throughout Europe is a distinct possibility.

2. Access to information statutes

As an appreciation of individuals' rights has taken hold, and people are less and less prepared to trust that those in a position of authority can be relied upon to protect their interests, various attempts have been made to allow people freedom of access to information held about them. Various statutes have been introduced all of which, from a consumer's point of view, have been more than necessarily protective of those holding information. The fact that such legislation had to be enacted at all is indicative of the power imbalance of the doctor/ patient relationship present at the time these statutes were passed. Three statutes grant specific rights of access to health information. These are the Data Protection Act 1984, the Access to Medical Reports Act 1988 and the Access to Health Records Act 1990.[2] These have all been amended so as to include osteopaths and chiropractors as relevant 'health professionals' to whom the Acts apply.

Although all of these statutes have wide exemptions in relation to health information,[3] the Acts do give patients statutory rights of access to information held by practitioners about them. Although these Acts do not specifically apply to non-statutorily regulated complementary health care practitioners, we recommend that respect for patients' autonomy requires that all therapists should follow the thrust of these Acts and permit their patients free access to their records as a matter of course (subject to practicability).

Given that the ideal of the complementary relationship is for therapist and client to be working together in a collaborative venture, there can be no justification for withholding details supplied by the patient. Practitioners who shudder at the prospect of clients seeing what has been written about them might need to consider the basis on which those notes have been made, and whether it is really constructive to include thoughts and ideas which could not be discussed with patients. One would hope that in a therapeutic alliance, clients should

---

[2] Similar statutory provisions exist granting access to particular social service records: Access to Personal Files Act 1987.

[3] All 3 statutes contain substantial therapeutic privilege clauses, allowing practitioners to withhold information which would, in their opinion, cause patients harm.

be seen as fully entitled to have access to records, not least of all to recap on goals of therapy and to be able to appraise what advances, if any, have been made.

3. Notification of diseases

The Public Health (Control of Disease) Act 1984 places registered medical practitioners under a duty to disclose certain notifiable diseases to the responsible authority.[4] There is no explicit statutory duty on complementary practitioners to report such information. Indeed we would argue that it would be dangerous to impose a duty on non-medically qualified practitioners to recognize, for example, amoebic dysentery or meningococcal septicaemia.

As in all cases, however, where a complementary practitioner thinks a patient may have a condition which requires medical attention, he or she should urge the patient to seek medical attention. The BCMA say that in this situation, a therapist should insist that a doctor is called in.[5] It is unclear whether by this they countenance that the therapist may breach confidentiality if the patient refuses to allow the GP to be contacted. As in all cases, practitioners must exercise professional accountability, and be prepared to justify their actions as being reasonable in front of their professional body.

4. Practice premises requirements

Various statutory provisions impose certain restrictions on practice, for example, the London Local Authorities Act 1991 makes it unlawful for premises to be used for certain purposes without a special treatment licence granted by the borough council. For the purposes of the Act, this includes premises to be used for acupuncture, massage, cosmetic piercing, light, electric, or other special treatment of a like kind.[6] The licensing requirements do not apply to premises where the special treatment is carried out by, or under the supervision of, a registered medical practitioner, or any *bona fide* member of certain bodies of health practitioners, or (in the case of acupuncture) a dentist.

The exemption to health practitioners applies to those practitioners

---

[4] For the diseases in question, see the Public Health (Infectious Diseases) Regulations 1988, SI No. 1546/1988.
[5] BCMA, June 1992, 4.43.
[6] London Local Authorities Act 1991, Part II, s. 4.

whose professional body has a register of qualified members, requires its members to hold professional indemnity insurance, subjects its members to a code of conduct and ethics (including a prohibition against immoral conduct in the course of their practice), and provides procedures for subjecting members to disciplinary procedures.[7]

B. Protection of title

1. Osteopaths Act 1993

In 1991, a working party on osteopathy was set up by the King's Fund Institute, under the chairmanship of Sir Thomas Bingham, Master of the Rolls.[8] The outcome was a highly influential report which found osteopathy to be the most widely used complementary therapy. The working party strongly supported the introduction of autonomous legislation and a draft Bill was appended to their report. In consequence, in 1993, osteopaths became the first complementary health care profession to be granted autonomous statutory status since the medical profession. This has been viewed as a significant achievement, and demonstrates the groundswell of Parliamentary support for complementary medicine. In the second reading of the Osteopaths Bill, Malcolm Moss, MP, said: 'The purpose of the Bill is to provide the profession with the statutory framework to regulate its own activities and chart its future development and growth'.[9] Having achieved this status, the osteopaths are, more than ever, noticeably distancing themselves from other, less organized, complementary therapies, preferring now to see themselves on a par with the medical profession.

(i) Background to the Act

The osteopaths had unsuccessfully sought statutory regulation since the 1920s. A 'kite-flying' Osteopaths Bill in 1986 had already established considerable all-party support for legislation, and the 1991 Report noted that the medical profession's attitude towards osteopathy had changed significantly. Legislators were undoubtedly persuaded that it would be appropriate to consider statutory regulation for osteopaths because they had a highly organized and long-established scheme of voluntary self-regulation administered by the General Council and

---

[7] Ibid., S. 4(b)(ii).
[8] *Report of a Working Party on Osteopathy* (King's Fund, 1991).
[9] 7 May 1993: 224 HC Official Report (6th Series).

Register of Osteopaths (GCRO), and required high educational and professional standards of members of the osteopathic profession.

None the less, the working party noted that practising osteopaths were dispersed among a number of different bodies, and that standards of education and training varied very widely. With no single body to govern and regulate all osteopaths, the public had no guarantee that an osteopath was competent. Equally, there was no single ruling body to prescribe or enforce standards.

The 1991 Report found that benefits to the general public of a statutory system of control would include:

(1) an assurance that in future all practitioners will be trained to a high standard of competence;

(2) a guarantee that appropriate standards of professional conduct will be enforceable by a single statutory governing body;

(3) the establishment of a suitable mechanism for dealing with complaints from the public concerning the conduct of practitioners; and

(4) a guarantee that all practitioners are fully covered by professional indemnity insurance.

Following on from the Report, Malcolm Moss MP introduced the Osteopaths Bill as a Private Member's Bill. The Bill received royal assent on 1 July 1993, although the Act is unlikely to be implemented before 1996. Effectively, this means that osteopaths are still a voluntary self-regulating profession, and will be until such time as their statutory councils are up and running.

(ii) Structure of the Act

Broadly speaking, the Osteopaths Act 1993 and the Chiropractors Act 1994 are modelled very closely on the Medical Act 1983, although they incorporate several significant amendments. Let us start by identifying some common features which all statutes regulating health professionals based on the Medical Act 1983 have in common. Amongst the notable characteristics of such legislation are the following

(1) A governing council consisting of elected members of the profession, various Government-made appointees, and lay representatives.

(2) The appointment of a registrar whose function is to maintain and publish a statutory register of qualified professionals.

(3) Various statutory committees including:

    (a) Education Committee—whose functions are to determine relevant training standards and qualifications required for entry onto the register and to license and inspect training establishments;

    (b) Preliminary Screening Committee—to consider complaints against practitioners and decide whether they need to be referred to a misconduct committee, referred to another agency or dismissed;

    (c) Professional Misconduct Committee—to consider allegations of misconduct against practitioners. This committee will have a range of penalties at its disposal, from admonitions to suspension or erasure from the register. The committee will be under a duty to prepare, and from time to time revise, a code of conduct;

    (d) Health Committee—where a practitioner's ability is seriously impaired due to ill-health, rather than being disciplined the Health Committee may limit practice and require appropriate medical treatment.

(4) Protection of title, backed up by criminal penalties.

One interesting point, which may have ramifications for any attempts at creating an overarching system of regulation is that statutes which grant protection of title do not define the therapy involved. Thus the Medical Act 1983 does not define what medicine is, beyond that which registered medical practitioners do. Likewise, the Osteopaths Act 1993 does not define what osteopathy is. This will be an interesting point for osteopaths and chiropractors who do not satisfy the requirements of the Acts and are thus unable to call themselves osteopaths or chiropractors, but who none the less practise those techniques.

The Osteopaths Act 1993 provides for the establishment of a General Osteopathic Council, charged with the duty of developing, promoting, and regulating osteopathy. Four statutory committees are established: the Education Committee, the Investigating Committee, the Professional Conduct Committee and the Health Committee, mirroring the structure of the Medical Act 1983.

The General Council must appoint a registrar to establish and maintain a register of osteopaths. Entry to the register is dependent upon the payment of a prescribed fee, in addition to proof by the

applicant that he or she is of good character, has a recognized qualification, and is in good health, both physically and mentally. The last
stipulation, an innovation in health care legislation, is particularly
important for practitioners working more holistically, and who, as a
consequence, will be dealing with patients on an emotional and
spiritual level, as well as on a physical level.

Provisions are made for conditional registration to allow osteopaths to come within the Act even where their length of practice
renders them ineligible for full registration. This grandfather clause,
debated long and hard in Parliament, was considered necessary to
allow a sufficient period of time for practising osteopaths to become
registered under the Act.

The General Council may make rules for provisional registration
during which period practitioners would have to work under a fully
registered osteopath. Although no such rules have been made at the
time of writing, this provision is extremely important, as it will place,
for the first time, a statutory obligation on complementary practitioners
to be supervised after qualification. Any suspension of a practitioner's
registration must be marked on the register (something that the GMC
are also about to introduce). The register must be available for public
inspection. The registrar must investigate any allegation that an entry in
the register is incorrect or has been fraudulently procured and has the
power to order the immediate suspension of a practitioner if this is felt
to be necessary to protect the public.

The Education Committee has a duty to promote high standards of
education and training, and to keep these standards under review.[10]
The General Council must consult the committee on matters relating
to education, training, examinations or tests of competence. The committee will have the power to appoint visitors to inspect existing or
prospective training establishments and report back to the council.
From time to time, the council must publish a statement of the standard of proficiency required for the safe and competent practice of
osteopathy. The council must maintain and publish a list of recognized qualifications which meet that standard.

The council can require osteopaths to undertake post-registration

[10] The working party recommended that the Council's responsibility for oversight of the education, training, and practice of osteopaths should include responsibility for determining the future of osteopathic education, having regard to:
(1) the changing requirements and responsibilities of clinical practice; (2) developments within the European Community; and (3) the need for a strong research
base.

training. Unlike the Medical Act 1983, but consistent with rules recently introduced under the Nurses, Midwives and Health Visitors Act 1992, continuing professional development will be a statutory requirement for osteopaths. A voluntary scheme is being developed to precede the implementation of the Act.[11]

The General Council must prepare, and revise where necessary, a code of practice laying down standards expected of registered osteopaths and giving advice about the practice of osteopathy. The requirement on the council to publish a statement of the standard of proficiency required for the safe practice of osteopathy, and, in addition, the duty, when varying that standard, to notify practitioners of how the previous standards have been altered, is also an improvement on existing statutes. As well as being extremely helpful in establishing boundaries of good practice, this provision may be very useful in determining issues of legal liability.

Where an allegation is made against a practitioner of unacceptable professional conduct, professional incompetence, that he or she has been convicted of a criminal offence, or that his or her fitness to practise is seriously impaired on the grounds of ill-health, that case must be referred to the Investigating Committee. If they decide that there is a case to answer, they must refer the case to the Professional Conduct Committee or the Health Committee as appropriate. If necessary, in keeping with other statutorily regulated professions, the Investigating Committee may order the immediate suspension of a practitioner's registration if this is thought necessary to protect the public.

As to the remit of the Professional Misconduct Committee, the Act contains a definition of unacceptable professional misconduct which embraces substandard practice and deficient performance. Thus, for the first time under any statutory scheme governing health professionals,[12] professional incompetence is specifically identified as a trigger point for disciplinary investigation. That it is included in the Act demonstrates the extent to which the osteopaths considered carefully the deficiencies of the Medical Act 1983, and the ways in which it could be improved upon.

[11] Although midwives have to date been under a statutory duty to undertake post-registration continuing professional training, new provisions which came into force on 1 Apr. 1995 will require all practising nurses, midwives and health visitors to undertake continuing professional development in order to maintain registration.
[12] (216 HC Official Report (6th Series) col. 1179; 15 Jan. 1993.)

Whilst the Professional Misconduct Committee will look at criminal convictions, the Act contains a specific statutory provision that a criminal conviction will not automatically lead to a finding of professional misconduct. The Professional Misconduct Committee may take no further action if it considers that the criminal offence in question has no material relevance to the fitness of the osteopath concerned to practise osteopathy.

Where the Professional Misconduct Committee makes an adverse finding against the practitioner, it has a variety of penalties at its disposal. It may admonish the osteopath, suspend registration, impose conditions on registration, or erase the practitioner from the register. As to the penalties which may be imposed, as with the medical profession, erasure is the ultimate sanction, which is only to be used exceptionally. The 1991 Report suggested that the legislation should opt for 'the widest range of penalties to enable the Professional Conduct Committee to tailor the penalty to the seriousness of the offence'.[13] The committee must publish an annual report setting out the names of the osteopaths found guilty of misconduct, the nature of the allegations and any steps taken by the committee.[14]

If the Health Committee finds an allegation well founded, it may impose conditions on the osteopath's practice, or suspend registration, if that is necessary for the protection of the public. Both the Professional Misconduct Committee and the Health Committee may order the interim suspension of the osteopath whilst investigations are in place, if this is felt necessary to protect the public. Here, as throughout the Act, the osteopath has rights of appeal. The General Council may appoint legal and medical assessors to give advice to the Investigating Committee, the Professional Conduct Committee or the Health Committee.

The Act makes it a criminal offence for any person who is not a registered osteopath to describe himself or herself as an osteopath of any kind. A person convicted of this offence could be liable on summary conviction to a fine not exceeding £5,000. Note that this provision would not stop manipulative therapists from employing osteopathic techniques; it would merely prevent them from using the professional title of 'osteopath'. The Act also makes it an offence to fail to comply with any requirement imposed by the Professional

---

[13] *Report of a Working Party on Osteopathy*, King's Fund.
[14] The GCRO has, for the past 2 years, published a digest of its Conduct Proceedings.

Conduct Committee, the Health Committee, or an appeal tribunal hearing against a Health Committee decision.

The General Council is empowered to require osteopaths to ensure that they are properly insured against liability towards patients. This will be the first time that complementary practitioners will have been statutorily required to carry professional indemnity insurance. The importance of this provision cannot be understated. Whilst this has been a stipulation of the more reputable voluntary organizations, the failure of many practitioners to carry professional indemnity insurance means that even if an aggrieved person were able successfully to pursue an action against a practitioner, there would be no guarantee that they would be able to obtain compensation.

Miscellaneous provisions amend data protection and access to information provisions so as to include registered osteopaths in their definition of relevant 'health professionals'. As with other health professionals, the Act exempts osteopaths from the Rehabilitation of Offenders Act 1974, so that practitioners must declare all convictions, including spent convictions, if asked, when applying for registration. This places osteopaths in the same position as other health professionals.

The Constitution of the Statutory Committees is set out in various Schedules to the Act. The General Council will consist of twelve members elected by fully registered osteopaths, eight members appointed by the Privy Council, three members appointed by the Education Committee and one member appointed by the Secretary of State. Of the twelve members appointed by registered osteopaths, at least one member must be both a fully registered osteopath and a registered medical practitioner. One of the eight members appointed by the Privy Council must be a registered medical practitioner appointed after consultation with the Conference of Medical Royal Colleges, and the other seven must be non-osteopaths, but any of them may be registered medical practitioners. The three members appointed by the Education Committee must be people qualified to advise on matters relating to education and training in osteopathy. The member appointed by the Secretary of State must be qualified to advise on matters of professional education.[15]

---

[15] At the time of writing, final appointments to the statutory committee were still being made, a year and a half after the Act received Royal Assent. Sources estimate that the register will not be fully operative until the summer of 1997 at the earliest.

It is clear that those involved in the drafting of the Act were aware that it would potentially serve as a model for regulating other complementary therapies, and a great deal of thought has gone into its preparation. Whether statutory regulation will benefit the profession of osteopathy remains to be seen. As we have suggested, if the diverse range of complementary therapies is regarded as constituting a spectrum, osteopathy is probably the most 'medicalized' end of the range. This is not only to suggest that the therapeutic techniques themselves are akin to orthodox medical practice, but also the fact that osteopathy, for some of the reasons we have discussed, is viewed as acceptable by the medical profession. It may be that there are benefits of statutory regulation for osteopathy which would positively hamper other therapies if the same model were applied to them.

The Osteopaths Act 1993 has not been universally welcomed by grass roots practitioners. There are several reasons for this. One is that there are many more schools of osteopathy than those recognized by the General Council. The likelihood, however, is that these will not be recognized as acceptable training establishments for the purposes of the Act. There will thus be a number of practising osteopaths and students whose qualifications will not entitle them to call themselves osteopaths when the Act comes into force. There is also a fear amongst the smaller establishments that the constitution of the governing council will be heavily loaded in favour of the more established training schools, who may not be as radical or alternative as some of the smaller schools. Of course, many osteopaths will wonder why, with such an effective system of voluntary self-regulation, it is necessary for them to be tied into a more rigid formalized statutory structure which, apart from anything else, will increase their professional membership subscriptions considerably.

2. Chiropractors Act 1994

We do not intend to set out the provisions of this Act in any detail, as the format of the legislation is virtually identical to the Osteopaths Act 1993. It is worth observing, however, that chiropractic has been awarded statutory regulation despite currently being a profession of only about 800 voluntarily registered practitioners (which is a fraction of the number of osteopaths).

As with osteopaths, a working party was set up, again chaired by Sir Thomas Bingham, to assess the viability of statutorily regulating chiropractic.[16] The report of the Working Party on Chiropractic found that although the profession was small, demand for chiropractic was growing and the number of students in training was increasing at such a rate that the profession was likely to double in size within five years. A significant impetus for approving statutory regulation for chiropractors was the favourable findings of a Medical Research Council randomized control trial into treatment of low back pain, comparing chiropractic with orthodox hospital outpatient treatment.[17]

The working party did not consider that it would be practicable to legislate for osteopaths and chiropractors under one piece of legislation, particularly since the Government has taken the view that legislation to regulate professions complementary to medicine is more suited to a Private Member's Bill than to a Government-sponsored Bill. Another factor which doubtless influenced the working party is the fact that chiropractic is statutorily regulated in most countries where it is practised.

Given the size of the profession and the burdens on practising chiropractors of financing the functions of a General Council, the steering group of the working party urged it to consider a reduction in the size of the General Council and its statutory committees. They, however, mindful of the likely expansion of the profession, and the disfavour with which Parliament would view repeated requests for amending legislation, determined that the size of the council, although slightly smaller than the General Osteopathic Council, should be sufficient to enable it to serve the needs of the profession for the foreseeable future. As with the Osteopaths Act, there are provisions to enable the size and constitution of committees to be varied by statutory instrument, rather than by amendment of the primary legislation.

C. Analysis of statutory model

Although the osteopaths and chiropractors have made certain amendments, the model is closely based on the Medical Act 1983. For those therapies considering autonomous legislation, this is the model to which they aspire. However, this model has significant drawbacks for all but highly medicalized therapies. In any event, it will only be a realistic option for the handful of therapies which are highly organized

---

[16] *Report of A Working Party on Chiropractic* (King's Fund, 1993).
[17] T. W. Meade *et al.* 'Low back pain of mechanical origin: Randomised comparison of chiropractic and hospital outpatient treatment'. 301 BMJ 1431–7 (1990).

therapies and have demonstrated a strong tradition of voluntary self-regulation. None the less, there are still reasons why other therapies might similarly aspire to statutory status.

At a time when purchasers are significantly influencing the provision of services within the NHS, a profession might feel that statutory status would enhance its attractiveness to health authorities and NHS Trusts. It is hard to assess the force of this argument. Certainly, purchasers will be more willing to deal with therapies which are taking accreditation and registration seriously.

There is also an assumption that a statutory basis would enhance a therapy's status and credibility in the eyes of the medical profession. Whilst most people welcome a more professional approach, the fundamental stumbling block will continue to be the need for complementary therapies to demonstrate clinical effectiveness. It will be interesting to watch the extent to which purchasers, if not the medical profession, will be satisfied by evidence of effectiveness from sources other than randomized control trials. One influential figure has written: 'the beneficial effects [of complementary therapies] are often so obvious, the side effects so rare and mild, and the duration of effect so variable after even a single exposure that perhaps observational studies may be enough to prove benefit'.[18]

The fact remains that without medical support, statutory regulation of any complementary therapy is unlikely. Certainly, the regulation of osteopaths was facilitated by a shift in attitude by the medical profession. Even if statutory regulation is granted, therapists should be aware that there is no guarantee that the medical profession will necessarily be more inclined either to refer or even to delegate patients to them. The GMC have given no indication that they will now formally approve referrals to osteopaths and chiropractors, falling back on the reasoning that any referral a doctor makes must be to a competent practitioner.

Autonomous legislation, then, may be appropriate for those therapies which seriously adopt a medical approach, and which do not threaten a biomedical understanding of disease. As we have seen, those therapies which are practised in a similar way to medicine, are likely to be regulated in the same sort of way and to an equally high degree. Statutory regulation will, however, be inappropriate for the vast majority of therapies, which are not amenable to understanding within

[18] Iain Smith, 'Commissioning Complementary Medicine', 310 BMJ 1151–2 (1995).

a scientific paradigm, which do not pose a danger to the public, and which would be better suited to voluntary regulation, fully supported by ethical underpinnings.

Is medicalization an inevitable consequence of pursuing statutory regulation? Certainly, it can be argued that osteopathy and chiropractic, provided they are practised in a reasonably mechanistic way, do not pose a philosophical challenge to the scientific community in the same way as, say, homoeopathy does. Would, for example, acupuncture have to shift its emphasis away from its traditional Chinese underpinnings to explanations expressed in conventional medical concepts in order to gain statutory recognition? We should not forget that a standardized and formalized curriculum is a central feature of statutory regulation, and acupuncturists who refuse to teach other than within a classical framework might find themselves marginalized or even excluded, were statutory regulation to be introduced.

Many have viewed osteopathy as a therapy which has become increasingly medicalized in order to achieve wide acceptance. Ward and Fisher refer to 'the osteopathic profession in America, which has virtually been assimilated into the conventional medical profession—so much that calls are now being made for it to "return to its original mission" '.[19] The perception remains that a therapy is likely to have to be deemed acceptable by the orthodox profession before being generally accepted. Thus the BMA accepted that there was 'an organised, reputable and coherent body of knowledge underlying osteopathy'.[20] Additionally, the osteopathic profession had the support of the Royal Colleges. In 1987, the Government said that one condition for statutory regulation would be that the medical profession were broadly supportive of that therapy's move towards statutory regulation.[21] Although there is far greater support for complementary therapies now, this statement is probably still germane.

The fact that a profession is awarded statutory status is no guarantee that orthodox medicine will embrace the therapy more willingly. As Margaret Stacey points out: 'State recognition does not, however, automatically confer the same status and power upon all professions who achieve it.'[22]

[19] Fisher, P. and Ward, A., 'Complementary medicine in Europe', 309 BMJ 107–11 (1994).
[20] *Report of a Working Party on Osteopathy*.
[21] *Hansard*, vol. 489, col. 1379–1416 (HMSO, London, 1987).
[22] M. Stacey, 'Therapeutic Collective Responsibility', in Budd and Sharma, *The Healing Bond*.

Although osteopaths and chiropractors are now statutorily regulated professions, it does not mean that GPs are necessarily more likely to refer patients to them. This will remain the case so long as the issue of regulation of various professions is divorced from the question of whether these therapies ought to be provided within the NHS. It will be interesting to see if the successful statutory regulation of all five of the complementary therapies currently seeking it would lead the Government to reconsider the issue of its provision on the NHS.

The Medical Act model is unlikely to be acceptable for any therapy which is unable to demonstrate its efficacy in scientific terms, or is not otherwise able to demonstrate efficacy in a way that would pass muster with the medical profession. In this context, the foreword to the King's Fund Chiropractic Working Party Report is extremely telling. It describes the Medical Act 1983 as the 'gold standard' in terms of regulation, and indicates that this will only be extended to those branches of complementary medicine that share certain key features with orthodox medicine. These features are:

(1) that the therapy rest on solid foundations in science and in examinable knowledge and skills;
(2) that it can be demonstrated by objective standards to cure or alleviate pain and suffering when practised skilfully, and that it has power to do harm in the wrong hands;
(3) that there is a significant public demand for it and that the public requires help in differentiating reliable from unreliable practice, and would be best protected by publicly accountable self-regulation by the profession concerned.

Robert Maxwell, Chairman of the King's Fund, continues: 'The legislation ... can provide a useful model for other branches of complementary medicine as and when they satisfy the same criteria as chiropractic and osteopathy now do'. If this genuinely represents the criteria which would be applied to further therapies seeking statutory regulation, few therapies would presently satisfy these requirements. The more interesting question is whether they would want to. To insist that complementary therapies justify themselves within a scientific paradigm shows no appreciation for the fact that there may be other equally valid ways of looking at healing and health, which do not lend themselves to quantification or proof in the same way as conventional medicine. Do therapists need or want to pander to the scientific community in order to validate therapy? Clearly, a considerable number of therapists do feel that statutory regulation is the way ahead. We must therefore look a bit more closely at the advantages and disadvantages that statutory regulation might confer.

D. Advantages of statutory regulation

(1) The indisputable advantage that statutory regulation has over other forms of regulation is the fact that statutes are backed up by the criminal law. Accordingly, in terms of enforcement, they have more teeth, in that few people are going to risk imprisonment or a fine for breaching the provisions of an Act. The main area where powers of enforcement are important is protection of title, where it is felt that the only real way to stop people professing to have qualifications that they do not have, and/ or holding themselves out to be something that they are not, is by threatening them with the criminal law.

(2) The other area where statutory backing is felt to be an advantage is disciplinary procedures. If there is only one statutory register per profession, and registration is a requirement for practice, then the ultimate sanction of deregistration is a major deterrent.[23] This can be contrasted with the current situation where for every significant therapy, there are often several major professional bodies. If a practitioner is removed from one of these registers, he or she is at liberty to register with another professional body and to continue practising, without disclosing evidence of misdemeanours. Thus, the Working Party on Chiropractic found:

Voluntary registering organisations have no effective sanction either against unlicensed, untrained practitioners, or against a practitioner who is adjudged to be guilty of unacceptable professional conduct. A voluntary registering body cannot prevent an unlicensed or professionally negligent practitioner from continuing to practice even though it is against the interest of the patients for him or her to do so.[24]

(3) Statutory status may offer therapists some protection where their therapy is under threat of medical colonization (this is more likely for mainstream therapies—most medical professions are not

---

[23] There is, however, the danger that disciplinary bodies might be more, rather than less reluctant to make a finding of serious professional misconduct because of the seriousness of removal from a statutory register.

[24] Para. 18, *Report of a Working Party on Chiropractic*.

interested in providing the more spiritual therapies themselves, even if they are happy for others to do so). It may also give them added bargaining strength to negotiate with purchasers, though this is not to suggest that purchasers will only deal with statutorily registered practitioners.

(4) Statutes are an extremely effective way of ensuring that training standards are met and training establishments are properly accredited. The advantage of having standardized training standards is that even though there is room for regional variation, there is an assurance that core competencies will have been acquired wherever the person trains.

E. Disadvantages of statutory regulation

(1) The Government will only consider regulation of therapies which can demonstrate efficacy. Until other, more qualitative methods of assessment are carried out and regarded as acceptable, only therapies which can prove themselves in scientific terms will stand a chance of gaining statutory recognition. In order to demonstrate this sort of efficacy, a therapy must be able to produce research of a standard which will be acceptable to the medical profession. Wherever possible, this will be in the form of randomized control trials. This overlooks methodological difficulties of applying randomized control trials to holistic therapies, and the fact that major funding bodies have never been prepared to fund significant studies into complementary therapies.

The requirement that a therapy will have to prove itself in scientific terms will rule out the validation of many therapies, particularly spiritual, energy, or vibrational therapies, which are not, as of yet, amenable to quantification in a way that scientists would find acceptable. It is not coincidental that the professions which have sought, or are seeking statutory regulation, have become more 'scientific' in their outlook. Therapists who reject the idea of pandering to the requirements of the conventional medical view should appreciate the extent to which the pursuit of statutory regulation could end up changing the nature of their therapeutic practice.

(2) Until a therapy is able to define its therapeutic remit, it will be extremely difficult to fit it within a statutory model. Statutory regulation is only appropriate for highly developed therapies with a strong theoretical base. Statutory regulation is not appropriate for therapeutic techniques which are small or marginal. A statute creating a

protected title is only going to be appropriate where a therapy can prove that it has something to protect. There are very few therapies sufficiently united in their views as to what it is their profession provides to be able, realistically, to seek statutory protection of title. Whilst statutory recognition confers professional status, it also carries with it professional responsibilities and a demand for high standards.

(3) Statutory regulation binds the therapy with legitimacy and interference from Government. All statutorily regulated health professions have appointments made onto their governing councils by the Secretary of State. Is this really what most alternative therapists are after? State regulation goes hand in hand with State control, as can be witnessed by the ceaseless battles between the Government and the BMA over doctors' pay and conditions. This may be a less desirable feature of State regulation, unappreciated by those practitioners who would like to see, for example, an Aromatherapists Act or Dowsers Act. Complementary practitioners should note that the functions of the Privy Council are exercised by the Government of the day. In effect, that makes statutorily regulated professionals accountable to Parliament. Practitioners should really ask themselves whether the legitimacy they perceive would flow from statutory regulation comes at too high a price.

(4) Statutory regulation imposes a standardisation upon practitioners which may not suit many therapies in which therapists operate in an individualistic manner. Statutory regulation is particularly restrictive on entry qualifications to a profession. This will be a significant disincentive for those therapies working in areas less amenable to formal systems of education, such as healing.

(9) Practitioners who administer statutory regulation may not necessarily represent the broad spectrum of views within that profession. This is thought to be a particular problem with the Osteopaths Act 1993, and would be an even greater problem for therapies where there are dozens of different schools of thought (for example, psychotherapy). Likewise, practitioners appointed onto statutory disciplinary bodies often become bureaucrats and may not have the best grasp of current trends, particularly if they are no longer in practice themselves.

(6) Statutorily regulated professions can become bogged down with regulatory detail which no one reads or knows about. The more formal statutory regulation is, the greater is the tendency for the profession to

ossify. Statutes can be rigid and inflexible. Also, the more formalized the disciplinary structures become, the more quasi-legal they are likely to be, which takes them into the realm of slow adversarial processes, where both parties will tend to require legal representation, bogged down with the same problems as litigation.

(7) Realistically, the Government is not going to regulate by statute any therapy unless the medical profession is behind it. Despite the growing interest of GPs, this approval will not be forthcoming in respect of most complementary therapies. Orthodox practitioners are aware that State regulation confers legitimacy. It can be expected that if the rights and responsibilities which come with statutory regulation are to be extended to complementary therapists, the medical profession will press all the more strongly for GPs to be retained as 'gatekeepers'. This will, of course, perpetuate the difficulties of referral/delegation discussed earlier. The Government is not behind mass regulation. In truth, the Government's avowed stance of benevolent neutrality is a cloak to hide behind. Parliamentary time is precious and the impetus is not there to regulate complementary therapies given the combined effects of the medical profession and the drugs industry on Government.

(8) Statutory regulation is more bureaucratic and much more expensive to administer than voluntary self-regulation. This would prove to be even more of a burden the smaller the therapy.

(9) Statutory regulation is only politically realistic for whole systems of healing. It is not appropriate for therapeutic modalities. It would make even less sense to have an Iridologists Act than an Endoscopists Act. Also new therapies emerge all the time. It would be pointless to suggest that Parliamentary time should be found every time responsible professionals develop a new procedure. Moreover, the whole purpose of professional autonomy is to allow practitioners to develop and monitor their own practices. This has to be at a pace set by professionals working within that field. It cannot be imposed from outside.

Despite the attractions of statutory regulation, there are considerable impediments to applying it to most complementary therapies. Few therapies have the sort of history of voluntary self-regulation which the Government would insist upon before considering legislation as a viable option, and even fewer therapies have the scientific evidence to hand which would satisfy the medical profession. Let us now consider how the common law is applied to cases involving complementary therapists, concentrating once again on whether the rigid formalism of legal mechanisms is best suited to the individualistic and humanistic ideals which characterize an holistic approach to health.

II. APPLICATION OF THE COMMON LAW

Unlike statutory and voluntary self-regulation the primary intention of which is to influence directly the way practitioners operate, the law acts in a more generalized way, regulating all citizens' conduct with the threat of legal sanctions for non-compliance. The success of the law as a regulatory mechanism depends on a number of factors. In terms of civil law, justice as between parties will depend most critically on access to the law. There is little comfort in telling aggrieved patients that they can sue their health care practitioners if, in reality, they cannot afford the process of going to law. Judicial attitudes also play a significant role, and in the past, judges have been reluctant to criticize professional medical judgement, although this is now changing to an extent. At a more fundamental level, the law is deeply conservative, with changes in public perceptions and morality sometimes taking a long time to be reflected in case law. This will be particularly relevant when it comes to entrenched notions of professional responsibilities, whereby duties such as the disclosure of risks, or patient confidentiality will tend to be analysed more in terms of professional duties than patients' rights.

We also need to look at the extent to which the common law, as opposed to statute law, is essentially a private activity, regulating affairs between individuals, rather than implementing change on a collective level. Given that many civil actions settle before they ever reach court, and only particularly lurid criminal cases receive media attention, we cannot assume that the effect of litigation filters through to the consciousness of non-affected practitioners. Is there a causal link between the degree of legal activity and the standard of professional conduct? Is the amount of litigation against doctors making them into better professionals, or simply making them more defensive? Is the increase in litigation a product of patients becoming more litigious or doctors being more careless? Within the NHS context, should the rising incidence of negligence claims be attributable to individual responsibility or are organizational difficulties at a much higher level to blame?

We shall need to see whether the law as it applies to existing health practitioners functions effectively when applied to complementary practitioners, or whether, as in the case of statute law, there are difficulties in applying rational, reductionist legal principles to systems of health care which are intuitive or holistic. Can synergistic therapies, which draw as much on the patient's resources as the practitioner's, be fitted within a negligence relationship which focuses entirely on professional responsibilities? We may find that law also requires 'scientific' proof of cause and effect which may simply be impossible to adduce in this context. As we shall see, establishing negligence requires proof not only that a practitioner was in breach of a duty owed to the patient, but that breach caused the alleged damage.

All health care practitioners must work within the law. Although professionals, unlike ordinary citizens, usually have the privilege of setting their own standards of conduct, they are subject to the full range of civil and criminal penalties for their wrongdoings. This is not to say that every professional mistake will attract legal sanctions. The law does not seek to punish all mistakes, only negligent mistakes.[25] Indeed, only a tiny proportion of medical mishaps end up in court.

In this section we shall be looking at common law provisions. By this we mean the range of cases which can be decided by judges. The common law is divided into civil law cases and criminal law cases. The bulk of our discussion will concentrate on the civil law of negligence, as this is the framework within which most actions for professional mistakes are made. Before we proceed further, it is necessary to spend a bit of time explaining some basic legal concepts.

A. Civil law

Actions in civil law will usually be brought in 'tort' or 'contract'. A tort is a civil wrong, which arises out of the relationship between two parties, whereas a contract is a more formal legal agreement between two parties which also gives rise to legal duties. In order to bring a case before a court, an aggrieved party must have a *cause of action*. This means that the wrong done to that person must fall within a

---

[25] In *Whitehouse* v. *Jordan* [1981] 1 All ER 267, Lord Fraser explained that an error of judgement may or may not be negligent, depending on the nature of the error. Thus, he said: 'If it is [an error] that would not have been made by a reasonable competent professional man professing to have the standard and type of skill that the defendant held himself out as having, and acting with ordinary care, then it is negligent'.

category recognized by the courts as one for which there is legal redress. In the civil law, redress usually takes the form of damages (monetary compensation); another important remedy is an injunction (court order) to prevent someone from persisting with the conduct complained of.

The law imposes a duty on practitioners of whatever discipline, to exercise a duty of care towards patients/clients. A breach of duty may give rise to an actionable tort. A common law duty of care arises irrespective of any other relationship between the parties. The right to sue operates independently of any other form of redress which an aggrieved patient may have against a practitioner. Thus, the fact that patients may also be able to bring a complaint against a practitioner's employers, or make a complaint to a practitioner's professional body does not prevent them from instituting legal action as well.

A patient is as entitled to bring a common law action against an unregulated practitioner as against a practitioner who is a member of a statutorily regulated profession. It may be harder to prove a case against an unregulated practitioner as there could be difficulties in establishing what would have constituted an acceptable standard of care in such a case. There is, of course, also the risk that such a practitioner does not carry professional indemnity insurance. In effect, there would be no point in suing a practitioner who could not pay damages in any event, especially if the plaintiff is ineligible for legal aid, and would risk having to bear his or her own costs.

Because most consultations with complementary practitioners take place in the private sector, where an individual patient makes an agreement with an individual practitioner, in return for an agreed fee, the relationship is usually a contractual one. A contract need not necessarily take the form of a formal written document. When most patients consult a complementary therapist they do not enter into formal negotiations and most commonly, terms relating to how much sessions cost, and how many sessions are likely to be necessary, will be discussed orally.

We can contrast this with formal, commercial transactions where there will be express terms or obligations on both sides of the negotiations. These form the substance of the contract. Often, in common contractual situations there will be standard terms, to which everyone will adhere. In principle though, parties are free to negotiate the terms of a contract as they see fit (although a contract to do anything which is against the law cannot be enforced). Few complementary therapists work in such a formal way. In a less formal arrangement, the substance of the contract will be implied. This means that the contractual obligations are not stated expressly, but there are certain responsibilities which the parties would be entitled to assume, or, in the event of a dispute, terms which a court would infer into the relationship. In respect of the practitioner's obligation, there will certainly be an implied term that the practitioner will exercise due care and skill when treating the patient.

The implied requirements of a contract, will, in effect, be identical to the requirements of common law, which also imposes a duty of care on the practitioner to act with reasonable care and skill. Failure to come up to that standard may amount to negligence. An action against a practitioner who fails to meet that standard may be brought either in contract, tort or both. Although the standard of proof is the same in each case, the main difference is in terms of damages, in that damages in tort will be restricted to those which are reasonably foreseeable, whereas in contract, all damages flowing from the breach may be recoverable.

B. Actions in negligence

In order to establish negligence, the patient (the *plaintiff*) must prove, on a balance of probabilities, that the practitioner (the *defendant*) owed her a duty of care, that the practitioner was in breach of that duty of care, and that as a result, the patient suffered harm. The patient must satisfy all three of these elements in order to make out her case. All three elements present unique difficulties for patients alleging negligence in a health care setting, which we shall examine shortly. Various procedural limitations may also bar recovery. Thus, even having satisfied the requisite evidential burdens, a patient may still lose her action, or recover only nominal damages, if the court determines that the harm suffered by the patient was too remote a consequence of the defendant's conduct. Let us now examine these three elements in turn, before going on to look at factors which may restrict recovery.

1. The duty of care

Any practitioner who enters into a therapeutic relationship with a patient assumes a duty of care not to harm that person. Whether such a relationship can be said to have existed will depend on the facts of the case. In a health care context, it is usually assumed that when seeing a patient in a professional context, whether by virtue of one's terms and conditions of service, a contract of employment, or by reason of entering into a contractual situation, one is entering into a professional relationship which will give rise to professional responsibilities.

Although NHS employees acting in the scope of their employment owe patients a duty of care, the creation of a duty may not always be clear cut. Does a doctor, stopped by a patient with her child on the street, who gives some casual advice, incur liability? If a qualified aromatherapist gives a massage to a friend as a favour, does a legal relationship exist between them? A contractual situation usually arises where the therapist offers to treat on certain terms, the patient accepts those terms and the patient gives 'consideration', usually in the form of money, in return for services rendered. Thus in order to establish whether or not a contractual situation exists, one may look to whether or not the person receiving the services has paid any money and then work backwards so as to infer a contractual duty. Although the determining factor is often the fact of payment, we must not forget that legal obligations exist alongside contractual obligations. This has particular implications for therapists who work voluntarily. If, say, healers regularly work in hospital, but receive no payment, they could still potentially owe a legal responsibility to patients they treat.

The basis of the tortious duty of care was set out in the landmark decision of *Donoghue* v. *Stevenson*,[26] which established the principle that people are under a duty not to harm those who are reasonably likely to be affected by their actions. If someone holds himself out as having a particular skill and gives advice, however casually, which someone relies on to his detriment, the courts might infer a duty of care if it was reasonable to do so. Such a duty is owed notwithstanding any additional contractual duty.

2. The appropriate standard of care

The standard of care required of any professional person is that of the ordinary skilled person exercising and professing to have that particular skill.[27] In the medical context, the standard of care is that of the

[26] [1932] AC 562, HL.
[27] The same standard is applied to all professionals, be they solicitors, doctors, surveyors or architects. On professional negligence generally, see Jackson, R. and Powell, J., *Professional Negligence* (3rd edn., Sweet & Maxwell, 1992).

Legal and Ethical Controls

reasonable person professing to have those skills. This is set out in the case of *Bolam* v. *Friern Hospital Management Committee*[28] by McNair J:

The test is the standard of the ordinary skilled man exercising and professing to have that special skill. A man need not possess the highest expert skill at the risk of being found negligent. It is a well-established law that it is sufficient if he exercises the ordinary skill of an ordinary competent man exercising that particular art.[29]

A practitioner does not have to demonstrate the highest level of skill, merely that of an ordinary competent practitioner. Thus, according to the *Bolam* test:

a doctor is not guilty of negligence if he has acted in accordance with a practice accepted as proper by a responsible body of medical men skilled in that particular art ... Putting it the other way round, a doctor is not negligent, if he is acting in accordance with such a practice, merely because there is a body of opinion which takes a contrary view.

Where there are two or more accepted bodies of competent opinion, it is open to a practitioner simply to follow one of them.[30] The school of thought followed does not have to be the most popular, it simply has to be rightly accepted as proper. One difficulty which besets complementary practitioners is that there are often dozens of schools of thought within any given therapy, and many therapists work in a highly individualized manner, so that it may be very difficult in practice, to establish whether the practitioner's actions represented the views of an *acceptable* body of professional opinion.

The *Bolam* test has been applied to every aspect of the conventional therapeutic interchange—to the treatment itself,[31] diagnosis,[32] and disclosure of risks.[33] The test applies not just to medical practice but to all professional endeavours. Cases of negligence against complementary practitioners would almost certainly be judged according to

[28] [1957] 1 WLR 582. [29] Ibid. at p. 586.
[30] *Maynard* v. *West Midlands Regional Health Authority* [1985] 1 All ER 635.
[31] *Whitehouse* v. *Jordan* [1981] 1 All ER 267, [1981] 1 WLR 246, HL.
[32] *Maynard* v. *West Midlands Regional Health Authority* [1985] 1 All ER 635, [1984] 1 WLR 634.
[33] *Sidaway* v. *Board of Governors of the Bethlem Royal Hospital* [1985] 2 WLR 480 HL [1984] QB 493, [1984] 1 All ER 1018. Other jurisdictions have successfully argued for a different standard to be applied in the case of disclosure of risks, and have moved some way towards patient-centred standards of disclosure.

the *Bolam* test as well, to the extent that therapists claim to have particular skills which are not accessible to the person on the street. This point is not uncontroversial, however, in that the anti-élitist rhetoric of many therapies such as touch therapy would tend to suggest that many of the skills that practitioners have can and should be passed on to individuals to use themselves. The same technical skills which may entitle practitioners to describe themselves as professionals will elevate their responsibilities out of the realm of normal responsibilities owed by all of us not to harm other people, and into the realm of professional legal responsibilities.

The standard of care relates to the speciality in which the person practises. Thus, an osteopath will not be tested against the skills of a chiropractor. However, an inexperienced practitioner will not be able to rely on his lack of experience as a defence to alleged negligence. Rather, juniors are expected to train 'on the job'.[34] This places a considerable responsibility on newly qualified complementary practitioners because there is very little post-qualification training, and not all practitioners work in supervised practice.

Whilst practitioners are under a duty to keep themselves apprized of new developments in their area, this is again subject to the bounds of reasonableness. Failure to read one article which might have averted the negligent act might be excusable, whilst failure to be aware of new techniques which have become widespread may be inexcusable.[35] For example, a failure of aromatherapists to notice one or two articles warning about the adverse effects of using a particular oil may be reasonable, whereas failure to heed warnings published in all major journals, over a period of time, against the use of a particular oil would not.

The closer the therapy to a medicalized model and the more formalized and the more standardized its techniques, the easier it will be for patients to establish a standard of care. In therapies which are more intuitive or esoteric, this may prove to be extremely difficult.

There are conceptual difficulties in applying legal standards of objective reasonableness to holistic practitioners. If the therapy is truly patient-centred it is not objective and, it could be argued that the therapy given was the only appropriate treatment for that particular

[34] *Wilsher* v. *Essex Area Health Authority* [1988] AC 1074, [1988] 1 All ER 871, HL.
[35] *Crawford* v. *Board of Governors of Charing Cross Hospital* (1953) *The Times*, 8 Dec. CA [1987] QB 730 at 778; [1986] 3 All ER 801 at 833.

patient at that particular point in time. So individualized can the treatment claim to be that it would be almost impossible for another practitioner who did not observe the patient at that time to say whether he would or would not have treated them in the same way. Individualized treatment may work against a patient, in that almost any treatment could be justified retrospectively by the practitioner. Thus, in practice, it could be very hard for a plaintiff to disprove the practitioner's assertion that what he did was the appropriate thing at that particular time (except, of course, in situations where the course of action was clearly one which no reasonable practitioner would ever have taken).

Obviously, it will be easier to establish the appropriate standard of care in some situations than in others. There would be little problem, for example, in establishing the negligence of an acupuncturist who used unsterilized needles, or an osteopath who failed to ask whether a patient was pregnant and gave treatment contra-indicated for pregnant women. The ability to establish a standard of care will depend on the extent to which the therapy has agreed competencies. Once a therapy has established what the basic competencies are, it can then ensure that every practitioner is trained in them. One of the biggest difficulties is that at present, many smaller therapies have not even begun to define what the competencies required of their skill are. The two main pan-professional bodies, the BCMA and the ICM, see their role as critical in guiding these newer, or less well-organized therapies to defining their skill base.

In orthodox medicine, the introduction of risk avoidance techniques designed in order to try to reduce costs, including the ever-increasing costs of litigation, has seen the standard of care required in given situations established and codified in protocols or clinical guidelines, which set out the procedures to be followed in various clinical situations. Guidelines may also make practical recommendations, for example, as to the need to record advice given in a consultation and to retain notes, so that if, for example, patients subsequently say they were never informed of a particular risk of therapy, practitioners have a contemporaneous note to which they can refer. Whilst we maintain that the need for complementary practitioners to keep good records is as crucial as it is for orthodox practitioners, even this may be more difficult for therapists who work on a largely intuitive basis, responding to subtle energy shifts.

In the United States, and to a growing extent in the United Kingdom, protocols are beginning to affect the litigation process in that if a practitioner has acted within the terms of a protocol that is *prima facie* evidence that he acted reasonably, and thus a defence to a charge of negligence. That does not mean that a practitioner may never deviate from a protocol, but that any such deviation would have to be justified in the light of the prevailing circumstances. Whilst there are certain advantages to having clear procedures, risk management is likely to be a less effective tool for practitioners working in an holistic fashion, whereas a radically different approach may be needed with each patient. None the less, there are definite benefits to protocols which remind practitioners to follow basic legal safeguards, such as the retention of clear, contemporaneous notes, for their own protection as well as the patient's.

3. Causation

Even when patients manage to establish that a duty of care was owed, and manage to ascertain what standard of care was owed, they must go on to prove on a balance of probabilities that the therapist's negligent act or omission caused them harm. Sometimes, another way of looking at this is to establish that the damage would not have occurred 'but for' the therapist's negligence. In many medical cases, this often proves to be an insuperable bar to claiming damages. Any number of factors may affect medical outcomes, particularly the patient's underlying medical condition, and it may be extremely difficult to show that the harm attributed to the practitioner's alleged negligence would not have happened in any event.

Both acts and omissions may give rise to negligence. As well as allegations that a therapist caused harm by virtue of what he or she did, patients might, alternatively, try to establish that because of the therapist's failure to act, for example, in omitting to refer, patients were deprived of conventional treatment which might have offered them a better chance of success. Cases of this sort will be extremely difficult to prove. Where, for example, an aromatherapist treats a patient for headaches and misses the fact that a patient has a brain tumour, then, in order to establish negligence against the aromatherapist, the patient would have to prove the following: that the aromatherapist had a duty to spot medical conditions; that even if the aromatherapist exercised that duty and had recommended the patient to see her GP, the patient would in fact have consulted her GP; that having consulted the GP, the GP would have made an accurate medical diagnosis; that had an accurate diagnosis been made, treatment would have been offered, which the patient would have accepted; and furthermore, that had treatment been given, the harm would not have occurred. Although the point may seen laboured, the court will look at whether the plaintiff would have acted any differently had the alleged negligence not occurred.[36]

Causation is particularly important in cases relating to failure to warn patients of possible risks involved in the procedure. Here, plaintiffs will be trying to demonstrate that had the appropriate warnings been given, they would not have gone ahead with the treatment. As we shall see, this line runs the risk of being self-satisfying when damage has, in fact, occurred. The difficulty for the court is to decide whether even if the warning had been given, plaintiffs would have acted any differently. In acute medical situations, it will be particularly hard for plaintiffs to establish that given the seriousness of their condition, they would not have accepted the risk even if they had been fully informed about it. Cases could thus arise where a court would be prepared to find a defendant liable because as a matter of good professional practice a warning ought to have been given, but for damages to be nominal on the basis that the plaintiff would not have acted differently in any event. We must bear in mind, though, that unlike the 'failure to warn' cases which generate litigation in the orthodox sphere, very few complementary encounters operate in the acute sphere. Given the diversity of therapies on offer, a patient with a non life-threatening condition may well 'shop around' for a treatment which poses fewer risks, or risks which that individual would find unacceptable.

The biggest problem in establishing causation is proving that an intervention has caused a specific effect. In this regard, problems experienced in ordinary medical cases are multiplied many times. In medical cases, a plaintiff may have an uphill struggle in establishing that one out of, say, three possible causes led to the eventual outcome. In truly holistic therapies, where so many factors are thought to affect the patient's well-being, tying down a specific change to a specific intervention will be nigh on impossible. It needs to be recognized that complementary therapy may facilitate changes in personality or emotional behaviour that are a lot harder to quantify than physical states.

Of course, one further argument is that if, as the harshest critics of complementary medicine would argue, most therapies are without any

---

[36] See, e.g., *Newell* v. *Goldenberg* (1985), *Medical Law Monitor* (1995) Vol. 2, Issue 4, pp. 1–2.

specific therapeutic effect and are incapable of causing any benefit, it may, conversely, be extremely difficult to establish in a legal forum that they have caused any harm.

4. Limitations on recovery

Although we do not intend to dwell on either of these issues, two additional constraints are placed on plaintiffs. The first point is that damages will be limited in negligence to those which are reasonably foreseeable. This principle is known as 'remoteness of damage'. Because it would be unfair and impractical for the law to attach blame to every consequence of a defendant's action, however remote, recovery for damages will be limited to harm which was reasonably foreseeable as a consequence of the defendant's action.

The second point to observe is that legal actions must be started within a set time from the date of the alleged incident. Because it is perceived as unfair and impractical to bring an action against someone many years after an event took place, time limits are placed on the period within which an aggrieved party may sue. In principle, the limitation period is three years for actions involving personal injuries and six years for all other actions in negligence.[37] Note however, that in personal injuries, the three-year period runs from the date at which the person had knowledge that the actions complained of caused the harm.[38] As a result, therapists could be well advised to keep all of their clinical records for at least six years.

5. Contributory negligence

What is the situation when the plaintiff has contributed to his or her own injury? In these circumstances, the law will apportion liability as between the parties. Section 1(1) of the Law Reform (Contributory Negligence) Act 1945 provides:

Where any person suffers damage as the result partly of his own fault and partly of the fault of any other person or persons, a claim in respect of that damage shall not be defeated by reason of the fault of the person suffering the damage, but the damages recoverable in respect thereof shall be reduced to such an extent as the court thinks just and equitable having regard to the claimant's share in the responsibility for the damage.

---

[37] Limitation Act 1980, s. 11.   [38] Ibid., s. 11(4)(b).

Section 4 extends the Act to damage for personal injury. To establish contributory negligence, the plaintiff does not have to owe a duty of care to the defendant. All that is required is that the plaintiff failed to take reasonable care of himself, and contributed, by this want of care, to his own injury.[39] Contributory negligence operates as a partial defence, reducing the amount of damages payable by the defendant where 'a man is part author of his own injury'.[40] The standard of care in contributory negligence is the same as that in negligence.[41] The courts may, however, impose a lower standard of care on the very young, the very old, and the infirm who are unable to come up to the normal standard of care. In practical terms, the same principle tends to prevent a patient from being held contributorily negligent in a med-ical negligence action.

6. Vicarious and direct liability

Ordinarily, actions against practitioners will be brought against the individual in question. Where, however, a practitioner is employed by a health authority or NHS Trust (as a small but growing number of complementary practitioners now are), it may be possible for an aggrieved patient to bring an action against the employing authority. Provided the therapist was acting within the scope of his or her employment at the time of the incident, the employing authority may be liable by virtue of its position as employer. This principle is known as vicarious liability.

A principle less well established in law is that an employing hospital can be held directly responsible for negligent acts affecting patients which have been committed by staff employed by the hospital. In the case of *Wilsher* v. *Essex Area Health Authority*,[42] Lord Browne-Wilkinson said as an aside: 'I can see no reason why, in principle, the health authority should not be directly liable if its organisation is at fault'. It may be that the employer's duty is limited solely to ensuring that competent staff are employed. Certainly, though, it is an additional reason why purchasers will only be likely to deal with responsible organisations whose practitioners work within a professional code of conduct, and who carry professional indemnity insurance.

[39] *Nance* v. *British Columbia Electric Railway* [1951] AC 601.
[40] Ibid., at 611, *per* Lord Simon.
[41] *A. C. Billings & Sons* v. *Riden* [1957] AC 240.
[42] [1988] 1 All ER 871.

C. Actions in battery

The other civil wrong we need to consider is that of battery. Common law recognizes the principle that every person has the right to have his bodily integrity respected, and the presumption is that a person should not be exposed to risk unless he has voluntarily accepted that risk, on the basis of adequate information and adequate comprehension. Broadly speaking, if practitioners touch patients in any way when they have no authority to do so, they lay themselves open to a potential charge of battery. The law of battery derives from the notion that adult persons of sound mind are entitled to have their autonomy respected. In a medical context this means that they have sovereignty over what should happen to their own body and that the law will protect them from untoward interference. The legal advice through which respect for bodily integrity is protected is the requirement, on the part of health practitioners, to obtain the patient's consent. Consent turns a potential battery into a legally permissible touching.[43]

Before practitioners can treat patients, they must have the patient's consent to treatment. Except in the context of compulsory treatment for mental disorder, the authority to provide treatment derives solely from that patient's agreement (or the agreement of someone acting on their behalf in the case of incompetent minors).

In order to make a valid decision, patients must be given sufficient information to make a proper choice. The law of battery provides that if the amount of information given is so unhelpful or so inadequate that the patients do not even understand in broad terms the nature of what is proposed, then their consent, for legal purposes is invalid, and they may have an action in battery. Because it is regarded as undesirable that patients should be able to sue their practitioners in battery, the amount of information which must be disclosed to achieve even that basic level of understanding is extremely low.

Where patients have been given enough information to understand what is proposed in the most basic terms, they may yet bring an action *in negligence* for failure to disclose risks. In such a case, the patient would be arguing that had they been informed of certain risks they would not have agreed to the procedure.

Actions in battery are rare in a medical context, but are certainly not unprecedented. In the orthodox medical field, actions in battery

---

[43] *Collins* v. *Willcock* [1984] 3 All ER 374; [1984] 1 WLR 1172.

have been successfully brought against surgeons who have exceeded the bounds of what the patient consented to by performing non-life-saving surgical procedures on patients whilst they have been unconscious. The other occasion when an action in battery arises is when the patient has expressly refused permission for one form of intervention or another and the practitioner none the less proceeds with it. Several cases have arisen concerning Jehovah's Witnesses and Christian Scientists who reject certain medical interventions. In a Canadian case, a Jehovah's Witness who was given a blood transfusion against her expressed wishes was awarded considerable damages, firmly establishing the concept of informed refusal.[44]

In battery, unlike negligence, there is no need to prove, in addition, that the intervention complained of caused harm. The harm is the unwanted interference itself. Thus, conceptually, the battery action might appear to be a strong mechanism for protecting the patient's right to control his or her own body. In practice, however, the courts are most reluctant to make a finding of battery against health professionals, save in the most flagrant of cases.[45]

As is the case with much litigation involving the medical profession, poor communication is often the root of the problem. Although the therapies provided by alternative practitioners are, on the whole, less invasive than in conventional medicine, there is no reason why, in principle, an alternative practitioner could not also face an action for battery as a result of failing to give patients information to bring them even to a basic level of understanding. Practitioners treating Jehovah's Witnesses and Christian Scientists should formally discuss these issues before agreeing to treat such patients. It ought to go without saying in supposedly patient-centred therapies that practitioners should explain what they are going to do to patients before they do it. The consequences of not doing so could be very expensive indeed.

D. Actions for failure to warn

Most cases of failure to warn are brought not in battery, but in negligence. Essentially, in negligence, the patient has to prove, on a

[44] *Malette* v. *Shulman* (1990) 67 DLR (4th) 321.

[45] Teff argues that the rhetoric of medical battery 'offers the worst of all worlds, exaggerating the virtues of full patient-self determination, and creating false expectations about the law's capacity or willingness to ensure it'. H. Teff, *Reasonable Care: Legal Perspectives on the Doctor/Patient Relationship* (Clarendon Press, 1994).

balance of probabilities that the practitioner was in breach of duty for failing to disclose material risks involved in the therapy which would have affected the patient's agreeing to accept that procedure.

It cannot be stressed highly enough that therapists must not proceed in the absence of consent. Whilst it is not necessary to have written consent for every procedure, it is highly advisable that practitioners write down any warnings given to their patients, so that they will at least have some comeback if the patient brings a complaint after the event. However, a written consent form, whilst useful as a document-ary record that certain warnings had been given, is no more than evidence that the information has been imparted. Consent should not be regarded by practitioners as a one-off 'tick in the box', which gives them *carte blanche* to treat as they see fit. Rather, consent should be viewed as part of an ongoing, dynamic process, which recognizes the patient's ongoing co-operation and willingness to participate in treatment.

1. Can consent ever be dispensed with?

In the medical arena, there are certain situations where it is not pos-sible or necessary to seek the patient's explicit consent. We shall not go into all of these situations, but mention a few of them in brief. Express consent need not be sought where the patient's consent can be implied. Thus, where a patient presents the acupuncturist with her arm, it can reasonably be expected that the patient is consenting to have her pulse taken. Consent may not be possible in an emergency situation, where practitioners are permitted to treat on the basis of necessity, guided by what is perceived to be in the patient's best inter-ests.[46] Few encounters with alternative practitioners present the need for emergency treatment. Only rarely, will the patient be unable to involve the patient as an active partner in treatment by informing them fully about all aspects of their diagnosis, prognosis and pro-posed treatment.

This leads on to the most controversial exception to the need to consent invoked in orthodox medicine—when doctors exercise their so-called 'therapeutic privilege'. This refers to a situation where a doctor decides that a patient would be caused such emotional

---

[46] The landmark decision is *Re F (mental patient: sterilisation)* [1990] 2 AC 1. What constitutes a patient's best interests is a matter to be decided in accord-ance with the *Bolam* principle, discussed *supra*.

distress by obtaining consent that it is kinder to withhold information, and proceed without consent. The sort of situation where this might arise is when a patient is suffering from a terminal disease and is found to have yet another problem which requires treatment, knowledge of which is likely to deflate the patient's spirits yet further. Although well-intentioned, it is impossible to reconcile a therapeutic privilege with the right of self-determination, and it is easy to see how therapeutic privilege might be abused within a paternalistic medical culture. It is impossible to imagine a situation in which a complementary practitioner could ever be justified in seeking to rely on this exception. Patient involvement is an integral part of complementary medicine. As we have seen, the healing process in complementary medicine is not necessarily affected by external agency, but by a practitioner stimulating the body's own self-healing mechanisms.

We cannot state categorically that there will never be situations when a practitioner feels compelled to withhold information. Complementary medicine, no less than orthodox medicine, is motivated by a desire to help people and not harm them. However, a therapist should avoid making generalized assumptions that certain patients would not wish to receive certain information, and should facilitate supportive dialogue wherever possible.

2. The right to refuse treatment

It should go without saying that if the right to consent to treatment is to mean anything at all, it must carry with it a corresponding right to refuse treatment. This principle was enunciated in the important Court of Appeal decision in *Re T*,[47] where it was affirmed that competent adults have an absolute right to refuse medical treatment, even if this leads to permanent injury or death.[48] A patient's right to self-determination outweighs the public interest in preserving life at all costs. A patient's reasons for refusing treatment do not have to be rational. The Court of Appeal said that what had to be taken into consideration was the true scope and basis of the refusal of treatment. Specifically, it had to be asked whether the refusal was intended to apply to the circumstances which had arisen. Patients should be made

[47] [1992] 4 All ER 649.
[48] The only possible qualification is where the patient's choice could lead to the death of a viable foetus.

to appreciate that they do not have to accept the treatment proposed. We take this as further support that a patient is entitled, legally and morally, to refuse allopathic treatment in favour of alternative medicine, and that this should not be regarded as *prima facie* evidence of incompetence. This does not mean, however, that alternative therapists can or should treat patients if they are concerned that they require conventional treatment, instead of, or as well as an alternative approach.

3. What needs to be disclosed?

How much information are practitioners obliged to disclose about the risks involved in any given procedure? Before answering this question let us remind ourselves that the avowed aim of regulation is to protect the public and promote their well-being. In answering this question, our focus should not be 'how little can practitioners get away with when informing their clients' and instead, 'how much information does the particular patient need to make a fully informed choice?' In the medical context, this is limited primarily to the amount of information a reasonable doctor would disclose to the patient, even in response to direct questions.[49]

This professional standard was modified slightly by the case of *Sidaway* v. *Board of Governors of the Royal Bethlem and Maudsley Hospital*.[50] This landmark decision modified the *Bolam* standard slightly, although it did not, as is commonly thought, introduce the concept of 'informed consent' into this country. In *Sidaway*, a majority of the House of Lords said that where the proposed treatment involved a substantial risk of grave or adverse consequences a judge could conclude that a patient's right to decide whether to consent to the treatment was so obvious that no prudent medical man could fail to warn of the risk, save in an emergency or in the event of some other sound clinical reason for non-disclosure. This would be the case even if there were a practice to the contrary accepted as proper by a responsible medical opinion. The case reinforced the principle that in relation to disclosure of information, it is the court and not the health professional who is the ultimate arbiter of what it was appropriate to disclose.

In assessing which material risks should be disclosed, practitioners

[49] *Blyth* v. *Bloomsbury*, CA, [1993] 4 Med LR 151.   [50] (1985) AC 871 HL.

should consider the degree of probability of the risk of materializing and the seriousness of possible injury if it does. A risk, even if it is a mere possibility, should thus be disclosed if its occurrence would cause serious circumstances.[51] Medical evidence will be necessary for the court to assess the degree of probability and the seriousness. A further medical factor upon which expert evidence will also be required is to assess the character of the risk—is it a risk common to all surgery or is it specific to the particular operation? Special risks inherent in a recommended operation are more likely to be material.

The House of Lords, applying this test to the disclosure of risks conceded that it was not enough to simply follow accepted professional practice on the justification that if other doctors would not have disclosed that information, a defendant doctor could not be responsible for also withholding it. In *Sidaway*, they said that the practice must 'rightly' be accepted as proper by the responsible body of medical opinion. It was for the court to have the ultimate say as to whether an established practice was proper or not. If this were not so, unacceptably low standards of care could be perpetuated merely by adducing evidence from other practitioners that they would have acted in a similar way.

However, the amount of disclosure is still decided primarily by reference to prevailing professional standards. This dogged adherence to the *Bolam* test has been criticized in other jurisdictions, most recently in the Australian High Court case of *Rogers* v. *Whitaker*.[52] Other jurisdictions look not to the amount of information that the reasonable doctor would give, but to the amount of information that the reasonable patient would want, or the amount of information that the particular patient would have wanted.[53] We shall not pursue the argument vigorously at this stage, but one might wonder how patient-centred therapies which seek to empower and involve the patient could realistically opt for anything other than the 'particular patient' standard of disclosure.

In orthodox clinical settings, it is generally accepted that in terms of risks, a higher standard of disclosure is probably required where

[51] *Hopp* v. *Lepp* [1979] 98 DLR (3d 464).

[52] (1992) 109 ALR 625. For a discussion of this case, see Chalmers, D. and Schwartz, R. 'Rogers v. Whitaker and Informed Consent in Australia: a Fair Dinkum Duty of Disclosure' (1993) 1 Med. L Rev. 139.

[53] In North America, the test for disclosure varies between the 'reasonable (or prudent) patient standard' and the 'particular patient' standard: *Canterbury* v. *Spence* 1972 464 F 2d 772; *Reibl* v. *Hughes* (1980) 114 DLR (3d) 1.

the patient has a choice whether or not to have the therapy. We reject this dichotomy in relation to complementary therapy on the basis that the patient always has the ultimate right to accept or reject even life-saving therapy. Moreover, where the patient's full knowledge and co-operation is vital to the success of the therapeutic endeavour, the patient should always be given as much information as he or she feels is necessary to come to the right decision.

4. Implications for complementary therapists

In the light of the above, therapists should seek to provide clients with as much information as they require to make an informed decision. This will include giving details of any major side-effects, as well as details of any that the particular client is likely to regard as significant. Therapists should also warn patients that it is possible, when they are being treated holistically, that their symptoms will get worse before they start to improve, and that the client should not feel unduly alarmed by this.

Whilst consent may be implied in certain situations, the therapists should always tell their clients if they are going to do something unusual or which will potentially distress or embarrass the client. Thus, specific consent needs to be obtained for certain procedures such as intimate examinations.

5. Information about treatment alternatives

As well as giving information about the treatment that is proposed, in order to facilitate a true choice, a practitioner must also give a patient information about treatment alternatives. Until now, a very narrow view has been taken of the duty that a conventional practitioner owes a patient to give information about alternatives to the treatment proposed. Invariably, this has been seen as options (including no treatment at all) within orthodox medicine. We put forward the idea that the more that is known about alternative therapies, the more plausible it is to make a case establishing a legal duty on the part of an orthodox practitioner to recommend an alternative therapy, if this is the most appropriate form of treatment for the patient. Although up until now, allopathic medicine has been the only system of health provided within the NHS, the more evidence that becomes available as to efficacy of certain complementary therapies, the less justifiable it will be for

GPs not to consider referring patients to an appropriately trained complementary therapist.

Patients certainly cannot force their orthodox practitioners to use any unfamiliar technique themselves, for example, hypnotism rather than anaesthesia. Any doctor who attempted to perform any procedure for which he had not been trained would lay himself open to a negligence action and possible disciplinary procedures. No one, including the court, can compel a practitioner to treat any patient in any particular way.[54]

6. Children and consent

Here we need to separate two distinct issues: the right of parents to make decisions on their children's behalf, and the right of competent minors to make their own treatment decisions.

(i) Parental decisions and the notion of best interests

In law, parents, or those acting *in loco parentis*, are charged with acting as proxy decision-makers on behalf of their incompetent children. By 'incompetent', we mean children who have not yet reached a sufficient maturity and understanding that the law would recognize as entitling them to make decisions in their own right. The principle which governs proxy decision-making is that of best interests. Parents are assumed to make medical decisions on the child's behalf which are in the child's best interests. Usually, the parents will follow clinical advice as to what is likely to give their child the best chance of a good therapeutic outcome, and will comply with that advice. There is thus an assumption that best interests refers to 'best medical interests'.

The law recognizes that parents have widely varying ideas as to how to bring up their children. Liberal tradition in Britain has always allowed parents a considerable degree of flexibility to bring children up as they see fit, including freedom of choice over matters such as religion and diet. On occasion, parental choice will bring them into conflict with the law.

What happens where parents' principles bring them into conflict with the medical profession? Although the situation is rare, several cases have come to court involving Jehovah's Witness parents, who do not want their children to receive blood products. In such cases,

---

[54] Neither patients nor the courts have this right: *Re J* [1992] 2 FLR 165.

the courts will exercise their inherent jurisdiction to protect children and will override the parents' wishes if they think this is necessary in the child's best interests.[55]

The ethical basis for allowing parents to make proxy decisions on their children's behalf is that they can be presumed to be acting with the children's best interests at heart. The purpose of exercising decisions on behalf of children is to enable them to reach a stage of development whereby they can exercise their own autonomy. The difficulty in relation to refusal of medical treatment is that parental decisions may frustrate a child ever attaining that degree of maturity. Whilst adults may have a right to refuse life-sustaining treatment, they do not have a corresponding right to refuse that treatment on their child's behalf.

Statute provides that parents are under a statutory duty to provide children under sixteen with 'medical aid'. Does the duty to act in their best interests impose a duty to provide allopathic medicine rather than alternative medicine, or is this an area where patients are also free to exercise choice? Clearly parents can and do choose complementary approaches to their child's health. The difficulty will arise, however, where the child is suffering from a condition which requires conventional treatment. In such cases, parents have not only a legal duty, but an ethical duty to act in their child's best interests. Both they and practitioners would be in an extremely vulnerable situation if a child were deprived of orthodox treatment and suffered harm as a result. Indeed, in one particularly tragic case, a father whose insulin-dependent daughter died for want of medical care was prosecuted and convicted of manslaughter.[56]

(ii) Minors and decision-making

Section 8 of the Family Law Reform Act 1969 gives children aged between sixteen and eighteen the right to consent to medical and dental treatment as though they were adults. Although the legal position has never been tested in the courts, we may assume that this would enable them to consent to complementary therapy.

As well as this statutory provision, mature adolescents under the

[55] See e.g., *Re O (a minor) (medical treatment)* [1993] 2 FLR 149, and *Re R (a Minor) (Blood Transfusion)* [1993] 2 FCR 544. Both cases confirmed that the court should not hesitate to order a blood transfusion for a child in the face of parental opposition, if this were necessary.
[56] *R. v. Harris*, unreported.

age of sixteen may also be capable of consenting in their own right. The *Gillick* case[57] established that, providing children are capable of fully understanding the consequences of what is involved in the therapy, they may give a consent to that treatment. Although that particular case involved contraceptive treatment, the principle it established applies to all medical treatment. Because complementary medicine involves far greater participation from patients themselves, and because there may be residual fears that children's best interests would be better served by seeking allopathic care, the standard of comprehension required of children to consent to alternative therapy would probably be substantially higher than that which would be required for them to give a valid consent to conventional medicine.

As outlined above, however, the ability to consent is related to patients' functional ability and their competence to understand what it is that is proposed. Whilst a nine-year-old would not generally be considered sufficiently autonomous to make decisions about his or her health, a mature fourteen-year-old might well be. It is for the practitioner to weigh up whether the patient is sufficiently capable of understanding what is proposed.

The duty to respect confidentiality also relates to the functional ability, and would be governed by the same principles established in *Gillick*. Where children have reached a sufficient stage of maturity, they should be allowed to make decisions in their own right. Part of the recognition of their autonomy includes respecting their confidences. In all situations where practitioners feel they must breach confidentiality, they should first seek to persuade minors to agree to the disclosure. A duty of confidentiality exists in law as well as ethics.

For this reason, in most situations, the consent of a parent should ordinarily be sought for patients under sixteen, even if this is not strictly necessary as a matter of law. Certainly many codes of practice, especially those modelled on the BCMA Code, adopt this more cautious approach.

7. Consent and the mentally incapacitated

We shall not dwell greatly on this topic, as the situation in which complementary therapies will be given to incompetent patients are somewhat limited. The guiding principle, however, is that such

[57] *Gillick* v. *West Norfolk and Wisbech AHA* [1985] 3 All ER 402, HL.

therapy may be legitimate, provided it is in the patient's best interests.[58] Although, as a matter of law, no-one is capable of giving or refusing consent on behalf of an incompetent adult patient, a practitioner should only act with the agreement of the patient's carers.

E. Criminal law

All therapists are subject to the criminal law. Criminal statutes apply as much to therapists as they do to individual citizens. One would hope that practitioners do not fall foul of the criminal law in their professional capacity. Meanwhile, prosecutions have been secured against health care professionals in the following areas in the past and could, by analogy, apply to complementary practitioners:

Although manslaughter cases against health practitioners are extremely rare, there may be situations in which a patient has died where the practitioner's conduct has fallen so far short of what could reasonably be expected as to attract criminal liability.[59]

In addition, there are particular statutory duties towards children. Parents and legal guardians have a duty to provide 'medical aid' for their children under sixteen by virtue of the Children and Young Persons Act.[60] 'Medical aid' is not defined, but it may be that a parent who insists on a child receiving alternative therapy when orthodox treatment could be more beneficial would be in breach of statutory duty. Arguably, a practitioner who treated a child in such circumstances, where the child suffered harm as a result, could be charged with aiding and abetting the breach of statutory duty.

The Misrepresentation Act 1967 may be of application where a person has been induced to enter into a contract on the basis of misrepresentation, and suffers harm as a result. Thus, if a bogus practitioner lied to a patient about previous successes in treating other patients in a similar way, and thus induced the patient to enter into a contract, the practitioner could be liable in damages unless he or she could prove that there were reasonable grounds to believe that the facts as represented were true. If misrepresentations were proved, a patient could recover damages for all personal injuries sustained as

---

[58] *Re F* [1990] 2 AC 1.

[59] *R.* v. *Holloway, R.* v. *Adomako, R.* v. *Prentice, R.* v. *Sullman* [1993] 4 Med LR, 304.

[60] Children and Young Persons Act 1933 s. 1(2)(a) as amended by the Children Act 1989, s. 108(4), (5), Sch. 12 para. 2 and Sch. 13 para. 2.

a result of relying on the fraudulent statement. A practitioner may also be prosecuted under the Fair Trading Act 1983.

III. HOW EFFECTIVE IS THE COMMON LAW?

Although in theory, the law is open to all, as we have seen, numerous factors make this a less than ideal basis for regulating complementary medicine. Let us now consider some of the specific advantages and disadvantages of relying on common law as our principal source of regulation.

A. Advantages of civil litigation

One advantage is that common law remedies co-exist with other forms of regulation. Thus, whether a therapy is statutorily or voluntarily regulated, patients will always have the option, at least in theory, of suing a practitioner they feel has been negligent. Law is universal in the sense that the therapist/patient relationship will always give rise to a duty of care in law, breach of which may give rise to a potential action for damages. Moreover, this duty of care exists over and above any contractual relationship between the therapist and patient.

Litigation has an advantage over disciplinary proceedings in that it can make an award of damages in favour of a successful litigant. Pecuniary damages seek, as far as is possible, to put the plaintiff in the position he or she would have been in had the negligence not occurred. No disciplinary tribunal has the power to compensate an injured patient in financial terms.

B. Disadvantages common to all litigants

Litigation has numerous shortfalls for the consumer. Many of the difficulties in litigating stem from problems inherent in the civil justice system, which is slow, cumbersome, inaccessible, and expensive. It is also a last resort in terms of dispute resolution, usually only worthwhile when all other routes have been exhausted.[61] These inefficiencies in the civil justice system are currently the subject of wide-scale

---

[61] In part, the unwieldy NHS complaints systems forces a number of dissatisfied patients to seek redress elsewhere.

review. Whether these changes will speed up the legal process remains to be seen.

Civil justice is expensive and compensates only a fraction of meritorious cases. A more radical approach to reform would be to abolish the fault-based system and replace it with a no-fault compensation scheme. Various unsuccessful attempts have been made to introduce no-fault legislation. Comprehensive proposals were put forward by the Association of Community Health Councils of England and Wales (ACHCEW) and the Action for Victims of Medical Accidents (AVMA) recommending the creation of a Health Standards Inspectorate to deal more speedily with medical negligence actions.[62] It is unlikely that either of these schemes will be adopted, certainly in the short term.[63]

Undoubtedly, high standards of practice and good communication are the two most effective barriers to legal or other problems. Much litigation is brought against doctors because of their inability to acknowledge when mistakes have been made, and the fact that they rarely say 'I'm sorry'.

Aside from these organizational problems, there are various substantive difficulties in the way the law operates. Procedural hurdles in bringing a negligence action, together with the dominance of the *Bolam* test of professional negligence, make it extremely difficult for a plaintiff successfully to sue a practitioner.

Another significant problem is that litigation is retrospective. The primary goal of litigation is to seek to provide redress for alleged wrongs in the past. Effective regulation should be preventative, striving towards the avoidance of harm in the future. Also, litigation is limited to the specific facts of the case, and the common law develops by a process of distinguishing seemingly similar cases because of small factual details. Because it is precedent-based, common law grows in a piecemeal fashion, each case being limited to its own facts. As such, it is ill-suited to the task of developing consistent and useful

[62] Simanowitz, A. and Miles, K., 'Complaints and Compensation—How the System Should Work', *Health Care Risk Report*, Nov. 1994.

[63] Holding and Kaye point out that recent procedural reforms, including the division of personal injuries actions as between the county courts for claims under £50,000, and the High Court for claims over that figure, as well as automatic directions and exchange of witness statements have made substantial improvements in the current system. *Damages for Personal Injuries: A European Perspective*, Holding, F. and Kaye, P. (Wiley, 1993).

policy. As Jacob says, the purpose of regulation should be to inform practitioners what they can and cannot do before they do it.[64]

The obfuscation of legal language and the complexities of the legal process mean that few lay people have the courage to negotiate their way through the legal process. Litigants in person are extremely rare, and the only real alternative is to engage the services of the legal profession.[65] As such, patients lose control of their case, and are disempowered. They become mere bit players in a drama over which, realistically, they have little direction.

The adversarial context of litigation is not conducive either to discovering 'the truth' about any factual situation, or to the acknowledgement of responsibility. Litigation promotes winners and losers.

Although litigation can exercise a deterrent effect, certainly in relation to the individual practitioner concerned, its ability to deter others is questionable, not least of all where cases are settled out of court, and thus, may not attract publicity. Rather, it is more likely to encourage defensive working practices whereby, rather than treating patients according to their best interests, doctors will operate in such a way as to cover their own backs. This may involve submitting the patient to unnecessary diagnostic tests, for example, just so that the doctor can fend off potential negligence claims. As well as being unhelpful to the doctor/patient relationship, in that it introduces an element of fear and distrust, it is also extremely damaging in financial terms and is something the NHS can scarcely afford. Unlike more constructive risk management strategies, it probably does very little to create safer working practices generally.

Damages, in the form of financial compensation, are the only way the law can recompense successful plaintiffs where a wrong has occurred. Damages do not satisfy a patient's desire to ensure that the same thing could not happen again, nor do they guarantee that the patient will get an apology or even an explanation of why things went wrong.

---

[64] Jacob, J. M. in *Doctors and Rules*, argues that because of its inability to achieve this, the law, as a regulatory mechanism is bound to be crude or coarse.

[65] This course of action is not without its own pitfalls. As with any profession, standards of lawyers vary enormously and complaints against the legal profession have also risen steadily in the past decade. Whether one wins or loses a case may depend on the strength of one's advisors as much as the merits of the case.

C. Disadvantages specific to complementary therapies

One introductory observation is that as with doctors, few complementary practitioners have any understanding as to what the law requires of them. Most do not have any awareness of legal issues such as negligence and consent, and these are not often taught to students in any systematic way. Because of this, practitioners either tend to think that they are above the law, or that the law does not apply to them, or, conversely, that the law is there to persecute them, and impose unreasonably high standards on them.

As we have seen, the *Bolam* test of the professional standard is ill-suited to holistic, individualized therapies. There is no point in appealing to a standard of reasonableness in an arena which, ideally, is honed to meet the needs of the individual. Admittedly, one interpretation of the law as it stands is that this practically gives therapists *carte blanche* to do anything they like.

The existing test of negligence will be almost impossible to apply to therapies which work on an emotional and spiritual level more than they do on a physical level. The more the therapy depends on the performance of technical skills, the easier it will be for a court to establish that the procedure should have been performed in a particular way. But the more intuitive the therapy, and the greater the emphasis is on spiritual and emotional well-being, the harder it is to say what the therapist should have done, or even what the expected outcome of the interaction would be. In this regard, useful parallels may be drawn between psychotherapy and the more humanistic complementary therapies. In each case, there are obvious boundaries as to what constitutes unacceptable behaviour, for example, an out-and-out veto on having sex with patients. However, in terms of therapeutic method, the picture is far less clear. One difficulty is that the goals of such therapy are highly individualistic. As Karasu points out: 'the proliferation of well over one hundred schools of psychotherapy, each presumably with its own theory of mental illness and health, therapeutic agents, overall goals and specific practices, reflects the massive nature of investigating therapeutic efficacy and the complexity of establishing "scientific" guidelines'.[66] It is no surprise that those cases which have been brought in psychiatry rarely challenge the psychotherapeutic approach employed by the therapist.

[66] T. Byram Karasu, 'Ethical aspects of psychotherapy' in Bloch, S. and Chodoff, P. *Psychiatric Ethics* (2nd edn., OUP, 1991).

IV. CRIMINAL PROSECUTIONS

A. Advantages

Because of the almost entirely unregulated nature of complementary medicine, the criminal justice system provides an important longstop to protect patients against the most unscrupulous of practitioners. The criminal law is particularly important in cases of alleged sexual exploitation, and may also have a role to play in stamping out blatant charlatanism through law relating to fraud and possibly even theft.

B. Disadvantages

Criminal law is particularly unhelpful in the context of raising standards for the following reason: health care professionals rarely act with criminal intent. Whilst it is proper that practitioners' intentional acts are treated no differently from anyone else's, the criminal law, with all its negative association of blame and stigma, may operate particularly harshly when applied in a professional context.[67] Punishing a dedicated professional with the penalty of the criminal law will probably only serve to ruin that individual's career. It will not necessarily prevent others from acting in the same way. Also, within a hierarchical setting, punishing an isolated individual, often at the most junior level, may well cover up the wrongdoings of others in a more senior position, and more specifically, may divert attention from defects in the system. Punishing an individual provides little incentive to deal with underlying problems.

The workings of the criminal justice system, particularly in relation to rape and other sexual offences, may deter victims from reporting crime. As with civil law, in all cases, the onus is on the plaintiff, who has to satisfy the even higher evidential burden in criminal matters of proving their case beyond reasonable doubt. Victims do not receive compensation as a result of a criminal prosecution.

---

[67] This is not to dispute the regrettably frequent allegations of sexual or other impropriety brought against doctors and other health professionals, nor to suggest that they should escape the rigours of the criminal law.

V. SUMMARY

Despite the massive increase in cases against medical practitioners there has been no corresponding rise in cases against complementary practitioners. Indeed, there are no reported cases against complementary practitioners (although this does not preclude the possibility that a small number of cases might have settled out of court). We should try to understand why this is the case. Is it because practitioners do not do anything blameworthy? Desirable an interpretation as this would be, it stretches credulity in an age of increasing litigiousness, particularly against the medical profession. Can we assume that whatever it is that doctors 'get wrong', complementary health practitioners 'get right'? Certainly, there are grounds for arguing that factors such as lack of good communication go a long way to explain why people sue, and it may be that, on this front, complementary practitioners avoid the possibility of future adversarial clashes with their patients by attempting to work with them and genuinely seeking their active involvement in the therapeutic process. Tempting though it would be to assert that the sort of people who consult practitioners are not, in the main, the sort of people who would sue, such a proposition can clearly be no more than an intuitive response, albeit one which is expressed by a number of people.

Whilst these factors may have some bearing on why complementary practitioners are rarely sued, the answer, we would suggest, lies more in the inapplicability of a legal framework which is shaped by, and designed to respond to, the prevailing doctor/patient relationship than to the relationship between complementary practitioners and patients. The way in which the law of negligence is framed makes a number of assumptions about the sort of therapeutic relationship involved which cannot be substantiated in relation to the holistic therapeutic relationship.

The law of negligence, as we have seen, imposes a duty of care, which translates, effectively, into a duty on practitioners not to harm their patients. Establishing harm, as we have seen, requires certainty and proof of a sort which may not necessarily be amenable to a holistic relationship. We are not suggesting that it is impossible to measure outcomes in complementary medicine, or that removal of symptoms is not a mutually sought end of therapy. We recognize, however, that a holistic practitioner may well be working at the level of more fundamental shifts, or shifts in an emotional and spiritual level, which cannot be measured on a graph. However, the law seeks to impose on complementary practitioners a system of 'scientific proof' in much the same way as orthodox medicine, for the law requires proof that a specific action did or did not cause the alleged harm.

As far as the law is concerned, if causation can be demonstrated scientifically in cases involving doctors (remembering that the bulk of evidence in a medical negligence action will often be of a highly technical nature), it will seek to apply this same standard to complementary medicine. Trying to explain the ramifications of the holistic relationship in a court of law will be as difficult as trying to convince die-hard scientists of the same. This will not prevent attempts to sue complementary practitioners in the future. It is right and proper that practitioners be held accountable when they have been negligent. The difficulty will lie, however, in trying to establish negligence against a holistic practitioner within a medical paradigm.

If, as we have suggested, there may be great difficulties in establishing that a therapist's acts caused harm, would a plaintiff be any more successful arguing that a therapist's omission, such as a failure to spot a serious medical condition, was negligent? It cannot be reasonable to attach liability to a practitioner for failing to work within an alien paradigm. This is a critical point, as this is the basis upon which most complementary practitioners are likely to be sued.

At the centre of the argument is the troubling issue of how much conventional medical knowledge therapists require to practise safely. Conventional wisdom says that a practitioner must have, at the very least, enough knowledge to recognize serious medical conditions and to be able to avoid doing anything to exacerbate the patient's symptoms. The missing link in this equation is the fact that the patient has deliberately consulted a practitioner who works outside that conventional paradigm. Every person is entitled to be registered with a general practitioner. When people are ill, they have a right to consult their GP and to receive free treatment. They may or may not consult their GP, and they may or may not take their GP's advice. This being the case, is it appropriate, in legal terms, to expect non-conventional practitioners to pretend to be mini-conventional practitioners and rule out anything really serious before they can ply their own treatment in their own frame of reference? This is an insult to non-conventional practitioners and it is an insult to patients who have to take responsibilities for the choices they make.[68]

Thus, inability to prove harm is certainly one hurdle which will make cases against complementary practitioners unlikely to be successful. We would suggest however, that there is an even more profound problem with the existing legal relationship, and this is that *the very structure of the relationship presumed by professional negligence is the antithesis of the model holistic relationship*. What do we mean by this? The law governing professional relationships presupposes that an expert professional has all of the knowledge, and the patient has none. In this model, professionals strongly suggest the appropriate course of action and patients meekly acquiesce to treatment, hopefully having been given sufficient information to consent in law. The law of professional negligence places all of the responsibilities of the relationship on the professional and none on the patient because this, historically, has characterized the power relationship between the parties.

If we doubt that this is the case, we can test the theory by asking whether the law is prepared to make a finding of contributory negligence against patients who exacerbate their own problems. If a doctor recommends certain advice and the patient only half complies, or entirely fails to comply with the advice, would it be fair to hold the doctor legally responsible for the patient's subsequent deterioration? If a patient had presented with a potentially serious condition but had then not come back for subsequent treatment, how far should a doctor be responsible for following that through and chasing up the patient? We would argue that, in both these situations, the law would impose a significant duty on medical practitioners. In short, the law shies away from holding the old, the young, the weak, and the sick contributorily negligent, adopting a paternalistic attitude that they should not be held responsible for their actions.

The ramifications of this are significant. By refusing to hold 'the sick' responsible for their own actions, the law perpetuates reliance on the all-powerful, all-knowing, medical professionals. This approach is harmful to both the medical profession and patients. This degree of paternalism in the law is sharply at odds with even an orthodox

---

[68] It is for this very reason that the BCMA's code of ethics emphasizes that complementary practitioners cannot and must not make a medical diagnosis, for to do so would be to lay themselves open to legal liability for omitting to spot a medical diagnosis.

profession which is trying to promote self-responsibility. It has even less place in a therapeutic relationship in which self-responsibility is posited as being integral to a successful outcome.

We shall come back to these arguments in Part III. For now, however, it is enough to realize that the existing legal framework cannot respond to a relationship which is based on fundamentally different premises to the conventional doctor/patient relationship. As such, its usefulness as a regulatory mechanism is extremely limited.

10

Voluntary Self-Regulation

Given the doubts expressed in previous chapters as to the suitability of either statutory control or common law mechanisms for providing an adequate basis for the regulation of most complementary therapies, we must now look very carefully at the existing voluntary mechanisms regulating complementary medicine. Since neither the Osteopaths Act 1993 nor the Chiropractors Act 1994 have yet come into force, the whole of complementary medicine is voluntarily self-regulated at the present time. The purpose of this section of the book is to look at some of the self-regulating structures that are in place and to investigate how successful they are at protecting the public and ensuring high standards of practice.

I. LEVELS OF VOLUNTARY SELF-REGULATION

(1) Pan-professional organizations (for example, BCMA, ICM and CCAM).
(2) Pan-therapeutic organizations (for example, the General Council and Register of Osteopaths, the Confederation of Healing Organizations, the British Acupuncture Council, the Aromatherapy Organizations Council and the Association of Massage Practitioners).
(3) Member organizations (for example, the Society of Homoeopaths and the National Institute of Medical Herbalists).

One of the major difficulties in making meaningful observations about voluntary self-regulation is that complementary medicine is organized at a number of different levels, with several overlapping schemes operating concurrently. This raises two distinct problems. The first is that the term 'voluntary self-regulation' extends from the almost quasi-statutory regulatory structures of the General Council and Register of Osteopaths, to the written aims of loosely banded together groups of practitioners. The second is that most therapeutic

member organizations produce some sort of code of ethics and operate some form of disciplinary procedures. Member organizations may
well belong to a pan-therapeutic organization, which also has a code
of ethics to which member organizations must subscribe, as well as a
separate disciplinary mechanism. Pan-therapeutic organizations may
themselves be members, or affiliated members, of one of the major
pan-professional institutions who also have codes of ethics and exercise a disciplinary role.[1]

Most commonly, disciplinary functions operate at the level of
member organization, although deregistration from one's member
organization should lead to deregistration by the pan-professional
organization, and should prevent a practitioner from joining the
register of another member organization of the pan-therapeutic
organization.

II. CENTRALITY OF CODES OF ETHICS

The development of a code of ethics is seen as a central function of
self-regulating bodies. These documents seek to set out guidance on
good practice. Codes enunciate professional requirements, usually in
the form of what practitioners should and should not do. Thus, they
are normative instruments, attempting to influence behaviour. The
fact that they are called codes of *ethics* suggests that they are based on
ethical principles. It is important to grasp this seemingly self-evident
point, as we shall go on to question whether the sort of advice
included in most codes can genuinely be said to be ethical advice.
One of the difficulties is that most codes are not explicit in the way
that they base their guidance on certain core ethical principles. Whilst
there may be a stated duty to respect client confidentiality, for
example, this will not be grounded in the principle of respect for a
client's autonomy. So too, many codes will include prohibitions on
engaging in sexual relationships with clients. However, they will not
spell out that this arises out of an ethical duty not to cause client's
harm. We will argue that for codes of ethics to work effectively, there
must be an explicit understanding of the ethical requirements on
which these recommendations are based.

---

[1] All of the pan-professional organisations are member organizations. In other
words, their members are therapeutic organizations rather than individual practitioners. The BCMA and ICM both require the agreement of member organizations to abide by their respective codes of ethics.

Professions have a particular knowledge base, which is a powerful instrument. For knowledge to be used to serve the public, rather than for professional self-aggrandizement, a strong ethical base is essential. Healing professions are characterized by trust. Illness may make people dependent and vulnerable. Patients invest a lot of faith in those caring for them. Health practitioners wield a considerable amount of power over patients, which could easily be used to the detriment of the patient, unless the practitioner works within a strict ethical framework. Whilst a practitioner's own internal ethics and sense of propriety are important safeguards against unethical behaviour, as we shall see in Part III, reliance on one's individual sense of ethics is an inadequate basis for dealing with the multitude of dilemmas one is likely to encounter in practice.

Codes of ethics attempt to set out how practitioners ought to behave. Their purpose is to codify the prevailing values of the profession. As such, they are dynamic, and should be capable of revision as those norms change over time. As well as concerning themselves with the individual practitioner/patient relationship, codes are also concerned with collective morality and the importance of not bringing the profession as a whole into disrepute. One of the problems with codes of ethics is that they rarely adumbrate the full range of ethical principles which practitioners need to be aware of. Concepts such as truthfulness, which give rise to intense discussion within health care, are rarely dealt with. Nor do codes tend to question justice issues, such as access to grievance procedures and compensation for harm. One of the main difficulties with professional codes is that they tend to be designed by professionals for professionals. As such, they face the criticism that is most frequently levelled against self-regulating bodies, namely that they are not independent, and that they do not involve the consumer. There is little evidence within any complementary therapy of any serious attempt to involve users at the level of designing either ethical codes or complaints procedures. The degree of lay participation on misconduct committees is woefully inadequate. To the extent that organizations have formal mechanisms at all, these are often *ad hoc* committees convened by a senior member of the organization, which usually sit in private, with one or two professional members. There is little attempt to synthesize professional responsibilities with users' rights.

Needless to say, there is a marked variety in existing codes of conduct. Again, there is a spectrum of approach, with the 'medicalized' therapies having codes of ethics which are modelled closely on the GMC's guidance. Outside these therapies, the codes produced by the pan-professional bodies, and in particular, that produced by the BCMA, tend to form the basis of the individual codes of therapeutic organizations, adapted, as necessary, to take account of the particular therapy.

There is a greater problem with therapies who have no code of conduct at all. This may be the case with very small or very new organizations. The difficulties involved in producing a code are the same as the difficulties which beset any new organization setting itself up from scratch, namely, lack of time and lack of money. This is not to suggest that all codes emanating from newer therapies are insubstantial. The Association of Massage Practitioners code is an excellent example of a helpful, if brief, code of guidance.

Let us now look at the BCMA and the ICM codes in turn.

III. BCMA CODE OF CONDUCT (1992)

In addition to setting out the scope of professional practice, many codes attempt to define the interface between complementary therapists and orthodox health care professionals. The emphasis of the BCMA's code is firmly that complementary therapists should be seen as an adjunct, and complementary, to orthodox medicine. Thus the introduction to the code states 'the term complementary medicine makes no pretensions of replacing conventional medicine and taking its place'.[2] The BCMA's position that practitioners are 'complementary' to orthodox health care practitioners is not universally accepted by therapists, and can be contrasted with the position adopted by the ICM.

Critically, the BCMA states that 'the registered medical practitioner must remain in charge of the patient's treatment and clinically accountable for the care offered by the complementary therapist'. It views the relationship between doctor and therapist as one of delegation rather than referral. It goes on to state that practitioners must not countermand instructions or prescriptions given by a doctor

---

[2] This is not to suggest that the BCMA does not recognize the legitimacy of alternative therapies where the practitioner is diagnosing within a different sphere to orthodox medicine. Rather, it sees these therapies as falling outside their remit, and coming within the auspices of the CCAM.

(para. 1.12). When providing treatment within a hospital setting, the practitioner must not undermine the patient's faith in their hospital treatment or regime, or treat without permission of the hospital authority and ward charge nurse (paras. 2.1–7).

Likewise, the BCMA's code insists complementary practitioners may not make a 'medical diagnosis', this being something which only medical doctors can do (para. 1.14).[3] The BCMA position is that new patients must be asked what medical advice they have received. If they have not seen a doctor they must be advised to do so (para. 1.11). Given, however, that a patient cannot be forced to consult an allopathic doctor, the BCMA cautions that this advice must be recorded for the practitioner's protection. Note that the code does not go on to say that practitioners must refuse to treat patients unless they have received a medical diagnosis.

There are obvious political reasons why an organization dedicated to stressing that use of these therapies is complementary to orthodox medicine, should stress, as a matter of territorial boundaries, that therapists do not make a 'medical diagnosis'. There are also the strongest consumer protection grounds for emphasizing this point. Without a full medical training, it would be highly dangerous for complementary therapists to attempt to give a diagnosis in medical terms, which is highly likely to be wrong and may be a diagnosis upon which the patient relies to his or her detriment. Moreover, from a legal point of view, complementary practitioners would place themselves in an extremely vulnerable position were they to make medical diagnoses, on the basis of which the patients did not receive urgent medical treatment and suffered harm. (This is not to suggest that diagnosis is a precise science, or that doctors, even if consulted, always make an accurate diagnosis.)

This point is obfuscated by the code conceding that 'many practitioners have a "*gift*" of diagnosing and discovering dysfunctions of the physical, emotional, mental and spiritual aspects' (para 1.14). However, describing the painstakingly acquired ability of fully trained practitioners to make a competent diagnosis within the confines and principles of their own therapy as a 'gift' is to obscure totally the fact that in practice, all practitioners are making a diagnosis, but within their own frame of reference. Whilst few practitioners, save those with an orthodox training, would be reckless enough to exceed the bounds of their competence by putting a firm medical diagnosis

---

[3] *BCMA Code of Conduct and Guidance to Practitioners* (1992) at para. 1.14.

to a patient's condition, to suggest that practitioners should not make a diagnosis is at variance with what practitioners routinely do and need to do in order to treat a patient. After all, how could therapists be expected to treat patients without first having decided what is wrong with them?

The advice also ignores the fact that the patient may already have seen a variety of orthodox practitioners, who are perhaps unable to make a diagnosis, or who fundamentally disagree as to the cause of the patient's illness. Does the BCMA's recommendation mean that it is enough that the patient has consulted one medical practitioner, or that it is essential that before a complementary practitioner treats the patient, the patient has been given a definitive medical diagnosis? Looking behind the purpose of this requirement, it would seem that the BCMA are more concerned about protecting the practitioner from potential *legal* liability rather than anything else. This stipulation is regarded by some as being primarily politically motivated.

As to conduct, the practitioner's duty is to act with due diligence at all times and not to abuse the patient's trust in any way. Practitioners must behave with 'courtesy, dignity, discretion and tact', and be respectful of the patient's religious, spiritual, political, and social views. The point about diligence is a good general statement of the duty of beneficence. The latter sentiment encapsulates the need to respect the patient's autonomy in general terms, although it does not specifically link this to therapeutic issues.

Practitioners must never claim to cure, and must never guarantee the patient's recovery (para. 1.16). Practitioners are reminded that false or misleading claims may give rise to prosecution under the Misrepresentation Act 1967 and the Trades Description Act 1968 (paras. 4.46–50). Practitioners must be medically, physically, and psychologically fit to practise (para. 1.7). Throughout the code, emphasis is placed on practitioners working within the limits of their competence (see, for example, paras. 1.8, 4.27–8).

The code sets out various things that practitioners cannot do, these being primarily those activities which are restricted to doctors and other registered health professionals (paras. 1.15–22 and 4.4–16). The code gives a rather patchy analysis of the legal duties incumbent upon practitioners. Inaccurately stating that the only risk under civil law is in negligence (whereas a civil action for battery is eminently possible if a practitioner treats a patient in the absence of consent), the code points out that all practitioners are under a duty of care to exercise the knowledge, skill, and care of an ordinarily competent practitioner of that profession. The code again highlights the need for practitioners to make clear that they are not doctors, and do not claim to possess the same knowledge or purport to exercise the same skill as doctors (lest they be judged according to the same legal standard of care). It also sets out various statutory requirements relating to product licensing legislation (paras. 4.38–42) and notifiable diseases (para. 4.43).

As regards treating children, the code states that no alternative or complementary therapy is approved as 'medical aid' under the law. In fact, as we have seen, nothing specifically precludes the provision, to minors, of alternative or complementary therapies—the law is silent on this. As parents or guardians are under a legal duty to provide medical aid for their children under the age of sixteen, the practitioner must advise the parent or guardian to seek medical aid (presumably this means, advise them to consult an allopathic doctor). Parents or guardians who refuse to do so must sign a statement to the effect that they have been so warned (para. 1.23).

Advertising must be dignified and should not contain testimonials or claim a cure or mention any disease (para. 1.24). Part of the duty of non-maleficence is not to raise the patient's hopes unrealistically.

Prior to the commencement of therapy, practitioners must inform the patient what will be involved in the therapy, how long the period of therapy is likely to be and fees to be charged (para. 1.26). This is an important point in respect of autonomy and one which needs to be amplified. Because the nature of individual therapists varies so dramatically, in order to respect the patient's autonomy fully, the practitioner should also be under a duty to give the patient some idea about his therapeutic background and training, and his therapeutic philosophy.

Practitioners must keep clear and comprehensive treatment records, which can justify why a particular treatment was given (paras. 1.28–29). The code stresses the practitioner's common law and statutory duties of confidentiality (paras. 1.30–31). All practitioners must be adequately insured with public as well as professional liability cover (paras. 1.33, 4.30), and must operate from suitable premises (paras. 1.34, 4.31).

IV. ICM'S CODE OF ETHICS AND PRACTICE (1994)

The introduction urges professional associations to use the ICM code as a basis on which to build their individual requirements (para. 1.4). The remit of this code does not extend to affiliated members, and only applies to practitioners on the British Register. Rather than focusing on the complementary nature of the relationship between practitioners and doctors, the ICM code states: 'Complementary practitioners who are members of the British Register offer a service to the public as *independent specialists* [our emphasis]. This independent status means that they may receive patients directly, with or without a medical referral'. (para. 8.1). In stark contrast to the BCMA's advice, it continues: 'Every practitioner irrespective of status or technique must make an initial medical diagnostic assessment of the condition of the patient/ client and note the result on a record card'. (para . 8.3).

The code continues by providing that practitioners should make a distinction wherever possible between potentially life-threatening conditions and chronic states. Although the patient may bring a medical history based on allopathic diagnoses, the code recognizes that 'the complementary practitioner will need to assess the case from different criteria and no attempt should be made to describe a complementary diagnosis in allopathic terms unless the practitioner is so qualified' (para. 9.1–2). Practitioners are urged to take particular care when making a diagnosis not to put an allopathic name to a condition, if that is outside their competence.

Within a hospital setting the code is less categoric than the BCMA as to who is in charge of the patient, saying: 'The medical practitioner in charge will usually retain overall charge of the patient's case and will give permission for the treatment to be delegated to the complementary practitioner' (para. 10.1).

The code defines the aim of the complementary practitioner as being 'to assist the client/patient back to full health, strength and well-being at physical, mental, emotional and vital energy or spirit areas of consciousness' (para. 3.1). The importance of professional development is stressed, with a requirement on practitioners to take 'all reasonable steps to monitor, develop and advance their professional competence to the highest level and to work within that competence' (para. 4.4).

As with the BCMA's code, practitioners are instructed to make clear contracts with patients to clarify the terms on which treatment is offered (para. 4.5). Likewise, practitioners may not describe themselves as doctors or use other protected titles or make any claim to cure any given disease. Practitioners must be aware of notifiable disease provisions and conform with any local laws. Advertising should be descriptive but not self-aggrandizing.

As to treating children, concerns are also expressed about treating children under sixteen, and the code provides that practitioners should not conduct a physical examination of a child under sixteen years of age except in the presence of a parent, guardian, or other responsible adult. (It seems somewhat bizarre, given the holistic nature of complementary therapy, to isolate physical therapy in this context.)

The code sets out some specific areas of likely difficulty. For example, it states at para. 5.5 that 'patients should be warned that a specific treatment requires the removal of clothing where this is not immediately obvious'. Likewise, genital examinations should not be given without a chaperon present unless written consent has been given (para. 5.8.d).

V. DISCIPLINARY PROCEDURES

The BCMA's code sets out a broad disciplinary system to be adopted by member organizations. A disciplinary committee must consider any complaint and submit a written report and recommendation to the ruling body of the therapist's organization. Where the member who is subject to disciplinary proceedings is also registered with another BCMA member organization, they too should be informed, as well as the secretary of the BCMA. A therapist who is expelled from one member organization will be ineligible for membership of any other BCMA organization. Practitioners in breach of the code are liable to expulsion. No other penalties are referred to, although, presumably this is a point over which member organisations would be able to exercise some discretion.

As to the ICM, in terms of disciplinary procedures, the code is not specific, and refers to guidelines which will be laid down from time to time. It talks about a disciplinary committee convened for these purposes acting in a 'judicial capacity', although it is not immediately obvious what this connotes. The jurisdiction seems to extend over a practitioner's fitness and competence to practise.

Few codes attempt to identify what constitutes 'professional misconduct'. This is not exactly helpful given that a function of codes of ethics is to help practitioners know what it is they may or may not do. To the extent that certain therapies have modelled their guidance on the GMC's Professional Guidance, they have also adopted the GMC's interpretation of 'serious professional misconduct'. This is not unproblematic, since the definition of serious professional misconduct is, in the same way as in law, framed with reference to the doctor/patient relationship. As we have been at pains to point out, just as the legal mechanism relevant to medicine cannot be transposed to complementary medicine, so ethical guidance must also reflect the very different basis of the holistic therapeutic relationship.

One measure of the success of voluntary self-regulation is to look at how well disciplinary mechanisms operate in practice. Such mechanisms as do exist often operate behind closed doors, and there is little published data to rely on. The picture, however, is somewhat bleak. In terms of their operation, disciplinary mechanisms reveal inadequacies across the board. We do not intend to single out individual examples, but shall point to some of the general themes that emerge.

(1) Organizations at all level report a very low level of complaints. The BCMA has had no disciplinary complaints since its inception, and the ICM only a handful. Is this because of the genuinely low risk of harm, or the fact that disciplinary mechanisms are either not sufficiently visible, or do not regard complaints as sufficiently serious to merit taking disciplinary action?[4]

(2) Where organizations have disciplinary mechanisms, they tend to be extremely *ad hoc* in comparison to statutorily regulated professions. It is rare for there to be a formal preliminary proceedings mechanism, and it is very difficult to ascertain on what basis complaints are deemed to be sufficiently serious to merit further action. Sometimes, a single individual, for example, the chair of a disciplinary committee, will make a unilateral decision to weed out 'frivolous' complaints. The

---

[4] The former interpretation is supported by the extremely low levels of insurance for complementary therapists. The commercial basis upon which insurance is offered would tend to support the contention that the risk of harm is very small.

basis for accepting or rejecting a complaint is rarely provided for, nor are these decisions subject to any external scrutiny.

(3) Outside the highly well-organized voluntary self-regulating professions, it is unusual to find lay representation at any stage of disciplinary procedures. Complaints tend to be dealt with by a small number of practitioners at the top of the professional organization.

(4) Only a handful of therapies publish a digest of disciplinary cases heard against members. It is rare for such information to be disseminated to professionals and almost unheard of to make this information available to the public.

(5) To the extent that therapeutic organizations do receive complaints, they assert that these are frequently against non-registered practitioners, and thus outside their jurisdiction. If this is the case, it is all the more reason for the public to ensure that they only consult practitioners who belong to a recognized, well-established professional body.

In conclusion, such information as exists points to an unsatisfactory array of procedures. The *ad hoc* basis of much decision-making is inadequate, unreliable and potentially unjust, particularly given the rapidly expanding numbers of practitioners over whom professional bodies preside. Whilst establishing professional disciplinary procedures may not have been seen as a first priority for newly emerging therapeutic organizations, the scale on which they now operate renders this an unacceptable state of affairs. Complementary medicine must be seen to take its disciplinary responsibilities seriously. Even if there are very few complaints brought, the structures should be in place and should be highly visible to the public.

Professionals should realize that in the event of a complaint being brought, it is as much in their own interests for them to be fair and open procedures as it is in the consumer's interest. The more a therapy prides itself on its professional status, the stronger its vested interests should be in weeding out unprofessional colleagues. Resources must be allocated to providing effective disciplinary structures which should be regarded by therapists in a positive light and seen as being vital if complementary medicine is to retain the public confidence upon which it relies.

Notwithstanding the proliferation of voluntary self-regulating bodies, the role of ethics is still under-appreciated and under-utilized.

Those organizations which rely on 'GMC-style' codes of ethics will show a greater concern for legalistic matters than for substantive ethical matters. This is inappropriate, in that the impetus for respecting autonomy and obtaining consent derives from the patient-centred nature of much of complementary medicine, and is not, as is arguably the case in orthodox medicine, driven by fear of litigation.

As with legal constraints, formal regulation of any kind will require questions of competence to be capable of being measured or quantified. We have already discussed the difficulties of measuring the subtle interchanges that are going on in synergistic, vibrational therapies. These rely on an interplay between the practitioner and the patient in ways which rarely translate into the substance of ethical codes of practice, particularly when they model themselves on codes of practice designed, again with the traditional doctor/patient relationship in mind.[5]

The training in many holistic therapies places such a high emphasis on respect for the patient that some ethical principles may well be inculcated as an integral part of the training, without being formally identified as such. Despite the fact that certain ethical precepts may be conveyed to trainee practitioners within the context of their *therapeutic* training, other important ethical principles can only be instilled through explicit teaching.

In terms of disciplinary mechanisms, complementary therapies require an even greater appreciation of ethical concerns, given the non-measurable, non-rational dimensions of holistic practice. Particularly in therapies which do not have a highly technical skill base, ethical, rather than therapeutic, complaints are likely to give greater cause for concern.

VI. ADEQUACY OF CODES OF ETHICS

In the absence of statutory provisions, as the situation currently stands, codes of ethics are the only formal mechanism for ensuring that appropriate standards of practice are met.[6] We should be quite

---

[5] Significantly, even the GMC recognizes that its previous form of *Guidance on Professional Conduct* is outdated. Their new *Guidance* reflects to a far greater extent the underlying ethical basis of good medical practice, with increased prominence for patient autonomy, and the fact that the underlying relationship in orthodox medicine should be that of a collaborative approach.

[6] Statutorily registered health practitioners using complementary therapies will also be bound by their primary registering body. The fact that existing health

explicit that the content of codes of ethics may not be an adequate or accurate reflection of what it is to act ethically. Equally, we are not convinced that there is sufficient congruence between codes of ethics and how practitioners actually work.

Many would argue that the effectiveness of professional codes is limited because in the absence of statutory backing they are unenforceable. We acknowledge that as with any normative statement, ethical codes can only indicate how practitioners ought to behave. Even the law cannot make practitioners behave one way rather than another, it can only threaten legal sanctions if they contravene legal standards. The question then arises: how likely is it that these penalties will be enforced and how much authority do regulatory bodies have? The effectiveness of codes of ethics will be called into question if they are either incapable of being enforced, or if practitioners know that although there are penalties, they are hardly ever imposed.

Moreover, one has to ask how realistic it is to expect that broadly drafted, generalized codes will be able to impart ethical instruction to practitioners. What can codes of ethics possibly hope to teach anyone if ethical principles have not been instilled during training? Codes of ethics are no more than a summary of general ethical requirements. Their importance in promoting ethical standards of practice has to be seen in this context. It is pointless trying to include legal responsibilities as well. This fosters the notion that compliance with ethical and legal responsibilities is to avoid liability, rather than to promote high standards.

Meanwhile, because at present formalized ethics teaching is not widely taught within training establishments, many practitioners will encounter ethical dilemmas for the first time when they go into practice. This greatly increases the need for such codes to be both accessible and easy to understand. Unless practitioners work in a team setting, or maintain close links with their training school, practitioners may have no formal guidance beyond their code of conduct and their own conscience.

Ethical codes, if they are to be of any use in shaping conduct must be widely available to practitioners and patients. To the extent that organizations do have a code of ethics, many practitioners may not know of its existence. Were a complaint to be made against a practitioner which resulted in legal action, it would primarily be to the code

professionals are already regulated by a statutory code is likely to be extremely persuasive to NHS purchasers.

of ethics that the court would look in determining the appropriate standard of care. It is thus critical that practitioners are familiar with their professional guidance. Professional bodies have a responsibility towards their members to advise them on what they consider to be ethical conduct. Assuming that the role of a responsible regulatory body should be to improve standards as well as maintain them, codes of guidance must be revised as often as is necessary to take account of changes in attitudes.

VII. ENFORCEABILITY OF DISCIPLINARY MECHANISMS

If codes of ethics are to have any value whatsoever in protecting the public, they must be capable of being enforced and actually enforced. This means that professional organizations must take their supervisory role seriously and be prepared to impose penalties where necessary. To be effective, a complaints system must be easily accessed by the public.

The concern most frequently voiced in relation to voluntary self-regulation is that without statutory backing, ethical codes and disciplinary mechanisms are not enforceable. In fact, this is only part of the argument, which is inextricably linked with protection of title. The point is not that effective sanctions cannot be applied by voluntary self-regulating bodies, but that in the absence of a protected title. there is nothing to stop a disqualified practitioner from setting up in practice either under a different regulatory body, or without being affiliated to any professional organization. Is this a realistic concern? Although practitioners could, in theory, carry on in practice, even after being deregistered, is there any empirical evidence to suggest that this is happening in practice? We must remember that even if this is occurring in a few isolated cases, it may not be sufficient reason to insist upon statutory regulation for all therapies as a consequence.

At least two arguments can be put forward to support this proposition. The first is that just as the law cannot compel anyone to act in a particular way, so statutory regulation cannot ensure that a deregistered practitioner would not still attempt to carry on in practice after having been removed from the statutory register. Whilst the threat of a heavy fine or imprisonment would deter most people from such a course of action, it could not guarantee that this would never happen. Indeed, one can envisage a situation where loyal patients might still wish to consult a practitioner even if he or she had been the subject of adverse disciplinary findings.

A second counter-argument concerns patient self-responsibility. We have already referred to the emphasis placed on self-responsibility in the therapeutic relationship itself. We would assert that a high degree of patient self-responsibility should also be exercised by patients seeking a therapist in the first place. As few complementary consultations are emergencies, patients should spend some time and energy choosing their therapist. Whilst it can safely be assumed that health practitioners working in the NHS will be suitably trained and qualified, the same cannot be assumed of non-statutorily regulated private practitioners.[7]

There is no reason why the onus should not be on the patient to establish a practitioner's credentials before entering into a therapeutic relationship with that person. If a therapist claims to possess certain qualifications, a patient should contact the relevant professional organizations to check that the practitioner is duly qualified and has not, as far as they can tell, been the subject of disciplinary proceedings. Obviously, this depends on professional organizations being approachable and forthcoming with this information, but one would hope that such organizations would respond favourably as this would assist their ability to regulate their members. Likewise, patients should ask where the practitioner trained and should judge for themselves whether the sort of training the practitioner had seems sufficient. Hypnotherapists and acupuncturists whose qualifications have been awarded by way of correspondence course should be consulted with caution!

We do not pretend that this is a perfect solution. To the extent that people are more dependent on others when they are ill, they may be more likely to trust therapists who make enthusiastic claims about their ability to provide relief. However, given the common law right which enables patients to consult freely any practitioner of choice, patients themselves have to exercise a degree of common sense and self-protection in choosing their therapist.

VIII. DO CURRENT MECHANISMS PROMOTE ETHICAL PRACTICE?

Our difficulties with voluntary self-regulation come from a different angle altogether. Until now, the interest in codes of ethics has been

---

[7] See Darina Flynn's article 'Regulation of Non-Conventional Medicine', *Consumer Policy Review*, Oct. 1993 Vol. 3 No. 4 (Blackwell, 1993).

linked to whether they are sufficiently capable of enforcement, that is, on their negative and punitive element, rather than enquiring whether they are sufficiently explicit about the ethical requirements of the practitioner/patient relationship. In our opinion, none of the existing codes truly identify what is required of practitioners in order to act ethically. The rudiments of what is required to obtain a valid consent from a patient are not even addressed in the BCMA or the British Register's codes, nor does it seem, from talking to therapists *en masse*, that this knowledge can be taken for granted. The point is, practitioners will not learn what it means to practise ethically from a code of ethics issued to them as they are about to embark on practice in their chosen discipline. Substantive ethical teaching must be a part of all practitioners' training.

All regulation should be working towards the promotion of high ethical standards of behaviour. A sound ethical base is at the heart of safe and competent practice. Consumer protection concerns would be met if all practitioners worked to a high ethical standard. Thus, whatever regulatory model is chosen, ensuring high ethical standards will always be of paramount concern. The point remains that regulation cannot be seen as the application of some external force. High ethical standards have to come from the way in which practitioners *choose* to practice. A preventative ethical approach is far more in keeping with the essence of complementary medicine than the imposition of retrospective disciplinary measures.

Contrary to the rhetoric, we cannot assume that all therapists do work in a patient-centred way. Complementary medicine has its fair share of autocratic, domineering practitioners. Nor do all practitioners adopt a holistic approach. Many therapists adopt a multi-therapeutic approach and wander into areas in which they are less qualified to treat patients. There is thus a discrepancy between how practitioners are actually practising and what their codes of ethics prescribe.

IX. REGULATION—THE MORE FORMAL THE BETTER?

We must examine closely the assumption that the more formalized regulation is, the better it will necessarily be. Part of the rush towards statutory self-regulation may arise from a lack of understanding of what *effective* voluntary self-regulation could achieve. All therapies should be working towards achieving the highest levels of technical competence performed within an ethical framework. This objective is entirely consistent with proper voluntary self-regulation. Complementary medicine is currently in a highly privileged position. Its popularity is blossoming, and it is a successful commercial enterprise. More importantly, it is not the subject of frequent complaints and litigation.

If practitioners want to retain this enviable position, it is up to them to ensure that their standards of conduct are sufficiently high to ward off threats of external control. To achieve this objective, a greater degree of professionalism will be required of many therapies than in the past. Therapeutic organizations should be concentrating their efforts on working towards developing national standards of education and competence, developing training modules on ethics and communication, organizing post-qualification education, support and supervision, developing complaints mechanisms which incorporate users' views, and participating in research. In this regard, greater professionalism is all about achieving high standards. This does not require statutory regulation. Not only is statutory regulation unlikely to be forthcoming for the reasons we have outlined, but even if it were, smaller therapies would do far better to put their resources towards improving and developing standards of competence within their therapy. We shall go on to develop the argument that until such competencies have been defined, statutory regulation is unrealistic.

Statutory regulation cannot guarantee high ethical standards— witness the number of complaints against the medical profession. As with the threat of legal sanctions, formal disciplinary mechanisms and the threat of deregistration will not promote high standards. Legalistic codes of practice tell practitioners little about the true meaning of acting in an ethically appropriate way. To the extent that voluntary self-regulation is a cheaper and more flexible means of achieving the same regulatory aims, therapeutic organizations should be concentrating on facilitating good standards of practice through training.

11

Redefining the Role of Ethics

We have now explored the major regulatory options. Each has considerable shortcomings in relation to complementary medicine. Although we have looked at how existing mechanisms are applied, or would be applied to alternative therapies, there is an incongruity between the intuitive, fluid nature of many of the therapies themselves and the rigid formalism of legal or legalistic constraints, which rely on quantification, certainly, and proof. All the regulatory options we have looked at are reactive not proactive, tend to concentrate on the negative rather than the positive, and focus on punishment rather than encouragement. We must not fall into the trap of assuming that because, historically, health professionals have relied on these existing models, they are a realistic paradigm for the regulation of complementary medicine. Although statutory self-regulation has characterized health professions in the past, we have seen why this approach is unsuitable for the bulk of complementary therapies. Likewise, the legal strictures which govern the doctor/patient relationship may be too insensitive a mechanism to take into account the nuances of a truly holistic relationship.

I. HOW USEFUL ARE EXISTING MODELS?

The pattern which has emerged in the preceding chapters poses something of a dilemma. Although we have established that a high standard of practice is the primary focus of regulation, none of the formal regulatory mechanisms we have outlined seem to provide an adequate means of ensuring that these standards are achieved. Although both the common law and statutory control impose legal deterrents to ensure compliance, as we have seen, these do not guarantee high standards or that patients will necessarily be protected from harm or abuse by their therapists. Certainly, data from organizations such as the Prevention of Professional Abuse Network indicate that statutorily regulated professionals also have their share of abusers. Threats of criminal sanctions do not ensure ethical conduct—this is something which only careful selection of candidates, a thorough ethical grounding as part of training, and self-motivation can ensure. Statutory regulation is not a panacea. Problems emerge even where a profession is statutorily regulated. Whilst every profession will have its share of bad apples, which no amount of regulation or deterrent will prevent, we should be more concerned about the therapeutic irregularities which can persist, even within a statutory framework. The dramatic increase, for example, in elective cosmetic surgery, the worst excesses of which seem to fly in the face of good medical practice, demonstrates the need to ground practitioners within an ethical framework, not merely a legal one.

Likewise, although umbrella organizations such as the ICM and the BCMA are attempting to bring diverse ranges of therapists under a common ethical code of conduct, the extent to which these organisations exercise pan-professional disciplinary functions is unclear. Since its formation in 1992, for example, the BCMA has not dealt with one serious disciplinary case. To the extent that member organizations have disciplinary mechanisms in place, none seem to have more than a handful of complaints in any given year, and many of these relate to abusive relationships between practitioners and their clients.

In all of our research thus far, one critical feature emerges—cases relating to therapeutic competence are practically non-existent. Such complaints as there are tend not to relate to matters of technical performance, save to the extent that the therapist is alleged to have exceeded professional boundaries, usually sexually or emotionally. Most complaints relate to extrinsic matters such as infringing disciplinary codes over advertising, or making therapeutic claims. Unless we are to take the virtual absence of formal complaints, that is, disciplinary and legal complaints, against practitioners as evidence of faultless performance, we have to reappraise the existing regulatory models to determine why none of them seem to be capable of responding to this particular aspect of the complementary therapeutic relationship. The point is simply that all regulatory models currently in existence are moulded by, and designed with, the conventional doctor/patient relationship in mind. How does this manifest itself?

We have seen how professional negligence, the legal mechanism which is most commonly invoked to challenge the propriety of professional conduct, is all about the concept of professional responsibility.

Health professionals are the 'experts' and the proper application of their therapeutic skills will make the 'sick' patient 'well'. The application of their technical skills is supposed to evoke a cure, or, at the very least, to prevent deterioration. Self-responsibility and the extent to which the patients help themselves are not part of the legal picture.

In the area of health, the law is not prepared to impose duties of self-responsibility on patients. Patients are not held personally responsible in a legal system which is shaped more by the Hippocratic medical tradition than one which sees the legitimacy of health professionals as deriving solely from the patient's rights and the patient's consent to be treated. As we have seen, there is little room for contributory negligence in a medical negligence action. Is there anything wrong with the *status quo*? The answer in relation to cases concerning allopathic medical practitioners is probably not. The technical expertise base of most of modern medicine is such that it probably is justifiable to regard the practitioner as the expert, and the patient as the grateful, and often passive, recipient of health care who expects not to be harmed by unreasonable errors, and expects to find legal redress should such errors occur.

If we extend this argument a bit further, the position we would seem to be arguing is that in areas where professionals assume a high degree of professional expertise, it is only right and proper that they should be held accountable when things go wrong because the person in receipt of that professional expertise cannot really contribute anything to professional wisdom, and is entirely dependent on the responsible exercise of professional judgement. Certainly, the more that power is held by one party and one party alone, the fairer it would seem to be to place all the liability on that one party because, in essence, the disempowered party is incapable of exerting significant influence on the outcome of the therapeutic exchange.

Can this same model be applied to a therapeutic relationship which depends for its success on the active participation of the client? Let us take, for example, psychodynamic psychotherapy. Here, the therapist is giving the client space to realize his or her potential. If the client fails to do so, we would not expect this sort of failure to find expression through the law. Psychotherapy, whilst outside the remit of this book, is a useful parallel, because it demonstrates the difficulties that the law has in intervening where the alleged harm is emotional, not physical. This is not to say that the law can never make awards of compensation when people have negligently caused another psychological injury. In recent years, for example, there has been a dramatic increase in awards for cases of post-traumatic stress disorder. The point to note, however, is that in those few cases in which damages have been awarded for psychological, rather than physical harm, the alleged injuries must fall within a category of recognized psychiatric disorders. In other words, *even emotional harm has to be measurable and quantifiable.* This is because of a perceived fear that in the absence of stringent safeguards, it would be open to any aggrieved person to sue for having been caused emotional harm.

Although recent developments in this area of the law demonstrate a gradual move away from Cartesian mind-body dualism,[1] the point is that the law will still require evidence of a formal psychiatric diagnosis within the system of international disease classifications. To be compensatable in law, harm has to be quantifiable within biomedical terms. The problem for holistic therapies is that at least two of the realms they operate in, spiritual and emotional well-being, are not quantifiable in the sense that the law requires. This being the case, can holistic therapies be adequately catered for by a legal system which is based firmly on an 'illness' model of health, rather than a holistic model, in which the therapist is trying to bring the whole of the patient's being into harmony.

It is, however, the twin themes of professional expertise and self-responsibility which account for the failure of existing regulatory models to deal adequately with issues of therapeutic competence. If, as is our assertion, the patient's active involvement is a successful part of the therapy, and the role of the therapist is to act not as a detached expert, but one who is guided by the patient, acting as a conduit through which self-healing can occur, an entirely new model of the law is required, which will be discussed in Part III.

II. ARGUMENTS FOR SPECTRUM APPROACH TO REGULATION

As we have pointed out throughout this book, the lumping together of all complementary therapies under one umbrella is more of a political device than anything to do with the therapies themselves. We do not pretend that therapies such as herbalism or acupuncture, taught over several years, with a highly formalized knowledge and skill base

[1] See, e.g., *Page* v. *Smith* [1995] 2 All ER 736.

will be able to be regulated in the same way as dowsing or bioenergetics. Therapies, as we have seen, range from highly 'medicalized', technical-based approaches at one end of the spectrum, to non-formalized, highly intuitive, vibrational approaches at the other.

As there is a spectrum of therapeutic technique, so must there be a spectrum of regulatory responses. It should be fairly obvious by now that statutory regulation on a therapy-by-therapy basis is the least desirable approach, conferring a structure and status on therapists which is inappropriate for reasons we have discussed. For most therapies, self-regulation is the preferred route. Notwithstanding the points we have made, we need to ask whether there are some therapies which will still require, or be attracted to, statutory, rather than voluntary self-regulation.

III. DETERMINING CRITIERIA

A. Risk of harm

Throughout the book, we have seen the emphasis placed on patient safety as a central theme in regulation. It has been suggested that the potential harm that certain therapies pose requires them to be statutorily regulated. We must scrutinize this argument very carefully, since it carried with it an assumption that statutory regulation is the best way to protect the public. But we have seen that this is not the case. Ultimately, the best safeguard is high levels of competence, ensured through high standards of training and supervision. The only function that statutory regulation provides over and above voluntary regulation is the ability to protect its register through criminal sanctions, hopefully ensuring that untrained, or insufficiently trained, practitioners may not use that professional appellation. All other areas of standard-setting, including the effective accreditation of training establishments and the teaching of an approved syllabus with appropriate methods of assessment, can be ensured just as well through effective voluntary self-regulation as the acupuncture and homoeopathy professions impressively demonstrate.

None the less, the question of direct harm to patients must be taken very seriously. Unfortunately, in discussing harm, two contradictory and polarized positions are taken. The first line, taken by opponents of complementary therapies, is that complementary therapies are so

harmful that they should either be banned, or at the very least, practised only by registered practitioners, and opposing position trades on
the public perception that natural medicine is inherently safe. We
reject both extremes. Every therapy has potentially harmful implications. The most appropriate thing to do is to look realistically at the
sorts of harms that may arise, and consider constructively how these
can be averted.

As we have seen, the 'harm' that is most often raised is the failure
of complementary practitioners to recognize medical conditions
leading to patients being deprived of conventional medical treatment. Yet, despite the persistence of this line of attack, there is no
evidence to support it. Moreover, the argument is untenable because
alternative practitioners are not trained in making conventional
medical diagnoses. With the exception possibly of manipulative
therapists, they are not working within a biomedical model, and
view the patient's symptoms within an entirely different paradigm.
Where, as we have argued, patients have exercised a specific choice
to consult this sort of practitioner rather than an allopathic doctor,
it is unreasonable to expect the same sort of treatment. This is not
to say that any therapist who lays hands on a patient should not be
able to spot contra-indications to treatment and that this may
require a degree of conventional medical knowledge (how much
knowledge they will require is something we shall consider later
on). For these reasons though, we do not consider it legitimate to
describe the consequences of complementary practitioners working
outside biomedical confines as a harm.

Let us look instead at some of the specific risks complementary
therapies may pose. We shall do so under the headings of toxicity,
manipulative therapies, invasive therapies, and emotional harm.

1. Toxic therapies

The therapies which may have problems of toxicity are product-based
therapies such as herbalism, Ayurvedic medicine, Unani medicine,
traditional Chinese medicine and aromatherapy. Toxicity is a problem for all therapies which are based on supplying a medicinal product. Homoeopathy is usually excluded from concerns over toxicity
because the dilution of remedies is so great that they cannot be toxic
in the conventional sense (even though remedies are capable of inducing spectacularly florid side-effects).

This is one area where the media seem particularly bent on scare-mongering, often printing misleading articles on the dangers of herbal remedies. It is not the place of this book to evaluate these claims, only to suggest that the same standards should be applied to non-orthodox therapies as to conventional treatments. Despite the difficulty of standardizing the active elements of natural herbal preparations, all commercially produced products are subject to statutory control. We are concerned about the degree to which regulation can best serve the interests of the consumer, and the number of unregulated Chinese and Ayurvedic remedies available in this country, do present real problems of quality control. It is anachronistic that United Kingdom herbal preparations are subject to statutory controls, but imported remedies frequently evade such control.[2] Problems of obtaining the right herbs of a sufficiently high quality are compounded by the inability of many traditional Chinese medicine practitioners in the United Kingdom to communicate with herbal suppliers in the country of origin.

2. Manipulative and touch-based therapies

Manipulative and touch-based therapies include osteopathy, chiropractic, shiatsu, touch therapies, and aromatherapy. Unskilled or inappropriate manipulation can lead to soft tissue injuries, sprains, fractures, damage to the spinal cord, and even death.[3] There are also certain medical conditions in which aggressive massage may be particularly dangerous.

3. Invasive therapies

The primary therapy raising concern in this area is acupuncture. Acupuncture carries various risks, some of which were luridly set out in the 1986 BMA Report. These include the risk of infection and disease

[2] On this point see the article by Peter A. G. M. De Smet, who suggests that practitioners should be obliged to report suspected adverse reactions: 'Should herbal medicine-like products be licensed as medicines' 310 BMJ 1023–4 (1995), A database has been set up by the National Poisons Unit. See V. S. G. Murray, 'Investigating Alternative Medicines' 304 BMJ 11 (1991).

[3] In 1994, a coroner recorded a verdict of accidental death when a man died from brain-stem damage 4 days after having been treated by an osteopath who massaged the patient's neck as a treatment for tennis elbow.

transmission, particularly through unsterilized needles; the risk of puncturing organs and the risk of needles breaking, which may produce granulomatous reactions, or even find their way to organs.

Certainly, the sorts of risks associated with acupuncture are more serious than, say, those associated with reflexology. Obvious safeguards are now universally in place amongst accredited practitioners, so that the risk of an acupuncturist using or re-using unsterilized needles is a thing of the past. Certain precautions must always be taken, such as treating patients in a prone position, so that they cannot be caused injury if, exceptionally, they faint or fall whilst acupuncture needles are in place.

4. Emotional harm

The influence of the biomedical model and its focus on physical harm is such that emotional harm is sometimes overlooked. One of the more serious risks of complementary therapy is the potential harm caused by untrained, unskilled therapists working with patients on an emotional level. Some counselling therapies, hypnosis, regression, and visualization expressly work on an emotional level. The concern is not just in relation to these therapists, who, one would hope, are specifically trained to deal with emotional crises produced in therapy, but as much by other therapists who view working holistically as enabling them to delve into their patients' psyche at more than a superficial level. This is not to suggest that this is always entirely inappropriate, provided the therapist is capable of working on this level. There may be concern, for example, with touch therapists, who do not confine their work to a physical level, but who enter into therapeutic dialogue with their clients. Likewise, it is important that energy workers practising on a spiritual or esoteric level are capable of distinguishing spiritual malaise from *emotional* imbalance. The point to note is that being a therapist does not, without more, equip practitioners to deal with people who are potentially in considerable distress, and who may require skilled counselling or psychotherapeutic intervention. The need to recognize, rather than diagnose, medical conditions must, if we are to avoid mind-body dualism, extend to being able to recognize psychological contra-indications as well as physical ones.

That potential risks exist is beyond doubt. The question for us, however, is to consider which regulatory response, or which combination of regulatory responses, will prevent those harms from materializing. In all of the above situations, the only case in which grounds for statutory controls rather than voluntary controls seem appropriate is in the licensing of potentially toxic products. In this area, we find it difficult to draw a distinction between conventional medicines and alternative medicines. This is not to suggest that all natural therapies should be brought within the Medicines Act 1968, involving licensing procedures which are prohibitively burdensome on most manufacturers. The threat to herbal medicines indicates once again that the knee-jerk regulatory response is to try to squeeze complementary medicines into the bio-medical framework even where this is unnecessary, inappropriate, and unworkable. Devising alternative mechanisms for the licensing of medicinal products is outside the scope of this book, although we recognize that to the extent that the products used in particular therapies are statutorily regulated, the less intense the calls may be to regulate the professions dispensing those products.

Thus, we can see that complementary medicine is not without its risks to the public. But how far should these risks of harm, many of which are extremely remote, influence the regulation debate. Is paternalism going to prevail, restricting people from taking informed risks, or should consumer choice determine the issue?

B. Reliance on specialized knowledge

Like orthodox medicine, many therapies are now based on a highly skilled technical knowledge base. This technical skill base, acquired through formal assessment and examinable skills, together with the nature of therapeutic interchange, places certain therapies much closer to the orthodox medical model. The reality is, despite language of self-responsibility, that the technical knowledge base that increasingly forms the basis of the 'big five' therapies means that the patient is still beholden on the professional's competent performance, in much the same way as recipients of 'high-tech' orthodox medicine are. Indeed, one can accept that the more technical the skills required for the competent performance of a therapy, the stronger the grounds are for needing to prevent inadequately skilled practitioners from treating the public. One of the most powerful regulatory pointers will be the similarity the therapy bears to an existing orthodox modality, the extent to which doctors already provide that therapy, or recommend it, and the likelihood of its incorporation into the NHS.

C. A strong medicalized faction

We recognize the very real tensions that exist in those therapies where there is a strong medical presence, in the sense that a number of statutorily registered professionals (be they doctors, nurses, dentists, etc.) also practice that therapy, whether or not as part of their orthodox treatment. As we saw in Part II, therapists who belong to a statutory profession will already be bound by a statutory code of ethics. They may reasonably regard themselves as more tightly regulated than their lay counterparts. Of primary importance is the issue of how much biomedical knowledge therapists require in order to practise safely. Medicalized practitioners may have the tendency to feel that only they, with their grounding in orthodox medicine, can fully protect patients' well-being. From the perspective of lay practitioners, there is a fear that where a strong medicalized branch of the therapy exists, they are more likely to be squeezed out, with a gradual medical colonization of that therapy and a medicalized practising of the therapy which denies the more holistic underpinnings and traditional basis.

Because of the mutual fears and concerns, it is highly likely that where there is a sizeable medicalized faction, both sides of the profession will seek to resolve internal difficulties and work together towards statutory regulation, so that all practitioners are working to high standards of practice with an enforceable protected title which will exclude untrained or inadequately trained practitioners from holding themselves out as qualified therapists.

IV. THE CENTRALITY OF ETHICS

In the above sections we have argued why we feel that statutory regulation is inappropriate for the bulk of therapies for the foreseeable future. We have seen however, that therapies which rely on technical skills may demand a statutory response, because of the similarities with medicine in terms of a highly technical skill base, therapeutic claims, and client expectation. It is our central contention that, whether voluntary or statutory regulation is pursued, a grounding in what it means to practise ethically is at the heart of either system of regulation.

For all other therapies, with the exception of toxicity then, all the other potential harms we have identified go to the training and competence of practitioners. Our contention is that the best way of ensuring the highest educational standards is through effective voluntary self-regulation. This, as we have seen, is the model upon which complementary medicine currently relies. Does this mean that the *status quo* is acceptable and that voluntary self-regulation as it currently stands is an adequate means of protecting the public? In some cases the answer is yes. For the main part, however, there is a failure truly to espouse the notion of ethics-led regulation which, we believe, provides the key to effective self-regulation. If complementary medicine does not evince a real commitment to translating its rhetoric into concrete, organizational structures it is likely to lose its popular support.

Throughout Part II, we have seen the critical importance of high standards of practice, achieved through appropriate selection procedures, educational standards, post-qualification education, supervision, and support. Alongside these vital components must be a commitment, on the part of practitioners, to use their skills in an ethical manner to the benefit of the patient and to the credit of the profession. Part III will focus on how to achieve this in practice. Unless practitioners are taught in an overt and explicit fashion what it is that ethical practice requires as part of training, regulation is relegated to an *ex post facto* role, seen primarily as a means of picking up the pieces when things have gone wrong. The endeavour of this book is to propose a regulatory framework in which unethical practice is unlikely to occur in the first place. To the extent that ethical codes continue to be couched in punitive terms, they will not promote the ethical climate which, we believe, is the only real way to best serve the public. Let us now explore what ethics-led regulation requires in practice.

PART III

A Model for Ethics-Led Regulation

12
Ethical Practice

What do we mean by ethics-led regulation? Essentially we envisage a system of regulation whereby the emphasis is placed firmly on instilling a practical basis for ensuring ethical standards of practice and on avoiding mistakes in the first place. As with the promotion and maintenance of good health, the emphasis should be on prevention rather than cure. As we have seen, the modes of regulation we have looked at operate retrospectively, centring on disciplinary mechanisms which only come into operation *when professional standards have already been breached*. Our first aim, therefore, is to suggest ways in which practitioners can attain high, ethical standards on an individual level. The hope is that an emphasis on preventing mistakes, and a sense of individual accountability, will greatly reduce the extent to which punitive disciplinary measures need to be invoked. However, it would be naive to assume that a thorough grounding in ethical behaviour would prevent all forms of misconduct and abuse. If high standards of regulation are taken as the first plank of regulation, then enforcing those standards in an open and accountable manner must be seen as the second aim.

Our aim in this section of the book is to describe a system of ethics-led regulation which is responsive to the holistic dimension of complementary medicine, and which promotes and enhances patient-centred values. Whilst the common law will continue to exercise a regulatory function, the primary purpose of Part III is to explore how to achieve regulation which places ethical conduct at the fore. This, we believe, is a radical approach to regulation, but it is the only solution which will ultimately produce optimal standards of practice and protect consumers from such harms as complementary medicine may pose in its current state of development. Whilst we do not underrate the impressive efforts which are being made by some of the more efficient self-regulating bodies, many therapies remain unsatisfactorily regulated. In devising an appropriate framework, we must recognize that regulation for the nineties and beyond presents new challenges and opportunities.

The historical perspective explored earlier has demonstrated that the form of regulation chosen by the medical profession in 1858 had, as its primary purpose, a desire to create a professional monopoly. Thus, the creation of the Medical Register was to effect professional closure and keep out the numerous other occupational groups who were plying healing cures at that time. Critically, statutory regulation, as conceived by the medical profession at that time was not concerned with standard-setting or professional ethics. These are constructs which have only been incorporated within the statutory framework relatively recently. Arguably, the difficulties being faced by the GMC are a product of its changing role in changing times.

Today's self-regulatory bodies are operating in a totally different climate. High standards, rather than professional status, are the only justification for formal registration. Within health care, there is a far greater recognition of purchasers' power. As such, self-regulating bodies setting up from scratch will have to demonstrate that responding to what the consumer wants is the highest item on their agenda. As Margaret Stacey urges, we should be looking towards a concept of professionalism in which the principle of service is high on the agenda but privilege and power do not dominate.[1]

As we have attempted to demonstrate, the absence of significant complaints against complementary practitioners is no cause for complacency. Whilst complementary therapies may be generally safer than allopathic medicine, there are anecdotal reports of adverse outcomes which have not translated into formal complaints and this, we would argue, has much to do with the absence of well-organized complaints mechanisms. Certainly, the larger voluntary self-regulating bodies report that many of the complaints they receive against practitioners are from members of the public complaining about therapists who are not registered with a registering body and thus fall outside their remit.

In designing an appropriate form of regulation, the low level of complaints should not be our primary focus. Rather than focusing on punitive aspects of regulation, we should look towards creating positive regulatory structures which actively promote ethical practice. The common law is ethics-led to the extent that legal standards are derived from what is currently regarded as good ethical practice. As to statutory and voluntary self-regulation, we have seen that

[1] Stacey, M., 'Potential of science for complementary medicine: some introductory reflections'. *Complementary Medical Research*, Oct. 1991, Vol. 5 No. 3.

codes of ethics attempt, with varying degrees of success, to delineate what constitutes good ethical practice, and to discipline members who fall below the standards thus identified. Whilst we recognize that codes of ethics play a useful role in setting out, in the broadest of terms, the basic prerequisites of professional practice, they are not framed in such a way as to provide guidance to practitioners on what it really means to think ethically and to practice ethically. Indeed the more formalized self-regulating bodies become, the more legalistic their codes of ethics tend to be, focusing largely on what is prohibited.

How, then, are notions of ethical practice to be instilled? Within the health care professions there is a dawning recognition that formalized ethics teaching needs to be part of the curriculum. At this juncture, we do not need to decide whether ethical precepts should be taught separately or integrated within training. It is enough to recognize that if practitioners are not given a reason why certain forms of conduct are prohibited and others encouraged, they are less likely to practice in a truly ethical manner.

I. INDIVIDUAL *V.* COLLECTIVE ETHICS

Although behaving in an ethical manner is ultimately a matter for individual conscience, we need to differentiate between individual ethics and collective ethics. All practitioners must be accountable for their own actions. We must recognize however, that instilling ethical values and providing mechanisms for redress is something which can only be orchestrated at a collective level if individuals are to have the tools to practice ethically. This is not to downplay the role of good conscience and a sense of internal morality. It is not enough though to rely on 'gut feelings' as providing sufficient insight into what it means to practice ethically. Internal morality is, we would argue, deeply subjective, representing the cumulative normative influences to which individuals have been exposed—from parents, teachers, role models, etc. Religious beliefs may also influence this process. The result is that what someone intuitively thinks is right or wrong is highly value-laden. Whilst, for example, strong religious beliefs may provide the healing inspiration for many health practitioners, the imposition of strongly held religious views may taint the services one is prepared to provide.

We can perhaps see this more clearly with reference to conventional health care practitioners. For example, doctors and nurses who hold deep religious views on the sanctity of human life often experience acute difficulties in working in controversial areas such as abortion or passive withdrawal of medical treatment at the end of life. Whilst it would be unusual for complementary practitioners to find themselves in this sort of situation, the point is that deeply held convictions *of whatever sort* may prevent therapists from dealing with clients in an open and value-free manner, and may indeed see practitioners trying to instil their own values on others.

When we go on to look at ethical principles, we shall need to look at how they apply both individually, and how they can be organized through professional organizations on a collective level. It will emerge that all the ethical principles we discuss have ramifications both on an individual and a collective level. Whilst, for example, individuals can take personal responsibility when errors do occur by being candid, offering an apology, waiving fees and/or offering reparation, this will almost certainly need to be backed up by policies at an organizational level, whereby members have to carry adequate indemnity insurance for the work they do, and would be subject to complaints mechanisms.

II. 'CONSUMER PROTECTION' *V*. 'PROFESSIONAL SELF-INTEREST'

Customarily, commentators on the regulation debate have differentiated between those regulatory aims directed towards consumer protection, and those concerned with developing and enhancing professional status. Whilst this division has a superficial appeal, it should become apparent that many of the issues relate both to consumer protection and professional self-interest. Even the creation of a protected title, potentially the most blatant manifestation of professional self-interest, serves the dual purpose of enhancing the status of practitioners thus qualified, whilst simultaneously protecting patients from unqualified or incompetent practitioners using that title.

In particular, many of the points which would tend to be described as professional self-interest issues, on closer examination, also have a consumer protection component. For example, practitioners could legitimately argue that it would be easier for them to promote the public interest were they able to attain a position of professional power within the medical hierarchy. We have seen why some of these claims need to be treated with caution, and have looked at whether the perceived power obtained through statutory regulation inevitably distorts the therapist/client relationship.

Our aim then is to approach this subject in a more constructive fashion, on the basis that the primary aim of regulation should be to produce competent practitioners, working within an ethical framework, using their skills to the benefit of the patient. Our endeavour is to synthesize the issues identified in Part I with the shortfalls in existing regulatory models explored in Part II, to create an holistic model of regulation which, we hope, can be translated from theory into practice.

13

Ethical Practice and the Individual Practitioner

The growth of formalized ethics in health care is, in part, a response to the consumer movement, and an emerging commitment to patients' rights. In the past, it was tacitly assumed that a professional training, in tandem with the possession of an upright character, was enough to ensure that professionals would act in an ethical fashion. The principle of beneficence, seen as caring for the sick, was assumed to be the overriding feature of the professional relationship, and characterizes the Hippocratic tradition. Whilst securing a patient's compliance was obviously desirable, it was not seen as a legal or ethical prerequisite, and the means to secure compliance ranged from coercive language and bullying, to the use of the therapeutic lie, were that deemed necessary to protect the patient. This approach is no longer acceptable. Nowadays, as we have already seen, the principle of respect for autonomy is given such prominence that there is a legal duty on health practitioners to obtain a patient's consent before treatment.

The assumption that the concept of disease is value-free is unsustainable, particularly when considering an holistic approach to health. One of the purposes of medical ethics is to separate 'technical' medical decisions from moral decisions. Whilst health professionals can rightly be expected to have a certain 'expertise' in the former, they do not have any similar qualifications when it comes to the moral dilemmas that their work may generate. Working holistically, it may not be possible to separate out the purely 'technical' part of decision-making. Whilst physical ailments are often sufficiently recognizable to apply a descriptive label, emotional disorders are more challenging, and spiritual difficulties particularly elusive. As Fulford and Hope point out, 'traditional bioethics has assumed a scientific, value-neutral model of disease to which ethical principles can be applied'.[1] Fulford and Hope

---

[1] Fulford, K. W. M., and Hope, T., 'Psychiatric Ethics: a Bioethical ugly duckling?' in Gillon, R. (ed.) *Principles of Health Care Ethics* (John Wiley, 1994).

highlight the problems this may cause for psychiatry in which, as they suggest, the concept of disease is itself ethically problematic. We would argue that such difficulties are compounded when one considers an holistic approach to health and disease.

Rather than a model based in inappropriate medical concepts which do not fit the circumstances, a different approach is required. This supplants the science-based view of illness as non-functioning or malfunctioning, with a model which focuses on the analysis of the patient's experience of illness, for example, in terms of lack of functional ability, or failure of intentional action. Were this approach to be followed, more weight would be placed on how the patient viewed the outcome, rather than looking exclusively to what the professional did or did not do.

So what do we mean by ethics and what does the pursuit of ethics seek to achieve in a health care context? Ethics is about acting morally and reaching moral decisions. It is about how people should behave, and what they ought to do. Can there be any objective agreement as to what constitute important moral principles? Remarkably, the answer seems to be yes, in that most societies and most cultures share certain basic principles, such as the avoidance of unnecessary pain, and respect for life, although the weight that will be attached to competing principles will vary from society to society.

As Schneider observes, in considering the wide variety of ethical dilemmas that arise in health care:

a rich vocabulary of ethical considerations, styles and approaches is necessary. Different bioethical issues arising in different contexts may demand a regime of rules or the flexibility of discretion, a rights discourse or a language of duties, public policy analysis or private preference, the salvation of religion or the neutrality of liberalism, the profits of principles or the insights of casuistry, the uses of utilitarianism or the devices of deontology, the rigors of economics or the consolations of philosophy. In my father's house there are many mansions.[2]

Before considering some of the ethical principles, we shall look at how these principles relate to ethical theories and how competing principles might be reconciled.

---

[2] Schneider, C. E., 'Bioethics in the Language of the Law', *Hastings Center Report* 24, no. 4 (1994), at 16–22.

I. ETHICAL PRINCIPLES AND ETHICAL THEORIES

In considering ethical principles, we are really talking about the values on which health care is based. Although some principles may have greater emphasis in relation to alternative medicine, the values we distil should be broadly similar in all areas of health care. Although the list is not exhaustive, ethical (or moral) principles relevant to health care might include compassion, respect for the patient's wishes, a duty to relieve suffering and not to harm patients, truth-telling, and keeping promises. Merely elucidating certain ethical principles is no guarantee that practitioners will thereby act ethically, but it enables them to identify those moral issues which need to be critically reflected upon in arriving at any decision.

An additional way of looking at the moral issues which arise in health care might be to ask 'what sort of people should practitioners be?' Here, we are concerned not with generalizable principles, but with the role of *individual virtues*. By this we mean acquired traits such as benevolence, humility, a sense of justice, and integrity. Note that when we use the term 'virtue', we are not talking simply about someone's character, or their innate qualities. As we have seen, in seeking to arrive at moral decisions, it is not enough to rely on 'gut feelings', however important intuitive responses may be.

As suggested above, there has been some reluctance in accepting health care ethics as a discrete discipline, particularly by those who think that provided all practitioners are well-intended, morally upright people, they will instinctively know the 'right' response in any given situation, and be able to resolve any dilemmas which emerge. The reason this position is untenable is that people's concept of what is 'right' may vary enormously. More than anything, a formalized approach to ethics connotes reflective thinking. Health care ethics is, as Gillon describes,[3] about ethically evaluating moral decisions underlying health care, and is thus a conscious activity.

A distinction needs to be drawn between ethical principles and ethical theories. Ethicists attempt to justify ethical principles by reference to one or more ethical theories. Whilst, for example, all practitioners would, it is hoped, recognize the need to take a client's

---

[3] Gillon, R., *Philosophical Medical Ethics* (John Wiley and Sons, Chichester, 1986); Gillon, R., *Principles of Medical Ethics* (John Wiley and Sons, Chichester, 1994).

wishes into account (and recognition of the principle of respect for autonomy now permeates official statements), what is the underlying justification for this position? The principle derives from the theory that people have an intrinsic value and should not be used as a means to an end. It derives from the Kantian notion that society is best served if respect is given to the autonomous choices of rational 'moral agents' to direct their own life in the way they think appropriate.

Ethical theories attempt to provide an overarching justification for pursuing various courses of action in reliance on various principles. Adherence to ethical principles should promote a better outcome because the aim of ethics is to bring about a better state of affairs not a worse one. One group of ethical theories, known as *deontological* theories, derive from the idea that there are certain fundamental rules which should be followed. This duty-based approach ties in strongly with the idea that certain groups of people may, by virtue of their position, incur additional duties towards others. The Kantian duty of respect for persons described above would be an example of this.

The other main group of ethical theories are *consequentialist*, that is to say, they assess the righteousness of an action by looking to the outcome that following that course of action will bring about. Utilitarianism is an example of this sort of ethical reasoning. In its most simplistic form, a utilitarian analysis would weigh up potential benefits and harms involved in pursuing any proposed action and say that the course of action that should be followed is that which maximizes happiness for the greatest number of people. For example, a utilitarian might argue that respecting confidentiality is a good thing because it enables patients to trust practitioners and provides them with the knowledge they require to diagnose effectively, and that this personal information would not be imparted if patients thought that practitioners would blurt this information out to all and sundry. Indeed, the primary justification for respecting confidentiality is that if people did not think their secrets would be preserved they would either not give vital information, or they might avoid seeking professional help at all.

Customarily, a variety of theories may be invoked to justify any given ethical stand. It is important to realize that ethical principles are not abstract concepts. Rather they apply in relation to the particular facts of any given case. In trying to analyse the best ethical decision, practitioners will need to be apprised of all necessary factual information. For example, in applying a risk/benefit analysis, the practitioner will need to have the best evidence available upon which to support the outcomes proposed. Whichever theory is invoked, real-life factual situations are complex, and ethical principles invariably conflict, giving rise to dilemmas. Much ethical reasoning is about attempting to solve these dilemmas on a case-by-case basis, starting with an ethical theory, and using it to justify various principles which are then applied to the facts of the case.

Trying to decide which ethical principles and which ethical theory to invoke is no easy matter. Beauchamp and Childress offer an approach based on the four ethical principles of respect for autonomy, beneficence, and non-maleficence, and justice.[4] Whilst these principles are all, undoubtedly, morally significant factors, the 'four principles' approach has been criticized for failing to offer any solution as to how these competing principles should be reconciled. In any given situation, the degree of emphasis given to one principle over another will inevitably be a subjective decision varying from practitioner to practitioner. If that is right, then even using the four principles, one would arrive at a better analysed, but still inherently value-laden decision.

A pertinent criticism of focusing on principles affecting the health practitioner as an individual is that this fails to address broader ethical questions. Moreover, the deductive approach outlined above may place too great a reliance on the duties and responsibilities of the individual practitioner in a given situation, and may pay inadequate attention to the context in which the ethical dilemma arises: the institutional setting, inter-professional issues, systems of reward and such like. In discussing ethical issues we must be sensitive to the political, economic, social, and historical contexts in which these moral problems appear.[5]

Ethical discourse is all about the values that shape any given enterprise. We have seen throughout that as well as a need to focus on issues arising within the individual therapeutic relationship, alternative medicine raises a host of more profound issues such as patient-empowerment, the extent to which therapists can or should work within existing institutionalized settings, and even what is meant by 'health' and 'disease'. It could certainly be argued that the limitations which have delineated the subject matter of 'medical ethics' deliberately keep the emphasis away from broader social issues.

[4] Beauchamp, T. and Childress, J., *Principles of Biomedical Ethics* (4th edn., OUP, 1994).
[5] This point is developed by Murray in his chapter 'Medical ethics, moral philosophy and moral tradition' in *Medicine and Moral Reasoning*. Fulford K. W. M., Gillett, G. and Soskice, J. (eds) (Cambridge University Press, 1994).

We suggest that there is a difference between criticizing the principles themselves and criticizing the way that they are applied. As with the law, we must avoid the trap of assuming that because certain ethical principles are given a particular weight within the doctor/patient relationship, they will have the same weight in the complementary setting. We appreciate the dangers of applying the 'four principles' framework in an uncritical way. None the less, we shall use these principles as a peg upon which to hang our discussion, mindful of the need to do so in as value-free a way as possible.

II. CONSIDERATION OF ETHICAL PRINCIPLES

Let us now consider the requirements of ethical practice by fleshing out these ethical principles with specific reference to complementary medicine. How, for example, does working (or professing to work) in a patient-centred way affect one's ethical responsibilities? We shall explore the way in which ethical principles have been interpreted within existing health care relationships and ask whether a certain re-ordering might not be required in the context of complementary medicine. Here, as elsewhere, we must appreciate that medical ethics discourse has also been framed with reference to the doctor/patient relationship. The primacy of the ethics of beneficence in the Hippocratic tradition encapsulates the inbuilt assumption that medicine and healing is something that is 'done to' patients. It has not, historically, embraced the concept that the best way to help people is to help them to help themselves. This is not to denigrate attempts made, particularly by primary health care practitioners, to convey public health messages to the population. If, however, medicine were to be sincerely committed to health promotion and the provision of a National Health Service (rather than a National Ill-Health Service) then preventive medicine and epidemiology would be the most illustrious medical specialities, rather than macho, 'high-tech' surgery.

A. The principle of beneficence

The duty of beneficence is seen by many practitioners as their overriding duty. Indeed, a desire to help people is often cited as a reason for entering into caring professions. Whilst wanting to help people is a worthy ambition, it is not always obvious what the best way of helping is in any given situation. In a health care setting, beneficence is most obviously connected with curing people and applying therapeutic skills to make sick people well. Increasingly though, in an era of highly technological medicine, it is accepted that keeping people alive at all costs may not be in their best interests. Ethical discussion increasingly focuses on *quality of life* rather than sanctity of life. This is an important development, because it recognizes that other factors, beyond the physical, must be built into any notion of effective healing.

The primary aim of healing is to help people who are suffering. This has been construed in medical terms as curing those who can be cured and caring for those who cannot. The relief of suffering is at the heart of Hippocratic tradition. In a complementary context, benefiting patients may take on a rather different meaning. 'Healing' (particularly with its connotations of making whole) is a wider concept than 'curing'. People may experience healing even if their symptoms persist. Reconciling oneself to illness may be the sole or primary aim of the healing intervention. As we have seen, beneficence does not necessarily encompass effecting a cure.

It makes sense to consider the duty of beneficence alongside its converse duty, namely the duty of non-maleficence. As well as the concept of not hurting patients deliberately, the principle of non-maleficence, which we shall explore shortly, taken in conjunction with the principle of beneficence should ensure that the risks involved in any given procedure are proportionate to the benefits. Thus, for example, in an orthodox medical setting, the use of highly toxic chemotherapy drugs has to be set against extremely distressing side-effects. In all situations, practitioners are engaged in a risk/benefit ratio, offering treatments which, on balance, will do more good than harm. We shall discuss in due course whether that analysis should rightly be performed by the practitioner or by the patient.

What constitutes benefiting a patient may not be immediately obvious. As we have suggested, law and ethics concur that keeping patients alive at all costs may not be the most beneficent course of action. Maintaining the lives of people who are suffering from terrible pain may merely be to prolong their misery. Thus, the concept of beneficence relates not merely to treatment for the physical aspects of disease, but also has something to do with benefiting that person as a whole, taking into account psychological benefit. Beneficence in a medical context has been construed as curing people whose condition can be improved and caring for them when they can no longer be cured.

Central to our thesis is the proposition that the nature of the relationship between complementary therapists and their clients is based on different premises to the conventional doctor/patient relationship. Unlike the conventional model, which sees patients largely as the passive recipients of beneficent practice, complementary medicine views the healing process as something substantially different. The therapist acts as a conduit to activate the patient's own self-healing mechanism. Within this relationship, greater reliance may be placed on self-responsibility, change coming from within patients themselves. Thus, the patient's consent and co-operation is not something which the therapist needs in order to be allowed to do something to the patient, rather, it is central to the process of healing, in which the patient is an active participant.

'Dis-ease' is seen as more than the symptom with which the patient presents; it is, potentially, evidence of a more fundamental imbalance within the patient. That imbalance may be physical, or it may be emotional or spiritual. Central to the notion of holistic practice is the idea of making patients whole and helping them to become integrated on a physical, spiritual, and emotional level. Seen in this context, we can begin to appreciate that a complementary practitioner who cannot deal with patients on anything other than a physical level cannot be a 'good' practitioner. Moreover, therapists' attitudes towards their clients and how they respond to the patient on a personal level may be as integral to the success of the therapy as the 'technical' side of the therapy.

One of the major differences between an holistic approach and an orthodox approach is that holistic therapists attempt to address health problems on a deeper level, looking at underlying causes more than symptoms, helping a patient to achieve a deeper understanding of the origins of their ill-health than is the norm in orthodox medicine. This is not to suggest that individual medical practitioners may not also rely on this approach, simply to contend that orthodox medicine is more directed towards providing symptomatic relief and less interested in why a person became ill in the first place. There are two distinct reasons why this might be the case. The first is that the dualistic nature of orthodox medicine is such that where a patient presents with physical symptoms, a doctor is unlikely to look for emotional reasons which might also have contributed to the illness. Another reason is that contributory causes of ill-health, such as bad housing and poor nutrition, have historically been treated as falling outside the scope of medicine. On a collective level, doctors have, until recently, distanced themselves from these determinants of health. Those who recognize broader concepts of cause of ill-health in principle, are rarely able to pay attention to these factors, or even to elicit the information because of the limited time they have to spend with patients.

In a holistic setting, helping the patient is a highly individualized process, which requires first-rate communication skills. Thus, a homoeopath faced with two patients with seemingly identical symptoms will probably prescribe two entirely different remedies on the basis of his assessment of their physical, emotional and possible spiritual state. This is the essence of patient-centred treatment—the therapy suits the individual, not the practitioner. Patients will not be prescribed a remedy because the manufacturers have been doing a particularly aggressive marketing campaign on arnica that month. Mostly, patient-centred treatment is about listening to patients and involving them at a profound level. Involvement requires the sharing of as much information as is necessary to allow patients to participate fully in their own treatment. Participation, in turn, requires a fundamental reconstruction of the duty of beneficence to embrace the notion that securing patients' participation is a central part of therapy.

1. Redefining competence

Beneficence presupposes well-trained practitioners who have the requisite skills to help their patients, and, therefore, to have undergone the necessary training to equip them with whatever therapeutic skills they are offering. In other words, in order to be able to act beneficently they must be able to demonstrate the competencies required of that therapy. As well as technical skills, the nature of the therapeutic relationship makes it important that the practitioner has good interpersonal skills as well. When analysing what constitutes high standards of practice, most people make the tacit, uncritical assumption that it only involves the acquisition of technical skills relevant to that therapy. Indeed, a technical skill base is one of the defining characteristics which sets professionals apart from other occupational groups.

To emphasize this point, we might begin by asking whether it is sufficient for a complementary therapist to be technically superb, but lacking in interpersonal skills? Could we call a practitioner who was bullish and dismissive of a patient's fears a 'good practitioner'. It is still not uncommon to hear of surgeons who are lauded for their technical wizardry, but roundly criticized for being better at communicating with anaesthetised patients than conscious ones. This situation is undoubtedly changing, and communication skills are now included within the curriculum of many medical schools.

In order to demonstrate that the competence required of a health practitioner amounts to more than the possession of certain technical skills, let us consider three different commercial scenarios which may illustrate this point.

(i) The plumber scenario

When people call out a plumber to mend a washing machine, they are not particularly concerned whether the plumber is cheery or morose, sympathetic to the trouble this problem has caused, or critical of the last plumber who did a bad job. The customer's concern is solely that the plumber will be able to do the job competently. Although most people would agree that it is always more pleasant to have dealings with congenial people, particularly when we are giving them money for providing a service, the plumber's attitude and disposition is not integral to the customer's sense of satisfaction. This is because the plumber is dealing only with a person's property. He or she is not dealing with the customer on a personal level.

(i) The hairdresser scenario

Consider, next, an appointment at the hairdresser. The atmosphere should put the client at ease, and be a relaxing and enjoyable experience. Having discussed what style the customer wants, the hairdresser will set about interpreting that request. A successful cut should improve the client's sense of well-being, albeit on a rather superficial level. In this scenario, the hairdresser's personality and attitude, as well as his or her technical skills, will directly affect the customer's sense of self. Already, a crucial distinction can be made in that because the hairdresser is dealing with an aspect of the patient's body, it is critical that he or she first elicits the patients wishes. Although this may seem a somewhat trite analogy, it could certainly be argued that a client who wants her shoulder-length bob trimmed would be justifiably angered if the hairdresser gave her a short back and sides. Whilst the effect of such an action would be temporary, and hardly life-threatening, the anger at having one's wishes overridden would be significant, and would almost certainly result in a refusal to pay.

(iii) The masseur scenario

For a final example, let us suppose that if we are 'stressed out', we might indulge ourselves in a relaxing massage. Here, we are entering into a still more intimate sort of relationship than the previous scenarios, where the demeanour and personality of the masseur will be as important as his or her technical skills. Moreover, we take it for granted that the masseur will act with decency and propriety, and would certainly desist from any intervention that the client is finding to be unduly painful or unpleasant. We would expect the masseur to preserve the client's confidentiality and not shriek to the neighbouring booth that this was the worst case of cellulite or varicose veins ever seen.

What can we glean from these three deliberately light-hearted scenarios? We can tell that as soon as an intervention is designed to improve well-being and affect people on an emotional level, more is required of the service provider than mere technical skills. In complementary therapy, the demeanour of the therapist is viewed as directly contributing to the efficacy of the therapy. In orthodox medicine, by way of contrast, any non-quantifiable benefit attributable to the personality of the doctor is dismissed as being 'mere placebo', rather than a useful therapeutic component in itself.

What, then, do we expect of health carers? Critically, we want to be responded to as individuals, not as faulty machinery. If all we expected from practitioners was 'medical plumbing', it would not trouble us to look to the first scenario, whereby it would be sufficient that the practitioner had technical skills, but no interpersonal skills. The whole point though is that we do experience human emotions, mortal fears and anxieties, all of which deeply affect our interaction with health care workers. The process of being ill may affect our autonomy and our decision-making ability. It may also make us more dependent on others than we are accustomed to. For these reasons, we hope that practitioners will deal with us on a humane and caring level, always taking account of our wishes and feelings.

We shall now look at the specific skills that are required to bring about a beneficial healing effect. These can be broadly categorized as technical skills and human skills. Competent practice requires the combination of both. It is necessary to make this distinction as different skills will be imparted in different ways. Whereas technical, or 'doing' skills, can perhaps be judged by observation and written examination, 'being' skills, that is, the attributes required of a good therapist, including compassion, humility, a strong sense of self, and a high level of self-awareness, will require more creative means of teaching and assessment. The acquisition of technical skills in isolation, does not guarantee that practitioners will be good with patients.

2. Acquisition of technical skills

We have identified that beneficence requires healers to be competent and that one aspect of this is the possession of certain 'technical skills'. What do we mean by technical skills in relation to complementary medicine? These may connote skills which are medicalized in nature, but they may also include or depend entirely on skills which orthodox medicine would not view as being relevant to a technical knowledge base such as, for example, knowledge of the healing energies of crystals or the healing vibrational potential of flower or colour energies. The more formalized the technical skills, the more appropriate a lengthy training would be. We should not assume though, that all therapists work from a formalized knowledge base in the way that orthodox doctors do. Spiritual healing, for example, works on a spiritual level and may not necessitate, or be amenable to, formal instruction, nor does it necessarily require a detailed knowledge of anatomy and physiology.

We have already considered the vexed issue of whether complementary therapists need to have a degree of medical knowledge in order to practise their therapy safely. For the sake of consistency, the requirement to have some medical basis should also extend to a knowledge of psychiatry, since therapists are dealing with the patient's mental health and there may well be situations in which a therapist might need to identify patients requiring orthodox psychological or psychiatric assessment or care.

Is the requirement to possess medical knowledge reasonable or indeed feasible? Here again, we can identify a spectrum approach, depending on the therapy in question. It may, for example, be a more germane requirement for therapists who have direct body contact with the patient, and who see and touch the body, to have some grasp of orthodox knowledge than, say, spiritual healers, who run their hands over a fully clothed patient. It might be reasonable to expect the former, but not the latter, to encounter physical manifestations of disease. It would also be reasonable to impose this requirement on therapists such as osteopaths or chiropractors who have undergone several years qualifying and whose training includes a considerable amount of anatomy and physiology. It would not, however, be either feasible or reasonable, to expect that same degree of knowledge to be imparted to crystal therapists, who may have undergone a few week-end training sessions, and whose philosophical underpinnings are entirely at variance with a medical interpretation of disease.

We must also constantly remind ourselves of *why it is that people consult complementary therapists* and what it is they expect from that therapy. Given that everyone has a right to be registered with a general practitioner, we do not think that many patients who are consulting a complementary practitioner would want, or indeed expect, that therapist to be the source of a diagnosis in orthodox medical terms. Often, it is precisely the limitations of conventional means of diagnosis that they are seeking to transcend. Increasingly, people are concerned with not simply the physical aspects of their disease, but also with trying to find an explanation for why they became ill in metaphysical terms. The search for spiritual understanding, seen by many as the inevitable product of an increasingly atomized and materialistic society, also accounts for the burgeoning interest in new cults and religions.

A prime ethical requirement is that practitioners who hold themselves out to have a particular skill have a legitimate basis for doing so. Healing involves helping people where possible, and above all, not harming them further. Much of the hostility towards complementary practitioners, especially at the more intuitive or esoteric end of the spectrum, is that practitioners are plying useless or dangerous interventions, dressed up as therapeutic procedures, to a gullible and desperate population. Apart from the discredit this does to rational adults and their ability to make reasoned choices, we need to disentangle how much of this attitude stems from a general discomfort felt primarily by the medical profession in allowing people to choose an unconventional approach to dealing with their own sickness. Critically, this is not to say that untrained or unskilled practitioners may not represent a real threat to the public. Good training and a realistic basis for making therapeutic claims are vital.

Practitioners must not make specific promises or guarantees as to the effectiveness of the potential therapy. The question of making claims about healing is central to the issue of regulation. Yet the question of who is entitled to make claims about being a holistic practitioner is far from straightforward. A massage given by a beauty therapist may be as beneficial to a patient as one delivered by a professional massage therapist. Wherein lies the difference? On what basis is one to make specific *health* claims? If we are adopting a broader concept of health, consistency would surely allow something which operates on a well-being level to describe itself as therapeutic?

The crucial question is how potential patients are likely to regard a therapy when it is described in medicalized terms of benefits to health. After all, many stress-relieving techniques undoubtedly have a significant role to play in reducing the stresses of modern living which are increasingly seen as a contributory factor in the cause of illness. Again, the issue of what constitutes health, and thus who may make health claims, is preconditioned by the biomedical model. A good example is the degree to which the public are protected against cancer cures. Here, we must ask who defines health, who defines harm and whose concept of relief is important—the medical profession's or the patient's. Whilst chemotherapy may attack cancer cells (and healthy cells as well), visualization techniques may legitimately be said to 'help' cancer if they make patients feel better. Each, in its own way, constitutes treatment for cancer. We must avoid being drawn in to the trap of accepting the medical view as absolute truth simply because we do not have the vision to countenance a different conceptual framework. It is precisely the strength of that argument that convinces the population that invasive techniques are the *best* way to tackle what is a multi-dimensional therapeutic issue.

Benefiting patients in most therapies requires high standards of education and training. In order to train competent practitioners, it is first necessary for each therapy to decide what the required competencies and skills in that particular discipline are. This is itself no mean feat. We acknowledge that within individual therapies there may be a far greater diversity of acceptable practice than in other health care areas. Once competencies have been established, therapies can work on the most appropriate way of instilling that knowledge and assessing whether the therapist has acquired the requisite skills. To this end, certain therapeutic organizations are beginning to work together in developing national standards and core competencies within complementary therapies. The Department of Further

Education and Employment is now part-funding the Project for the Development of National Occupational Standards for Complementary Therapies. The project, which is concentrating on homoeopathy, aromatherapy, hypnotherapy, and reflexology, is under the aegis of the Care Sector Consortium which is the Occupational Standards Council for Health and Social Care in the United Kingdom. This project has three interlinked strands, the other two being Health Promotion and Professions Allied to Medicine. It is anticipated that this project will be completed by February 1997.

3. Acquisition of human skills

The ability to bring about healing is enhanced by the possession of certain personal attributes. Humility and the ability to acknowledge the limitations of one's competence are also prerequisites. These skills cannot necessarily be imparted in the same way as technical knowledge, and training is a continuous dynamic process. Thus, Aveline describes psychotherapy as 'a purposeful activity in which trainees and trainers have a professional and ethical commitment to evaluate and refine their work'.[6]

All therapists, be they orthodox or complementary, need to cultivate qualities such as basic empathy, genuineness, warmth, and an ability to communicate. Some trainees are more talented in these areas than others. It is debatable how far these things can be formally taught. Various educational approaches are possible. These might include the intellectual approach, the didactic approach, the experiential approach, or a model which integrates all these approaches.[7] A number of complementary courses specifically include counselling skills as part of the curriculum. A truly skilful diagnosis depends on intuition and listening to what the patient does not, as much as what the patient does, say. These powers of observation may take many years to hone.

Insight and self-awareness are also necessary prerequisites of being a good counsellor. As Nelson-Jones observes: 'A number of trainees may themselves require counselling to work on their own lack of self-acceptance and possible need to control and direct others'.[8] Whilst

[6] M. Aveline 'The training and supervision of individual therapists' in Dryden, W., *Individual Therapy: a Handbook* (Open University Press, 1990).
[7] For a fuller discussion of these models, 'The Fundamental Counselling Relationship' in Nelson-Jones, R., *The Theory and Practice of Counselling Psychology* (Cassel, 1988) ch. 11.   [8] Ibid., 216.

this point is commonly recognized in relation to counsellors and psychotherapists, it may not be regarded as that important for other complementary therapists. We would argue that to the extent that holistic practitioners are, by implication, working on an emotional level with patients, their training should equip them with specific skills in counselling. So too, as Aveline points out, the phenomenon of transference and counter-transference, a critical concept in analytic therapies, is, to a greater or lesser extent 'part of any human interaction and, certainly, of any therapy where the participants have a close relationship'.[9] These too are matters which should be addressed in training.

4. Limits of competence

The duty of beneficence also requires practitioners to know when they are out of their depth and to recognize the limitations of their competence. In hierarchical situations, such as medicine and nursing, this will often involve recognizing when to seek the assistance of a superior colleague. Alternatively, it may require the practitioner to refer patients to practitioners who are better equipped to deal with the problem.

All therapists must recognize the limits of their competence and know when problems or symptoms are either outside their range of expertise or are patently not responding to treatment. In such circumstances the therapist must consider referring the patient either to a more experienced therapist in the same field or to a therapist working in a different therapeutic modality. This may or may not be a mainstream orthodox practitioner, depending on the nature and the severity of the condition.

It would be as unethical and irresponsible for complementary practitioners to seek to turn their patients against their orthodox practitioner as it would be blinkered of orthodox practitioners to deter patients from seeking alternative therapy where this might be able to help them. Because most patients are registered with a general practitioner, and it is helpful for one practitioner to retain information about a patient, wherever possible, complementary practitioners should actively encourage the involvement of the GP, and keep him or her informed of treatment given

As we have already discussed, the ability of complementary practitioners to recognize serous medical conditions which might require acute intervention is an extremely vexed question which raises a

[9] Aveline, *op. cit.* (above, n. 5), 316.

number of legal and ethical concerns. Notwithstanding the fact that complementary practitioners may be working in a different paradigm, they bear responsibility for the patient's overall welfare. As such, they must facilitate the patient receiving the most appropriate form of treatment. We have already considered the inappropriateness of un-trained practitioners attempting to make medical diagnoses and the legal risks to which they expose themselves should they attempt to do so. At this stage however, we are concerned less with issues of attract-ing legal or professional liability and more concerned with ensuring that patients receive the best treatment available.

There is a real danger of practitioners analysing every ailment that is presented as one which falls within the parameters of their own therapy, for example, nutritional therapists diagnosing all ailments as being due to deficiencies in the patient' diet, where, more realistically, this might be a contributory factor. Unlike orthodox medicine, where a patient's problem may be hawked from one specialist to another until an explanation is found, complementary therapists tend to dia-gnose within their own paradigm, and do not necessarily refer to another complementary practitioner who uses a different approach.

Complementary therapists do not necessarily have knowledge about therapists practising in other disciplines. There should be much greater awareness by all therapists of the major registering bodies in other therapies, so that patients can be assisted in this regard. There are also grounds for arguing that complementary therapists' training should include a broad overview of other complementary therapies as well.

Do complementary practitioners, like general practitioners, have a broad knowledge across a wide area, or, are they closer to allopathic 'specialists', who are as ignorant in other areas of complementary medicine, as say an orthopaedic surgeon would be of ophthalmology? It should not be assumed that complementary therapists are well in-formed about other complementary modalities outside their own areas of practice. There is as wide a variation within complementary medicine as within orthodox medicine. Moreover, therapists do not all work within the same philosophical confines merely because they eschew the biomedical model.

5. Practising in more than one discipline

Many therapists practise in more than one discipline. A therapist may, for example, be trained originally as an osteopath, but also offer some acupuncture and hypnotherapy as a sideline, or may combine all therapies. This seems to be more of a feature in complementary medicine than in orthodox medicine, where super-specialization means that practitioners may have a highly technical, but somewhat narrow area of expertise.[10]

Cross-specialization is ethically acceptable provided practitioners are adequately trained in each of the disciplines they are using. What is adequate will vary. Practitioners should avoid acquiring a superficial knowledge of other therapies and applying them randomly without an adequate understanding of the theoretical underpinnings of that therapy, thereby potentially jeopardizing the patient's safety. Again, certain therapies and particularly certain therapists, will be more open to incorporating different techniques.

6. Balancing risks and harms

There are risks involved in any therapeutic encounter. Any treatment option involves a careful balancing of risks and benefits. Part of this process is about reconciling the duties of beneficence against duties of non-maleficence. Sometimes in a medical context it is thought to be permissible to cause a degree of harm to the patient if this is necessary to avert a significantly greater harm. For example, it might be appropriate to recommend the amputation of a patient's gangrenous foot if failure to act will result in the patient's death. (This does not mean that the practitioner is solely responsible for weighing up risks and benefits, nor that a doctor would be justified in amputating the foot without the patient's consent.)

Certainly beneficence would require practitioners to ensure that the therapies they use are as safe as possible. Practitioners are under a moral obligation, as well as a professional one, to minimize the possibility of harm. This duty manifests itself in different ways according to the therapy. In product therapies, practitioners should assure themselves of quality control as far as they are able to, by only using products from reputable suppliers. Acupuncturists should likewise ensure their needles are of a good quality and should make sure that any electrical equipment they use is regularly maintained. Manipulative therapists should make sure that their massage tables are able to withstand the client's weight. The duty of beneficence requires

---

[10] We note, however, the development of specialization within some of the more medicalized therapies, such as paediatric osteopathy.

practitioners to be in good health themselves. The duty not to harm patients means that they must be scrupulous not to carry out invasive procedures if they have any infection which could be passed on to the patient, and, of course, predicates that they be in robust, psychological health.

7. Establishing the efficacy of therapies

Another principle of beneficence is that the therapies offered to a patient are of proven efficacy, and that the practitioner has some basis for suggesting that it is likely to have a therapeutic therapy in the particular instance. Usually, this will require some sort of empirical evidence, based on research. The difficulties involved in conducting research, and in particular the difficulties (although not impossibility) of conducting randomized control trials are frequently voiced by those within complementary medicine. However, they will lose credibility unless they can develop other means of establishing efficacy. It is incumbent upon practitioners, however, to establish by whatever means appropriate that there is some reason to think that the therapy should work and that the client should hand over money on that basis.

B. The principle of non-maleficence

The ethical imperative not to cause harm requires practitioners to refrain from any behaviour, professional or personal, which would be detrimental to the patient's health and well-being. This would include issues like the careless or wanton breach of a patient's confidentiality, either by failing to secure information relating to the patient, or by engaging in idle gossip. It would also involve exerting undue influence over a patient, for example, persuading a patient to alter a will in the practitioner's favour. But this duty also involves not abusing patients in a variety of ways. Thus, practitioners should refrain from becoming sexually involved with patients or members of the patient's family because of the detrimental effect this is understood to have on the patient/therapist relationship. The duty would also prohibit emotional or financial exploitation of patients. We shall look at some of these issues in greater depth.

1. Protection from abuse

(i) Sexual exploitation

Unfortunately, sexual abuse of patients by therapists is not uncommon, although because so many therapists are not registered or regulated in any way, it is impossible to specify figures with any accuracy. Sexual abuse permeates all therapies, and is as much a problem within orthodox medicine. It is thus an ethical problem which is not prevented by the existence of statutory regulation (although the powers to deal with an offending practitioner will be greater where there is an effective disciplinary system in place).

The problem of sexual abuse by therapists is well documented.[11] There have been various alarming press reports, for example the reported case of a 'hypnotherapist' who used hypnosis to abuse female patients.[12] Several organizations exist specifically to help patients who have been abused by therapists.[13]

Given the intimate nature of a consultation, there are certain precautions that it would be wise for any practitioner to take. These would include practitioners making use of chaperons when they are carrying out intimate examinations, and ensuring that where a physical examination is required, particularly one which may involve the genital area, the patient's written consent has been obtained prior to conducting the examination, and that this is documented on the patient's record. Thus the code of ethics of the ICM's British Register of Complementary Practitioners states: 'Complementary Practitioners on the British Register may not conduct a genital examination of a patient without a chaperon being present unless written consent has been given' (para. 5.8.d).

One of the biggest barriers to preventing abuse is that sexuality is

---

[11] See, e.g., Peter Rutter's book *Sex in the Forbidden Zone* (Unwin, 1990) and Derek Jehu's *Patients as Victims: Sexual Abuse in Psychotherapy and Counselling* (Wiley, 1994).

[12] Referred to in a letter from P. J. Whorewell, urging for greater regulation (307 BMJ 327 (1993)). He goes on to stress that hypnotherapy does not have to be confined to the medical profession as a medical qualification is not a prerequisite to being a good hypnotherapist and that 'some lay therapists are better than their medical counterparts'.

[13] Prevention of Professional Abuse Network (POPAN) and Abuse in Therapy Support Network are two such organizations. POPAN estimates that at least 35,000 people have been abused by health care workers in this country, and that the overwhelming majority of these people will have been seriously affected by the experience. Source: POPAN Development Plan 1994–7.

still regarded as a taboo subject, and is not addressed in training. This is an extremely unhelpful approach. Therapists may experience sexual feelings towards clients from time to time and the issue must be tackled, particularly when training body-work therapists.[14] Rather than ignoring the issue, some codes of ethics deal specifically with the issue. For example, the Association of Massage Practitioners's code states quite firmly that practitioners should not touch the genital area.

Given the numbers of practitioners who do have sexual relationships with their patients, we might reasonably ask whether sexual relationships are ever permissible between therapists and patients whilst treatment is ongoing? The overwhelming consensus is that this is potentially extremely harmful to the patient. Jehu lists the following reasons for proscribing sexual activity: breach of trust, violation of the role of therapist, exploitation of vulnerability, misuse of power, absence of consent, impairment of the therapeutic process, iatrogenic effects, and bringing the profession into disrepute.[15] Although the position is less categoric in relation to former patients, there are still strong reasons why sexual relationships are to be avoided.

Training bodies and professional associations should be trained to respond sympathetically to patients who make allegations of sexual abuse against their members.

(ii) Financial exploitation

Again, one of the reasons abuse persists is that the issue of charging for services is not openly discussed. A number of points need to be addressed. How much should practitioners charge for a session? Whilst market forces determine this issue to a great extent, is it possible to say what a fair price might be? Between £20 and £40 is common for a one-to-one session lasting about an hour, although a number of therapists offer concessionary rates for clients who cannot afford to pay the full rate. Arguably, the longer and more arduous the training, and the more technical the knowledge base (that is, the closer to a medical model), the more appropriate it would be

[14] See, e.g., Tanya Garrett's article, 'Grasping a hot potato: how understanding sexual feelings in therapy could help to prevent therapist–client sexual contact.' *Clinical Psychology Forum*, April 1993.

[15] Jehu, *Patients as Victims*, p. 23. Given the avowed holistic nature of complementary medicine, we feel justified in extending this rationale to all therapies. We recognize that there may be particularly strong arguments against sexual relationships when the patient is presenting in state of emotional distress.

for the fees charged to reflect the time and money that the practitioner has invested in acquiring those skills.

Private NHS practice is not a very helpful analogy in this context, as orthodox private practitioners tend to be consultant level, or practitioners who have had considerable NHS experience, including many years of supervised practice. Also, in orthodox medicine, there is a viable and comprehensive alternative in the form of the NHS. Whilst the accessibility of specialist services may take longer than in the private sector, the standard of medical treatment should be the same in the NHS as in the private sector. People pay to go privately primarily for reasons of speed and convenience. There is no parallel availability of complementary services within the NHS, which is why complementary practitioners can command the fees they do. In the absence of a single trade union body, it is impossible to set an appropriate level.[16] As a general point though, if complementary practitioners are going to charge for a skill, they should be competent to provide that skill. At present, whether they are or are not is a matter for personal conscience.

Where the healing powers are a gift, and are bestowed upon the healer other than by formal training, should the practitioner charge at all, and if so, how much? No one would deny that healers who dedicate a substantial amount of working time to their healing need to be able to support themselves. In a way, there are parallels here with miracle healers, especially American evangelical healers—there is no reason why healers should not make a living out of what they do, but were they to start earning millions of pounds, there would inevitably be allegations of exploitation and trickery,

The practice of unnecessarily prolonging therapy for financial or emotional reasons is a major ethical issue. After an initial evaluation, a therapist should give the patient as good an idea as possible of how long the course of therapy is likely to go on. Even if a period has been set, if the therapy is not appearing to have the desired effects, or is causing the patient harm, the therapist should consider stopping treatment and consider what other therapeutic approaches might be more successful.

It is unethical to foist unnecessary products and preparations on patients, all the more so when the practitioner is trained by a school which is directly linked to the manufacturers of such products. This

---

[16] Cf., the BMA's Private Practice and Professional Fees Committee which sets suggested fees that doctors in private practice can charge.

is a particular problem, for example, in the training of aromatherapists and nutritional counsellors, where training establishments are often tied up with manufactures. There is a possible pressure to promote these products over others which could be more beneficial. Additionally, certain therapies may, by their vary nature, expose their patients to a greater risk of exploitation than others. Hypnosis, for example, is an area where therapists must be extremely vigilant about not exploiting their patients.

(iii) Emotional exploitation

Healers must avoid exploiting their power over vulnerable patients (this is neither to suggest that all practitioners are seduced by power, or that all patients are vulnerable). None the less, the power imbalance between therapist and patient opens the door to the possibility of abuse. Is this power differential different from other professional relationships? Does a lawyer's professional expertise lead to a power imbalance in the same sort of way? One would expect the response to be that the same issue does not arise, because ultimately most legal disputes boil down to money, whereas health practitioners are dealing in an infinitely more precious commodity. The power imbalance in health relationships is, we would argue, more significant, because the consequences of abuse of that power are more important. The healer is offering potent stuff, and abuse cannot be adequately recompensed by way of financial damages.

The power to offer to heal someone is extremely persuasive when a patient is in pain, distressed, and possibly confused. Patients invest a lot of faith in healers, believing that they can do what they claim to be able to do. This is why it is so critical that therapists do not make unrealistic claims. Quite apart from the legal folly of guaranteeing a cure, it would be ethically inappropriate to do so. Thus the BCMA's code states firmly: 'Practitioners must never claim to "cure". The possible therapeutic benefits may be described; "recovery" must never be guaranteed.'[17]

An additional factor is that many complementary therapists have a much more open and friendly demeanour than their medical counterparts. Most encounters with orthodox doctors are somewhat constrained. Doctors often cultivate an air of detachment and objectivity,

---

[17] *BCMA Code of Conduct*, para. 1.6.

which patients pick up on. Complementary therapists may, on the other hand, seem genuinely interested in the patient as a person. They may be more emotionally or physically demonstrative with patients than orthodox practitioners, and would not, for example, shy away, if the patient clasped them in a hug of appreciation at the end of a session. Boundaries may thus appear more blurred to the patient than in a conventional relationship, and a patient may mistake therapeutic concern for something more than that.

Complementary therapists can emotionally exploit or abuse their patients in the following ways:

(1) They may bully patients into accepting their particular theory of health and disease. This can be particularly damaging to patients where therapists are of the 'victim-blaming' variety, who tell patients that they have brought disease upon themselves. In such an environment, practitioners can easily go on to convince the patient that if a therapy has not worked, or has not been as effective as might have been hoped, that this is down to the patient's resistance and that on a fundamental level, the patient doesn't really want to get better;

(2) They may be inadequately skilled to cope with any emotional distress the therapy might unleash;

(3) They may allow a patient's dependence to develop to satisfy the therapist's own ego, or shortcomings. Problems are likely to arise if therapists are insecure, neurotic, or selfish, and bring these characteristics to the therapeutic relationship. This may manifest itself by therapists prolonging therapy unnecessarily in order to satisfy their own emotional needs, such as dependency on the patient, or their own need to be needed.

Therapists must be particularly aware of the additional responsibilities they incur by working with patients on an emotional level. Unless practitioners have specific counselling qualifications, there is a limit to the amount of emotional advice they should seek to give patients. The need to discuss these issues becomes all the more critical when the practitioner holds himself out as a holistic healer, as most complementary practitioners do. All healers are involved in draining and sometimes traumatizing work and they must be sufficiently psychologically suited to such work, with their own safety valves and access to supervisors. Commenting on psychotherapy, Holmes writes: 'a not insignificant proportion of those who are drawn to the therapy profession may also be beset with their own emotional difficulties.'[18]

Therapists are beginning to recognize what has been described as the 'rescuer syndrome',[19] that is, a desire on the part of healers to make others feel better whether or not it is appropriate. Here, the compulsion to help others may be masking the practitioner's own psychological needs. Greater attention needs to be paid, also, to the need of some therapists to be needed by their patients and clients. Few health professionals are taught to deal with the fact that they may derive something from their patients' reliance on them. Because, as we have observed, doctors and complementary therapists have little specific preparation to equip them to deal with the emotional issues thrown up by their work, training must discuss how therapists meet their own personal needs in this regard.

We are also aware of the unhelpful double standard that it is acceptable for patients or clients to suffer from depressive disorders, but unacceptable for health professionals to do so.[20] The existence of health committees within disciplinary mechanisms ensures that practitioners whose performance is affected by ill-health will be dealt with sympathetically and not in a punitive fashion.

2. Harmful therapies

Non-maleficence requires therapists to refrain from using techniques whose harms outweigh benefits. A primary endeavour of regulation is to ensure safe therapies. If we look at orthodox medicine, we realize that therapeutic techniques are not regulated individually. It would be unworkable to design statutory controls over therapies rather than therapists. Rather, the emphasis is on assuring the competence of practitioners, and allowing them the discretion to act within the limits of that competence. Given the somewhat unorthodox nature of many complementary therapies, we need to evaluate how potentially harmful therapies may be, as the capacity to cause harm will no doubt be a

[18] Holmes, J. and Lindley, R., 'Ethics and Psychotherapy' in *Principles of Health Care Ethics*, ed. R. Gillon (Wiley, 1994).
[19] See, e.g., McNeil, D. and Williams, K., 'Keeping Vibrant'. *International Journal of Alternative and Complementary Medicine*, Sept. 1992.
[20] Examples of this are described in 'Wounded Healers—Mental Health Workers' Experiences of Depression', Rippere, V. and Williams, R. (eds) (Wiley, 1985). The authors point out how 'suffering' as a patient may help practitioners to break down the 'them versus us' distinction, and how experiences of depression may contribute to improved social and professional functioning.

major influencing factor in determining the level of regulation that is required.

Side-effects are an inevitable consequence of all therapies, as the huge number of patients suffering from iatrogenic illnesses demonstrate.[21] The benefits of any treatment have to be set against their risk of harm. Historically, orthodox medicine treats the most serious illnesses with the most aggressive therapies. Side effects of chemotherapy are often perceived by patients to be worse than the symptoms of their cancer. Generally speaking, complementary therapies tend to be 'softer' (hence the French term '*douce*'), with less severe side effects. However, this is not to suggest that all complementary therapies are safe and can be given without supervision. Complementary medicine has, however, been subject to a sustained media campaign inflating one-off incidences of harm in a biased and unhelpful manner. Reports, for example, of an isolated patient dying after taking traditional Chinese medicine will fail to mention that the patient had an end-stage illness. Were the media to report every incidence of patients dying as a result of orthodox medical intervention, such stories would run to several pages a day. None the less, patient safety is paramount. Side effects must be minimized. Therapists must be fully cognizant of contra-indications to a particular therapy, and thorough records should be kept of any treatments given.

Who should decide whether the benefits outweigh the risks? Although doctors cannot proceed without consent, they may have already made prior decisions about the range of options to offer the patient.[22] In orthodox medicine the risk/benefit analysis is traditionally seen as part of the doctor's function, in other words as a technical decision. Given the emphasis we have placed throughout on the need for patients to be active partners in decision-making, we may need to rethink whether deciding on risks and benefits is most appropriately a matter for practitioners, or patients, or both acting in conjunction. In this, as in all matters, the duty of beneficence has to be tempered by the duty to respect the patient's autonomy.

---

[21] Illich provides the most forceful exposition of 'what has turned health care into a sick-making enterprise' in his book *Limits to Medicine* (Penguin, Harmondsworth, 1978).

[22] The likelihood of success will influence the decision to even suggest certain therapies. Whilst this used to be an area where clinical autonomy was rarely challenged, increasingly, the cost of various therapeutic options also forms part of the equation.

C. Principle of respect for autonomy

In contrast to the beneficence-based, Hippocratic model of health care, within the last twenty-five years, the principle of respect for autonomy has taken root as the cardinal principle of medical ethics. The word autonomy is derived from the Greek *autos* (self) and *nomos* (rule of governance). Beauchamp and Childress offer a definition of autonomy in this context as: 'personal rule of the self that is free from both controlling influences by others and from personal limitations that prevent meaningful choice, such as inadequate understanding'.[23] Statements promoting the rights of competent adults to make their own decisions about health care permeate official statements at the highest level.[24] Although the law's commitment to the right of self-determination is questionable, respecting the patient's autonomy is now recognized as a fundamental part of good medical practice, if only at the level of rhetoric.

Complementary medicine is traditionally thought of as being more 'patient-centred' than orthodox medicine. But what exactly does this mean? Orthodox medicine can also claim to be 'patient-centred' in that its primary endeavour is the alleviation of suffering by the patient. How is complementary medicine different? Is being patient-centred the same as respecting the patient's autonomy, and is it the same as treating the patient holistically?

The concept of autonomy is one of the strongest ethical precepts, and can be justified on the basis of numerous ethical theories. The ethical requirement of respect for autonomy is so strong that it has found legal expression through the mechanisms of the law of battery, and, in negligence, through the law relating to consent. One might imagine that the principle of respect for autonomy is at its highest in relation to patient-centred therapy.

The term patient-centred is usually used to connote therapy which respects patients' wishes and accords with patients' views of themselves. It is therapy which matches patients' own belief systems as to what constitutes well-being. It suggests therapy which proceeds at an acceptable pace for the patient, and doesn't impose change on the patient at a faster rate than the patient can cope with physically or emotionally. Critically, patient-centred medicine implicitly rejects

[23] Beauchamp and Childress, *Principles of Biomedical Ethics*, p. 121.
[24] See, e.g., 'A guide to consent for examination or treatment'. NHS Management Executive (HC (90) 22).

the idea of doctors imposing their belief system and values on the patient. Note that all of these ideas are consistent with respecting the patient's autonomy.

It is important to evaluate the meaning of 'patient-centred' critically, because it is used in such a way as to suggest that it is something that complementary medicine is very good at, and orthodox medicine is very bad at. If we can understand the term better then we can see whether orthodox medicine falls short in this area, and look at ways of incorporating the patient's perspective into all healing consultations.

If patient-centred does mean some of the things indicated above, do all complementary therapists claim to treat in this way? If there is any broad difference between a complementary therapist and an orthodox doctor, it is that whilst both have therapeutic skills and a particular knowledge base, orthodox medicine tends to apply the same treatment to all patients alike, on the basis that the therapy is objectively verifiable and can be expected to work in much the same way for patients exhibiting relevant symptoms. If we were to apply this model to complementary medicine, we would soon come unstuck. The whole basis of, say, homoeopathy, is that symptoms may be a manifestation of much broader problems than one might initially suspect. Treatment must look to the patient as a whole, to all manner of influences and stresses on the patient, in short, looking at the patient as a whole person, and beyond the presenting symptoms. In this regard, whilst both complementary practitioners and orthodox doctors are concerned with helping the patient, the former is genuinely patient-centred, whereas the latter is generally symptom-centred,

What of respect for autonomy? What does that require of practitioners in practical terms? It requires listening to patients and trying to understand their perception of their symptoms, respecting their confidences, accepting their treatment wishes, including the right to resist any particular treatment (and, of course, ultimately, the right to reject therapists themselves), and providing as much information as they need and require in order to make an informed choice (patients may not wish to receive information, which would be a legitimate exercise of their autonomy and should be respected).

Although the goals of therapy may be somewhat less clear-cut than treatment for, say, a broken leg, principles of autonomy demand that the practitioner attempts to discuss and evaluate these goals with the patient both before and during the course of therapy, when those

goals might have changed. Where personal growth or change is actively sought as a goal of the therapy, the pace must be realistic given
the patient's capabilities. It would be highly unethical to set unrealistic goals or move the goalposts in order to prolong the therapy. Likewise, the therapeutic relationship must have a facility for the patient
to be able to express dissatisfactions, either of the therapist, or the
way the therapy is proceeding.

Respecting people's wishes, or respecting their autonomy is, we
would argue, an integral part of helping them, and should be seen as a
function of beneficence. Were this to be the case, respect for autonomy would become a fully integrated part of the definition of good
medical practice. To the extent that ethical standards determine legal
standards, respect for autonomy would come to represent the *Bolam*
standard of reasonableness, derogation from which would render a
practitioner liable in negligence.

1. Consent

The practical implications of the principle of respect for autonomy is
that, in law, before practitioners may carry out any therapeutic procedure they must have the patient's consent. One of the reasons consent is so important in orthodox medicine is that the potential risks of
invasive forms of treatment and chemotherapeutic agents are such that
the patient has to decide whether he wants to be exposed to them (this
is not to suggest that simply because complementary medicine carries
fewer risks, the practitioner has *carte blanche* to proceed without consent).

As we have seen, in law, the amount of information that has to be
disclosed is determined, primarily, by professional standards. Effectively, this means that a doctor will not be negligent if he discloses as
much information as any reasonable practitioner would give. Framed
that way, we can see that an ethical ideal may require rather more of a
practitioner. We contend that in all dealings with patients, not just
when obtaining consent, practitioners' standards of care and respect
should be of the very highest, not simply the minimum standards to
avoid being found negligent in law.

Applying this to consent, the amount of information a patient
should be given is the amount of information that the particular
patient wants. All patients are different, and practitioners should
avoid assumptions about what risks the patient would or would not

find relevant. This immediately becomes complicated, in that practitioners may reasonably ask how remote the risk has to be, and what sort of chance there is of the risk materializing. There is no pat answer to this question, and lawyers have vexed over whether it is necessary to disclose, say a 1 in 10,000 possibility of a risk occurring. Broadly, it is not just the chance of the risk occurring that matters, but the magnitude of that risk, and whether the particular patient would find that risk material in deciding whether to accept or reject the treatment. A lot of people would want to know if there is a risk of death, however small the risk may be.

Given that the risks associated with complementary medicine are not usually thought to be anywhere near as significant as those of orthodox medicine, there should be no excuse for deliberately withholding information, as doctors have done in the past, on the basis that the knowledge would scare the patient from having treatment.

Information should include what the treatment entails, what risks are involved, how many sessions it should take for the therapy to work, and information about the therapist, including the therapist's background, qualifications, training, and experience. This is crucial if we are to have enough information to choose a therapist they feel comfortable working with. This contrasts with orthodox medicine on the NHS, where patients cannot exercise any significant choice as to who treats them[25] (although some mobility is permitted in choosing one's general practitioner). In a holistic setting the patient needs, and is entitled to, this information, as the patients have a far better idea of the sort of therapist they think they will be able to respond to.

Often, in a medical setting, consent may be implied. If, for example, the patient willingly sticks his arm out to have blood taken, it would be reasonable to infer consent. There is a risk, however, of practitioners being self-serving in this regard. It is one thing to imply consent when patients are on familiar territory, but quite another to imply consent in situations where, if asked directly, the patient may well withhold consent to something being done. Few patients, for example, would necessarily appreciate that a manipulation therapist might need to carry out a genital examination in order to feel the

---

[25] Note, however, that the revised GMC *Guidance on Good Medical Practice* specifically acknowledges that to establish and maintain patients' trust, respect must be given to patients' right to a second opinion.

lower vertebrae. In such a situation, a practitioner should always seek specific consent, in writing.

2. Reduced autonomy

A number of factors may reduce a person's autonomy. To be fully autonomous requires freedom of thought and freedom of action. A patient may be rendered temporarily non-autonomous by unconsciousness or by the influence of drugs. A more controversial question is the extent to which a patient's autonomy is affected by illness. Features of illness such as pain, confusion, anger, and despair may influence a patient's competence to make a rational decision.

However, we must recognize that we are all subject to pressures and controlling influences which may reduce our ability to make fully autonomous decisions about our health. Although autonomous choices should, ideally, be voluntary, and made free from coercion, none of us is truly autonomous. We are all limited by our various constraints, perhaps by commitments to defendants or even employers, and to an even greater extent by our cultural expectations. We must avoid suggesting that illness, *per se*, reduces people's autonomy to such an extent that practitioners should no longer rely on their expressed wishes. All that we can expect is that patients make as rational decisions as they are capable of, given the fact that they are ill.

There are particular dangers in assuming that all patients are necessarily vulnerable. This is important, because this labelling is used to undermine the valid decisions people may arrive at when they are ill, never more so than when they reject orthodox treatment in favour of alternative therapies. Homogenizing and labelling patients is particularly inappropriate in relation to complementary medicine, which is often invoked to promote well-being, rather than to cure ill-health. People do experience a range of emotions when they become ill, particularly when they discover that they have a serious condition. They do not, however, automatically lose their rationality. In a society where suicide is legal and patients have the ultimate right to refuse life-sustaining treatment, it is insulting and anachronistic to think that all those faced with serious illness ought to expose themselves to the most invasive, and highest risk forms of medicine, and that if they are going to try gentler approaches, they should only do so as a last resort.

Labelling all patients as vulnerable cuts both ways. If, for the sake of argument, we accept that seriously ill people are vulnerable, they would be as vulnerable to the influences of scalpel-wielding surgeons as they would to complementary practitioners. This issue goes beyond the legitimate fears of out-and-out quacks exploiting the desperate, and has far more to do with prejudices that complementary medicine is not 'real' medicine. In Part I we saw how allopathic medicine has come to symbolize legitimate medicine. It must not be forgotten that these prejudices are a cultural phenomenon as much as anything else. In China, for example, where acupuncture is used to shrink and destroy tumours untreatable in the West, such hostilities do not exist. In our culture there is a silent assumption that people can be allowed to dabble provided nothing is too seriously wrong, but that when they are diagnosed as having a serious condition, they should really be per-suaded to have 'proper' medicine.

This is not to deny the successes of scientific medicine in treating certain diseases. Neither is it to pretend that there are no unscrupu-lous practitioners waiting to exploit sick people. But what we must accept is that not every patient views serious illness as a mortal enemy which can only be defeated with the might of aggressive procedures and aggressive drugs. Many people interpret their illness in a more holistic way. People may accept illness as a warning bell and a reason to review previously unhealthy patterns of behaviour. Such construc-tions do not necessarily imply that people are themselves to blame when they become ill, or that had they behaved differently, their bodies would not have succumbed to illness. Increasingly, people think that illnesses may be related to high levels of stress in our society. Complementary practitioners might legitimately argue that to try to tell people how they should conceptualize meaningful events in their own lives is supreme arrogance as it usurps people's individual-ity. People should be treated as sufficiently responsible to make health care choices accordingly.

3. Confidentiality

As well as obtaining consent, respect for patient confidentiality is a function of respect for patients' autonomy. As part of controlling their lives, patients have the right to direct how personal information about them should be used. Patients disclose certain personal information on the basis that it will be kept private by the practitioner and only be used for the specific purpose for which it was given, namely in the interests of their own health. It would be highly unethical, if, for example, a health practitioner extracted confidential information from patients and then passed it on to a third party for commercial gain.

Confidentiality issues arise in relation to disclosure of information to other health care professionals. For complementary practitioners, a difficult question is the extent to which they should seek to keep the patient's general practitioner/orthodox health carers informed about any treatment they are giving the patient. Because of the way that health care is delivered, there is increasing reliance on a team approach, with several health care professionals being involved in a patient's treatment. It is generally understood, though rarely explicitly stated to the patient, that information about him, whether in his records or otherwise, may be divulged to other people involved in his treatment who reasonably need to know that information. In the context of a complementary practitioner, does that extend to divulging information to the patient's GP? Ideally, there should be a flow of information between complementary practitioners and GPs and vice versa. Certainly, this would be expected in a referral basis. Without such a flow of information, both the GP and the complementary practitioner lose out on the opportunity to monitor how successful or otherwise the therapy has been. Wherever the practitioner is in doubt, he should seek the patient's explicit consent to disclosure.

One situation requires comment. For various reasons, including a fear of a dismissive response, patients may be reluctant to tell their GPs that they are going to see a therapist. If practitioners feel that it is important that the GP be involved in the case management, or if they require additional information from the GP, would they be entitled to go against the patient's wishes and approach the GP? This is a very delicate situation. Practitioners may genuinely feel unable to provide the appropriate treatment without that liaison. Although practitioners have a strong duty to respect their patients' autonomy, they also have a duty to themselves, and cannot be expected to respect patients' autonomy if it infringes their own. Equally, practitioners could lay themselves open to legal action if a clinical situation arose in which the GP should have been informed and was not, and the patient suffered avoidable harm. In such a situation, practitioners would be well advised to seek to persuade the patient to disclose the information personally. If that is not possible, then practitioners should make it clear that they are not prepared to continue to treat unless the patient involves his or her GP.

D. The conflict between beneficence and autonomy

One of the difficulties about applying ethical principles is that in real life, conflicts will arise between various principles. The most persistent tension, however, is that between the principle of beneficence and the principle of respect for autonomy. Historically, orthodox medical tradition has placed greater weight on the therapeutic purpose of medicine, namely to help or cure wherever possible, and at the very least, to do no harm, than on respecting a patient's autonomy.

The clash between these two principles arises when what the practitioner thinks as a matter of technical wisdom constitutes 'doing good' for the patient is at variance with what the patient wants or is prepared to accept. When practitioners override patients' wishes purportedly in their best interests, they are acting paternalistically. Buchanan offers the following definition: 'Paternalism is interference with a person's freedom of action or freedom of information, or the deliberate dissemination of misinformation, where the alleged justification of interfering or misinforming is that it is for the good of the person who is interfered with or misinformed.'[26] A spectrum can be identified, at one end of which is medical paternalism, and at the other end of which is consumer choice. Unlike the former, which relies on a model of the patient as a passive recipient of health care, the latter concept treats the patient more as a client, capable of exercising choice on the basis of relevant information, choosing between various therapies, and, quite possibly, rejecting intervention altogether.

Are health care practitioners more prey to paternalism than other professional groups? After all, the basis of a profession is arguably the specialist technical skill of its members. Lawyers too would be dismayed if clients, having sought their advice, then chose to ignore it completely and pursued a course of action which would lose them several thousand pounds. Unlike doctors though, they would not be so outraged if clients failed to accept their advice that they might contemplate having them declared incompetent and pursuing the course of action which they felt to be in their clients' best interests.

The tendency towards paternalism in medicine is often justified on the basis that the consequences of going against the doctor's advice may be extremely serious for patients and even fatal. Information is

[26] A. Buchanan, 'Medical Paternalism', 7 *Philosophy and Public Affairs*, 49 (1979).

thus withheld on the basis that patients might be too scared to undergo procedures if told of the side-effects, and that as the treatment is something they need it is legitimate to withhold it. This, set against the duty most doctors feel that they are under to save life and prevent illness wherever possible, has meant that in the past at least, doctors have felt justified in resorting to fairly heavy-handed techniques in order to ensure patient compliance.

Equally, information may be withheld on the basis that giving the patient certain information would cause him considerable harm. As Buchanan points out though, the essence of a paternalistic judgement is that it assumes that the damaging consequences of giving the information will outweigh the harm involved in withholding it.[27] Usurping patients' right to decide not only overrides their autonomy, but is likely to be based on assumptions made by practitioners as to how patients will react to receiving bad news, which may or may not apply in the case of specific individuals.

Paternalistic behaviour is no longer regarded as ethically appropriate, save in the most extreme of cases. It may, in addition, be unlawful if the extent of a doctor's coercion vitiates the patient's consent. The law, however, perpetuates medical paternalism in the context of disclosure of risks by allowing a doctor to exercise a therapeutic privilege and withhold information which might be harmful to the patient. Whether it was appropriate so to act is decided, as always, by reference to the professional standard of whether other doctors would have acted in a similarly paternalistic way.

Paternalistic behaviour is rarely justified in orthodox medicine. In complementary medicine it strikes at the heart of patient-empowerment and self-responsibility, and will rarely, if ever, be defensible. Especially given the non-acute setting in which most complementary consultations take place, few situations will demand that a practitioner acts against the expressed wishes of the patient. Likewise, for there to be a truly collaborative relationship between therapist and patient, there must be full and frank disclosure which facilitates the patient making decisions on the basis of all information available.[28]

This is not to suggest by any means that complementary therapists

[27] Ibid.

[28] In his chapter on 'The Collaborative Approach' Teff draws attention to the literature which supports the notion that 'collaborative autonomy' has distinctive *therapeutic* benefits: Teff, H., *Reasonable Care*, p. 121.

do not also exhibit paternalistic attitudes from time to time. It would be foolish to pretend that all therapists favour an autonomy-based, rather than beneficence-based, approach to their work. Commonly, it has been the charisma and persuasive power of a single individual which has led to the formation of new therapies, with founders acquiring a guru-like status. Indeed, many practitioners routinely demand the same sort of unquestioned respect reminiscent of old-style orthodox medicine, where the opinion of the doctor was unassailable. Whilst beneficence is clearly an important ethical duty for all healers, and a robust confidence may reassure some patients, the power disequilibrium they may foster can create an environment where paternalistic decisions seem justifiable.

It would be unhelpful, however, not to look beneath the surface and appreciate the very real tension between autonomy and beneficence which leads to paternalistic behaviour. The tension goes to the heart of healing. Paternalists would argue that the central purpose of any therapeutic endeavour is to make the patient better. Complementary practitioners, no less than orthodox practitioners, may, on occasion, feel that disclosing certain information to patients may be premature or unhelpful, if not positively harmful. This may be the case particularly in relation to intuitively acquired information, or information based on observational skills.

Practitioners may feel that they have the skills to improve the patient's condition and should be allowed to get on with it. The prevalence of this school of thought has led to a considerable backlash against patients' rights. Although increasingly few in number, there are still practitioners who reject patients' actively participating in decision-making, relying, when pressed, on therapeutic privilege to justify their failure to disclose information.

The counter-argument, however, is that practitioners only have the authority to treat people when they have consented, and even then, only within the confines set by the patient. This extreme 'patient as consumer' view is rarely mirrored in practice. The reality is that patients who are ill are usually needy and possibly scared when they consult a practitioner. To suggest that practitioners are merely at the beck and call of consumers reduces them to the level of mere technocrats. The notion of a collaborative venture looks to a paradigm within which there is scope for the patient to rely on the practitioner, safe in the knowledge that the practitioner will not exceed the bounds of his or her authority and will only act in accordance with the patient's consent. To deny the dependence that a patient has on a practitioner is unrealistic, and may itself, be damaging to patients.

Although few studies exist to confirm this proposition, it would seem that a large part of the healing process is triggered by patient's confidence in the practitioner, orthodox or alternative. Although respect for autonomy is now firmly enshrined as a key concept in medicine, there may be disadvantages in concentrating on autonomy to the detriment of the patient's well-being. Also, it cannot be assumed that all patients want their doctors to treat them as active partners in therapeutic alliance. Some patients will always wish to defer to professional expertise. As suggested above, however, the interface between beneficence and autonomy need not be conceptualized in terms of conflict if one adopts an interpretation of beneficence which embraces respecting the patient's autonomy within its definition. On this basis, to fail to respect a patient's wishes would constitute harm. This argument has utilitarian force in that if patients believe that practitioners are going to override their wishes they will stop consulting them and deprive themselves of necessary treatment.

E. The principle of justice

We might imagine that a duty to act fairly would be an obvious starting point in ethical discussion. Yet of the four ethical principles put forward as providing a starting-point for ethical discussion, it is the principle of justice that is least well defined. Much of the debate on justice issues centres on questions of distributive justice and access to health care. Consideration of allocation of resources is increasingly part of the health care debate. The principle of justice, even more than the other three principles listed, highlights how inappropriate it is to divorce consideration of ethical principles, and the ethical theories which underpin them, from their wider political context.

As Seedhouse points out,[29] in the area of health care provision, the principle of justice is interpreted by people in very different, and sometimes contradictory ways: 'There are those who think that the key to understanding "justice" is to treat people first and foremost in accord with what they *deserve*; others disagree—arguing that the basic criterion is *need*, and there is a further group who believe that justice can only come about when peoples' *rights* are upheld'. Space

---

[29] D. Seedhouse, 'An Ethical Perspective—How to Do the Right Thing', *Nursing Law and Ethics*, J. Tingle and A. Cribb (eds) (Blackwell, 1995).

precludes a detailed consideration of distributive justice but one important point must be made. At present, complementary medicine is provided almost entirely within the private sector. This means that availability is limited to those who can pay. From a welfare rights position, it could certainly be argued that the benefits of complementary medicine, to the extent that they can be established, should be freely available to all as part of a *comprehensive* National Health Service.[30] Leaving access to complementary medicine to the vagaries of market forces, in contrast to allopathic medicine which increasing numbers of people are beginning to reject, could in itself be unjust.

To date, complementary therapists have paid scant attention to wider issues relating to availability of complementary medicine, save to the extent that they may express preferences about greater integration within the NHS. We suggest that as practitioners are now beginning to grapple with ethical precepts, they should recognize that they too have a responsibility to enter the debate as to how health services should be provided, to whom, and on what basis. These are issues which could legitimately be pursued on a collective level, through the aegis of therapeutic, or even pan-professional, organizations.

The other concept of justice relates to compensation for harm. Principles of justice should ensure that people who have been harmed have access to complaints mechanisms and means of obtaining compensation, where appropriate. In Part II we saw how access to compensation via the courts is something of a lottery. This, we would argue, makes it all the more critical for therapies to take responsibility for bringing their own members to task. Whilst we would not wish to inhibit attempts made by individual practitioners to make amends for any harm they have caused (for example, by refunding a client's fees), we feel that this is such a critical area that it requires organization on a collective level.

F. Balancing competing ethical principles

In real life, equally important principles may often conflict with one another. Equally, clashes may occur when parties are asserting the same right. For example, a patient may exercise autonomy by requesting a certain form of treatment which the practitioner feels is inappropriate to provide, and which would infringe his or her own

---

[30] National Health Service Act 1977, s. 3.

autonomy. Beauchamp and Childress[31] suggest that principles can be balanced, by thinking of them only as a starting point for decision-making. In this way, principles are not seen as absolute, but must be balanced or must yield if they conflict with a more pressing overriding principle.

If the purpose of moral reasoning is to arrive at the best outcome, how can we guarantee that the decision taken will not be as subjective as if no deliberation had taken place? Beauchamp and Childress propose that practitioners have to be able to adduce good reasons for following a particular course of action. The outcome sought by overriding a principle must have a strong chance of success and not be merely speculative. For example, breaking confidentiality by telling the police that the patient has confided an intention to kill a named person must be linked to a strong possibility of avoiding that outcome. Wherever possible, the infringement must be the least possible commensurate with achieving the primary goal, and the practitioner must seek to minimize the negative effects of infringements wherever possible.

[31] Beauchamp T. and Childress, J., *Principles of Biomedical Ethics*.

14

Collective Ethical Practice

Ethical conduct, first and foremost requires a practical understanding of what it means to practise ethically. Although one would trust that practitioners come to healing professions with certain internal standards, a theoretical understanding of what is meant by behaving ethically is something which will be instilled during training. This presupposes the existence of an infrastructure by means of which this can be achieved. As well as practical training in the technical skills required of therapy, it will require a commitment to the incorporation of training in the ethical dimensions of practice.

Certain issues, however, go beyond the scope of individual practice. Determining efficacy depends on co-operation of large numbers of therapists. Likewise, funding and commissioning and carrying out research are things which require input at an organizational level. In addition, requirements of justice demand the provision of effective complaints mechanisms and the means of ensuring accountability. These two are matters which need to be organized on a collective level. By 'collective', we envisage the developing and strengthening of professional organizations which, we believe, will be most efficiently organized on a therapy-by-therapy basis.

The concept of ethics-led regulation presupposes high standards of practice at two distinct levels—first, at the level of pre-qualification training, both technical and ethical and secondly in professional organization, in areas such as professional registration, complaints mechanisms, and misconduct procedures. We shall explore each of these levels in turn.

I. TRAINING ETHICAL PRACTITIONERS

A. Assessment of competence

The most obvious way of assessing competence is to ensure that a candidate wishing to practice a therapy can demonstrate skill and

ability in certain areas of knowledge deemed to be essential to practise that therapy. Certainly, demanding examinations have characterized the training of orthodox professionals. As we have seen,
the curricula for many complementary therapies have become a lot
tougher in recent years. Courses are often longer, more technical, and
often more scientific than in the past. Herbalism, osteopathy, and
chiropractic may, for example, require three to four years' of undergraduate training and students are subject to rigorous examinations.

B. Assessment of human skills

It may not be possible either to teach or to examine many of the
attributes of a good complementary therapist in the same way as it is
possible to impart technical knowledge. Many complementary therapists rely on intuitive, not just rational, knowledge. This may not be
able to be taught in the same way as rational scientific fact. As to
examining non-technical skills, an interesting parallel can be drawn
with the architectural profession. Thus Johnson writes:

> The leaders of the architectural profession were particularly resistant to
> the idea that entry to the profession could be based on technical com-
> petence measured by formal examination, arguing that architecture
> was essentially an artistic pursuit involving individual talent which could
> neither be learned nor effectively examined.[1]

Whilst it is certainly possible to teach communication skills, is it
possible to imbue would-be therapists with characteristics such
as empathy, a capacity to respond in a non-judgemental fashion etc?
Many of these doubts have been expressed in relation to psychotherapy.[2] We would argue that these skills are critical for complementary
therapists, and go to the heart of why people seek a complementary
practitioner, rather than an orthodox doctor. The problem is, these
skills cannot necessarily be taught or examined. This is not to say that
technical skills are not also extremely important.

It is of course fundamental that practitioners acquire a sound therapeutic knowledge base and master the skills that a therapy has to
offer in a safe and competent way. Two points emerge: first, certain

---

[1] Johnson, T. 'The state and the professions: peculiarities of the British'. In
Giddens, A. and Mackenzie (eds.), *Social Class and the Division of Labour*
(Cambridge University Press, London, 1982).
[2] See, e.g., Jeffrey Masson, in his impassioned rejection of psychotherapy
Against Therapy (Collins, 1989).

therapists will have a considerable intuitive approach. People may be outstanding at what they do, even though they have no formal training, or if they cannot succeed at exams. A second point is that it may be harder to assess competence in a highly individualized responsive form of therapy than in a rigid mechanistic approach to healing. This is not to suggest that either competence cannot be defined or that it cannot be measured, it is simply to acknowledge that a more creative approach is likely to be needed.

This is particularly so of any examination system. Just as the information taught should be relevant, so the system of evaluating that information must be capable of recognizing what is truly important to that therapy. The skills which will be necessary are linked to the skills that the therapy professes to offer. Here we run into particular problems with the concept of holistic therapy. We presume this to be therapy which treats the person not the symptoms—a recognition of emotional and spiritual needs, as well as physical. As we have seen, orthodox medicine also recognizes the need to place the patient in context, and to look at that person in the totality of his or her environment. The problem for complementary medicine is one of credibility. It is all very well to pay lip-service to treating emotional needs and spiritual needs, but are most complementary therapists equipped to do this? Even if they have some training in counselling skills, which would seem to be a prerequisite if attempting to work on an emotional level, what training is given, or can be given, to respond to a patient's spiritual dimension? The issues goes to the heart of orthodox scepticism of complementary therapy, and is a matter which sooner or later, will have to be addressed on a collective level.

C. Pre- and post-qualification training

Undoubtedly, appropriate education is the central requirement in ensuring the quality of present and future practitioners. Many of the shortcomings of orthodox medicine can be attributed, directly or indirectly, to medical training. That biomedicine has adhered to a scientific, reductionist path is largely due to the imbalance of the medical school curricula. The GMC's document *Tomorrow's Doctors* demonstrated full awareness of the shortcomings of the medical school curriculum. However, the protracted timescale over which reforms are being introduced by medical schools demonstrates further the inability of the GMC to respond effectively to the regulatory needs of the profession. In this critical regard, the statutory self-regulation by the GMC has not worked in the interests of either patients or practitioners.

Complementary therapy courses should make every attempt to contextualize the teaching of their therapies. Unless training touches on issues such as gender assumptions, cultural expectations, and the politics of health, practitioners will be deprived of the opportunity of developing a deeper understanding of the philosophical basis of complementary medicine. Students should be encouraged to challenge assumptions rather than accept what they are taught as unquestionable truths.

D. Selection criteria

A point which is so fundamental that it may sometimes be overlooked is that people have a variety of motives in becoming therapists. Some of these may be functional and borne out of a genuine and healthy desire to empathize and help others, but other motives may be dysfunctional, including the trainee's own unresolved difficulties, perhaps a desire to control and dominate, and an unhealthy need to care for others. Training establishments have a significant responsibility in selecting appropriate candidates, and not merely those who are able to pay course fees. This is an ethical prerequisite not merely to protect those who are not suited to becoming therapists, but also to protect the public against potentially abusive therapists.

E. Agreed core competencies

This will require a far greater degree of co-operation between schools of therapies than currently exists, so as to be able to define core training requirements within each therapy. As well as deciding what these competencies are, therapies need to decide what is the best way to impart that knowledge, as well as how to assess skills.

F. Strong research base

There must be a recognition at a collective level that therapeutic interventions must be able to demonstrate efficacy. Research skills should be included as part of therapists' training. If complementary therapies are not amenable to randomized control trials, then other research methodology must be developed. A central research base is critical, ensuring, amongst other things, that research is not dupli-cated.[3] This is particularly critical given the scarcity of funds for research into complementary medicine, particularly from the major funding institutions. Guidance should be given in how to make proper research applications, and research methodology and research ethics should be taught as a formal part of training. Research findings should be made known, whether they generate positive outcomes or not. Given the methodological problems of conducting randomized control trials in certain complementary therapies, there should at least be an emphasis on the importance of audit, with students being taught how to record outcomes of their practice in a systematic way.

G. Inclusion of orthodox medical knowledge

Although the amount of biomedical knowledge that practitioners require is the subject of fierce debate, a basic level of orthodox med-ical training is necessary for all practitioners so that, at the very least, they will be capable of recognizing contra-indications to their therapy and situations in which urgent, acute medical care is required. How-ever unpalatable, we believe this is a necessary concomitant of comple-mentary practitioners holding themselves out as providing therapies with specific health benefits. This may be assisted by co-operation with GMC and Royal Colleges. The more medicalized a therapy is, the more medical knowledge students will require. Needless to say, where a therapy has a medical faction, the self-protective stance of its medical practitioners will push for a high degree of medical train-ing for 'lay' practitioners

Because of the practical and philosophical problems in including a significant amount of biomedical knowledge in complementary therapists' training, and the problems which this raises in terms of practitioners' ability to spot serious underlying conditions which may require conventional treatment, therapists should be encouraged to work as closely alongside GPs as possible. Greater integration of complementary therapy at a primary care level will no doubt be the best way of increasing understanding between practitioners working within a different conceptual framework.

[3] The Research Council for Complementary Medicine is part of an initiative currently involved in making an application for a complementary medicine field within the Cochrane Collaboration, a worldwide research network, committed to maintaining and disseminating systematic reviews of randomized control trials of health care interventions.

H. Educating the medical profession

Therapeutic organizations should also see it as part of their role to increase and enhance understanding of their therapy by the medical profession. To this end, they should co-operate in the development of basic programmes on theories of complementary medicine for orthodox practitioners. (In some other countries, such as Germany, complementary medicine is a compulsory part of the undergraduate curriculum.)

Bearing in mind the fact that complementary therapies are provided by a variety of existing health care practitioners, a sensible alternative might be an integrated modular approach to complementary therapies, from which doctors, nurses, and other health care professionals could all benefit, rather than each of them incorporating separate training courses into their tight teaching schedules. This could be more effective in achieving a broader, standardized level. If therapies wish to attain this goal, they will have to become professionally organized and be able to present a united front if they wish to appear credible before the GMC, the UKCC and the boards established under the Professions Supplementary to Medicine Act 1960. Genuinely protecting consumers' interests will only be possible when all 'sides' recognize the contribution they make in maintaining and improving health, and equip themselves with basic knowledge about the healing modalities which their patients are using concurrently.

I. Post-qualification experience

As well as continuing education, the concept of continuing professional development, which is only just beginning to be recognized in the context of orthodox medicine, should be a requirement of continued registration with a regulatory body.

J. Supervision

Supervision has a number of vital functions. It provides therapists with the much needed space to explore their own emotional and spiritual needs, it provides a forum to discuss ideas and talk through ethical dilemmas which have arisen in practice, and it reduces the isolation of therapists working on their own, which can lead to insecurity and self-doubt. Supervision also allows trainees to evaluate their development. One approach to supervision which may have a useful role in complementary medicine is the development of 'buddy' systems whereby colleagues work in pairs providing co-teaching and assessment. Not only is this useful in training, but can be an important source of support once therapists are in practice, particularly if they work in isolation.

Increasingly within orthodox medicine there is a tendency to work in a team, with respect for individual professionals who all have distinct responsibilities. This is in contrast with the previous pyramid structure placing consultants at the top. This team approach is not mirrored in complementary therapy, and means that individual therapists may not have the peer support they require, and may lack the peer review central to any self-regulating enterprise. Structured measures are required to counter this. In this regard, there may be merit in establishing a 'mentor' system, whereby inexperienced practitioners have access to a more senior, highly experienced practitioner to whom they can turn for advice on therapeutic and ethical issues. In the absence of such initiatives it is all the more important that training bodies should be accessible to those they have trained, and be prepared to provide ongoing advice and support.

Complementary medicine is not like orthodox medicine where seven years' training is deemed, rightly or wrongly, to equip medical students to start treating patients in a supervised capacity. Without the hierarchical infrastructure of NHS medicine, the therapist bears sole responsibility for determining whether he or she is ready to start accepting patients. Practitioners need to feel confident and secure in their training. In choosing their training establishment, students would be well advised to opt for a course which provides ongoing support and supervision, particularly after qualification. The Society of Homoeopaths, will not accept practitioners onto their register even when they have successfully completed their exams and training until they have also completed one year's supervised practice. We regard this as an extremely wise precaution, and one which should be followed by other registering bodies.

K. Support for therapists

In order to be effective healers, therapists must be in good physical and mental health. Working with patients on an emotional and spiritual level as well as a physical level may give rise to a lot of uncomfortable issues for the therapist as well as for patients. If therapists are attempting to work with people on these levels, they need to have worked through their own psychological issues, and developed a high degree of insight and self-awareness. The concept of 'burn-out' is well known and well documented amongst healing professionals, and usually arises because of a failure to develop self-protective devices and boundaries.

L. Post-training education

Obviously, as with any area of human endeavour, therapeutic techniques develop and change with time. In order to benefit patients and fulfil duties of beneficence, all practitioners must keep abreast of developments in their own field, for example, by reading the appropriate journals, attending training meetings, and maintaining contact with practitioners working in the same area. Clearly, this will place a different duty on different therapists. The more formalized the technical skill base, the more onerous it will be to keep up to date.[4]

M. Teaching ethics

There has been considerable debate as to how ethics should be taught. There are strong grounds for arguing that rather than separating ethics and hiving it off as a discrete discipline in the same way as anatomy and physiology, its teaching should actually be integrated throughout a practitioner's training. In medical schools, one approach is to have ethical training sessions throughout clinical training, so that students will learn about ethical and legal issues pertaining to the particular specialty in which they are working. Another method is to look at particular clinical cases and discuss the ethical issues that are raised. Michels and Kelly, writing on psychiatry, point out the danger of this approach in that there may be a tendency to concentrate on unusual or hard cases, 'rather than to recognize the universality of ethics as a framework for understanding professional functioning'.[5]

---

[4] There is a corresponding legal duty to keep apace of changes, so that, e.g., an aromatherapist could be excused for failing to notice one article in a journal suggesting contra-indications about the use of a certain oil for treating certain conditions, but could not be excused if a series of articles over a period of time, based on recent research, firmly recommended avoidance of use of that oil.

[5] Michels, R., and Kelly, K., 'Training in Psychiatric Ethics'. In Block, S. and Chodoff, P., *Psychiatric Ethics* (2nd edn., OUP, 1991).

On the whole, complementary medicine seems to prefer an integrated approach to the teaching of ethics. In this way, rather than being taught about the principle of respect for autonomy, this will be taught as part of how therapists should work with their patients, and how they should learn to elicit the patients' wishes and expectations of therapy. It may well be that terms such as autonomy and beneficence are not even used in training.

The teaching of health care ethics as a discrete discipline is a relatively new phenomenon. Within the last five to ten years though, there has been a pronounced tendency to introduce health care ethics into the training of health care practitioners, along with an awareness of relevant legal issues. We are beginning to see a corresponding interest amongst more formal training programmes for complementary therapists. A number of schools now offer modular courses on law, ethics, and good practice. Whilst it may be possible to teach ethics as an integrated subject, we feel that the centrality of understanding ethics is so central to good practice that some time must be spent in teaching certain theoretical ethics as part of training.

II. CREATING EFFECTIVE DISCIPLINARY STRUCTURES

A. Registration

In order to ensure that practitioners have been trained to a high standard, it is necessary to develop some registration system to separate those who have been qualified from those who have not. Currently, hundreds, if not thousands, of qualifications are awarded. Unlike orthodox medicine, where the major qualifications such as MD or FRCS are recognized by the public, in the case of complementary practitioners, patients cannot assume that the more letters a practitioner has, the more rigorous his or her training. On an individual level, in order to respect prospective patients' autonomy, practitioners should assume the responsibility of explaining to patients prior to treatment what their qualifications mean.

On a collective level, the more unified a therapy becomes, the more it will be able to determine acceptable standards of training within that particular therapy. This is not to say that all courses will have to be the same, or lose their individuality. What it would ensure, however, is that minimum requirements for ensuring safe standards of practice apply across the therapy. This may not prevent the 'six week-end training school' phenomenon, but it would certainly make it harder for such schools to attempt to issue 'qualifications' on the basis of which people could set up in practice.

The difficulty is that until each therapy is unified, any division will potentially lead to public confusion. (The current state of affairs may additionally make it very difficult for a prospective student to know where best to train.) Where, say, a therapy has five separate registering bodies, it is virtually impossible for a patient to wade through the differences between all five before choosing a practitioner. It may be that amongst those five, there is considerable variation in relation to, say grievance procedures, which a patient may only discover in the event of something going wrong. Because the emphasis of self-regulation should be on protecting the consumer, rather than protecting professionals, regulatory bodies should be accessible to public requests for information. Lists of registered members should be given to the public free of charge.

B. Codes of ethics

Rather than the punitive, rather legalistic documents that certain professional organizations use, a shift of emphasis is required so that ethical advice to members concentrates on good therapeutic practice. To the extent that codes continue to be couched in a negative list of prohibitions, they will not reinforce practitioners' training as to what constitutes ethical practice. The need for codes to be drafted in positive, rather than punitive terms is recognized by the GMC whose revised guidance to doctors, *Good Medical Practice*, represents a substantial departure from the form of ethical guidance it has disseminated in the past.

In addition to producing dynamic codes of ethics, regulatory bodies should also exercise an educational role to the profession. As the ultimate sanction of deregistration may remove a person's livelihood, regulatory bodies should give practitioners as much guidance as possible on the limits of acceptable conduct, especially in sensitive areas.

Ideally, professional organizations should be prepared to provide members with ethical advice when they are facing a dilemma. Professional bodies could do this by employing advisors experienced in ethical dilemmas, who can provide an accessible service to members as well as advising the regulatory body on developments in ethical thinking. Customarily, professional regulatory bodies shy away from saying whether proposed conduct would or would not be unethical, in the same way that the police do not field enquiries from the public as to whether a proposed course of action would or would not be unlawful. Whilst it may be inappropriate for a regulatory body which exercises disciplinary functions to give members advice over a specific scenario, they should be able to advise on ethical matters *in general terms*, so as to prevent problems from arising. If this is unrealistic then, at the very least, professional bodies should regularly disseminate to practitioners examples of conduct which have been found unacceptable.

C. Complaints

A primary function of self-regulating bodies is to establish effective and accessible grievance procedures. Complaints systems must be tied in to a system of risk avoidance so that mistakes can be prevented in the future. This is best achieved by disciplinary bodies working in close conjunction with educational establishments. Complaints mechanisms must endeavour to respond to aggrieved clients as speedily as possible, not least because of the length of time involved in attempting to get redress through the courts.

A complaints system should be as accessible to the public as possible. Given that the primary function of any self-regulating body is to protect the public, there should be easy access to complaints mechanisms and people should not be deterred by unnecessary bureaucracy. Specially trained staff should be available to deal sympathetically with complaints at each stage. Ideally, regulatory bodies should take an active part in informing the public of their rights in facilitating the bringing of complaints before the appropriate authority.

D. Rehabilitation

As a general starting point, disciplinary procedures should, so far as is possible, be seen in a positive light, and not as a purely punitive mechanism designed to deprive practitioners of their right to practise. A professional ethos must be developed in which it is recognized that weeding out poor standards of practice is to the advantage of the profession as a whole. The main way that this can be achieved is by designing flexible sanctions with an emphasis on retraining and rehabilitation wherever possible.

E. Composition of disciplinary committees

In order for self-regulating bodies to be genuinely accountable to the public they serve, they must have a significant lay presence. We do not think that this is achieved by having one, nominal, lay member on a disciplinary committee. Given the problems of credibility that all professional groups seem to have in bringing their members to task, it would not seem inappropriate for half of any committee to be made up of lay persons. As we have already identified, it is not sufficient to have a lay presence, unless lay members are allowed to participate fully and their views given equal weight to those of professional members.

As to professional members, it is important that these are drawn from practising therapists who have an up-to-the-minute grasp of current standards. In order to attract members of the highest calibre, the profession should be prepared to pay members who sit on regulatory committees, on the basis that it is in its own interests to be presided over by professionals who are not out of touch with the day-to-day reality of therapeutic practice.

One of the difficulties with the GMC is that the procedural rules are such that hearings have most of the trappings of litigation. There is a danger of making proceedings so formalistic that members of the committee are in effect judge and jury, but without having the legal skills to analyse situations in a legalistic way. In order to be accessible to both the complainant who, out of courtesy, should be kept fully informed of the progress of any complaint and should be invited to attend the proceedings, and the practitioner who has been accused of wrongdoing, procedural formalities should be kept to a minimum. This is not to say that practitioners should not be allowed legal representation, but that the system should be sufficiently informal that they should not need it. To accord with the rules of natural justice, the practitioner should have a full opportunity to put forward his or her case, and should have a right of appeal against an adverse finding.

F. Deregistration

Ultimately, disciplinary tribunals must have the right to deregister or disaffiliate someone as the ultimate sanction. Again, the problem of effective disciplinary procedures is, as we have seen, affected by the existence of a multitude of professional registers. Deregistration ceases to be an effective sanction as long as practitioners can merely join a separate register. The solution to this does not necessarily require statutory regulation. To the extent that a therapy is unified and there is only one professional register for that therapy, deregistration would have the desired effect of withdrawing the status of professional membership. We recognize that the absence of statutory protection of title would mean that the practitioner could continue to practise 'bare', but we would argue that in this regard, patients should exercise self-responsibility by checking whether the practitioner is registered with that therapy's professional body.

G. Compensation

Although complementary medicine is relatively harmless (although by no means harm free), there needs to be a mechanism outside the common law, by which a person who has been injured can be recompensed. Evidence suggests that in the context of health care, compensation is not the most important issue for the vast majority of complainants.[6] In their proposals for a Health Standards Inspectorate, the Association for Community Health Councils for England and Wales and Action for Victims of Medical Accidents identified the prime concerns of patients who believed something had gone wrong in their treatment as wanting to establish: what happened, why it happened, whether anyone is to blame, if so, what action will be taken against them and what action is going to be taken within the system to ensure that it does not happen again.

III. TRADE UNIONS

To the extent that practitioners are beginning to move out of the realm of private practice and into working within the NHS, therapeutic organizations will need to involve themselves in trade union activities. Because the aims and aspirations of different therapies are so great, realistically, it is hard to imagine how this can be handled other than at the pan-therapeutic level. As well as negotiating terms and conditions for their members, therapeutic organizations will have

---

[6] *A Health Standards Inspectorate.* A Proposal by the ACHCEW and AVMA (1992).

to start addressing themselves to the legal implications of their members working within the NHS, and be in a position to provide their members with legal advice and representation.

IV. PAN-PROFESSIONAL ORGANIZATIONS

Consumer protection, we have argued, will be best served when complementary medicine organizes itself on a therapy-by-therapy basis, and each individual therapy unites to make combined decisions on matters specific to that therapy. The advantages of registering qualified practitioners will be severely limited until this is the case. Bearing this in mind, is there any residual role for a pan-professional organization? Were all therapies to organize themselves, would there be any remit for such an organization? To the extent that there is now far greater professional organization, have the existing pan-professional organizations outlived their usefulness?

We do not dispute that historically, pan-professional organizations have had an important role to play, not least of all in establishing the credibility of complementary medicine. Whilst therapies have been in the process of developing self-regulating bodies, it has been important to have a pan-professional code of ethics and an ovearching disciplinary function. In reality, though, the role of pan-professional bodies in exerting disciplinary functions has been marginal. Now that many therapies are really starting to get to grips with self-regulation, and professional structures are beginning to emerge, the need for an umbrella organisation of this sort is questionable.

An explicit statement made by Baroness Hooper in 1990 reinforced that complementary medicine needs to organize itself on a therapy-by-therapy basis. Speaking of the Government's changed stance on umbrella bodies she said:

At one time, we were of the view that there might be advantages if all the natural therapies came together in mutual understanding. But, given the diversity, practice and aspirations of those professions—coupled perhaps with their increasing proliferation—we now believe very firmly that it must be for each therapy group to determine its own future development.[7]

In terms of an educational role, we recognize the vital part that

---

[7] *Hansard*, vol. 518, no. 82, col. 1431–2 (HMSO, London, 1990).

pan-professional organizations have played in helping establish educational standards, and the ongoing role they have in the National Vocational Qualifications arena. But as therapies become better organized and more clearly defined, can such bodies realistically have anything other than an advisory role? The need to develop core competencies within a therapy is essentially a matter which will have to be organized on a therapy-by-therapy basis.

A. Limitations of pan-professional role

1. Impracticality of a single statutory scheme

Outside those professions which have now achieved autonomous statutory recognition and those which are likely to be awarded statutory status in the foreseeable future, would there be any merit in a pan-professional organization attempting to unite all other therapies under a single piece of legislation? The conclusion of our arguments must surely be no. Bearing in mind the problems experienced by the Council for Professions Supplementary to Medicine whose jurisdiction is limited to seven professions, the idea of bringing together over a hundred therapies is totally unrealistic.

At a time when most complementary therapists are striving to protect their common law right to practise, we would question what support there would be to introduce occupational closure across the entire range of complementary therapies. Would not the opposition to the Osteopaths Act 1993 which we are now witnessing from osteopaths who fall outside the statutory scheme be replicated in every therapy such an Act would seek to cover?

In addition, an overarching scheme would have to be capable of being amended every time a new therapy emerged. Moreover, existing complementary therapies are at such disparate stages of therapeutic and professional organization that it would be absurd to attempt to unite them under a single statutory scheme, even if they uniformly wanted to pursue statutory regulation, which clearly many therapies do not. As we have suggested, it is not feasible to regulate therapies before they have even established therapeutic credibility. It would also be positively harmful to grant statutory status to a therapy which had no tenable basis for making therapeutic claims.

However, the most important objection to a single statutory scheme is that statutory regulation, as we have seen, does not guarantee high standards of practice. These can only be achieved through an ethics-led approach to regulation, which encompasses not only the highest standards of therapeutic training, but also a real understanding of the requirements of ethical conduct.

2. Disciplinary functions

As long as complementary medicine remains, primarily, voluntarily self-regulated and therapists are free to practise at common law, any attempt to register all complementary practitioners on a single non-statutory register will be defeatist, on the basis that practitioners cannot be compelled to register themselves and the public cannot be deterred from seeking out unregistered practitioners. Although a single qualification, such as membership of the British Council of Complementary Practitioners, could serve as a kitemark of quality assurance, presumably in most cases this would be in addition to other therapeutic qualifications that a practitioner holds. As such, the same problems will arise with duplication of qualifications, and the public will still have an array of qualifications to decipher.

3. Mandate

Whilst it might be useful for a single organization to be able to negotiate with central government or the medical profession, the reality is that without the support of all sectors of complementary medicine, it would be hard to establish a legitimate basis for a pan-professional organization to exercise such a role on behalf of the whole of complementary medicine. Most other major health care professions have both a regulatory body and a separate body exercising trade union functions. It is hard to imagine how a single body, even if democratically elected, could effectively negotiate on behalf of the broad spectrum of therapies, some of whom may have competing agendas, and all of whom have different aspirations. This is rendered all the more unlikely by virtue of there being three major pan-professional organizations and a host of smaller pan-professional bodies. Arguably, unless these bodies are able to rationalize their functions to a far greater extent than at present, they are in danger of losing their credibility with both therapists and consumers.

B. Future role for a single pan-professional body

The above concerns do not rule out the need for a pan-professional organization. We propose a framework within which a single pan-professional body would play a more restricted, but critically important role. Primarily, such a body would have three main functions. These would be:

(1) the development of a module for ethics training;
(2) pan-professional disciplinary functions;
(3) a public information service.

C. Development of an ethics module

Our central proposition is that consumer protection is best promoted by an ethics-led approach to regulation. As we have seen, the role of ethics is underappreciated and underdeveloped at all levels. There is considerable merit in suggesting that a pan-professional body should develop and oversee a standardized training module in ethics and communication, which all therapists would have to complete in addition to their therapeutic training. In addition, such a body could be empowered to ensure that ethical standards are met, and to exercise a disciplinary function, primarily in relation to *ethical* breaches of conduct.

Currently, only a handful of training establishments teach ethics in any formal sense. We have seen that an explicit understanding of ethical principles is vital if practitioners are going to work in an ethical manner. Given the huge numbers of training schools and the huge divergence in standards, we do not think it is feasible that they will be able to develop the expertise to teach ethics in a systematic or sufficiently rigorous way. Given the highly fragmented nature of most therapies, it would be inappropriate to leave quality assurance to individual training schools in this most critical of areas. If the public is to be reassured that practitioners have ethical as well as technical competence, this will require organization at a central level.

Existing pan-professional bodies have considerable experience in setting educational standards. This experience should be harnessed and used to develop a standardized approach to ethics training, so as to provide all practitioners, from whatever therapeutic discipline, with a core competency in ethics as it affects complementary medicine.

A valid argument against this proposal is the fact that unless such a body had a statutory backing, with statutory powers of registration, it would be impossible to enforce this training requirement upon practitioners. Complementary medicine has no equivalent body to the GMC, which, as we have seen, has now recommended that ethics training must form a part of the undergraduate training of all medical students alongside their clinical studies. For the reasons we have outlined, however, a *compulsory* statutory scheme for all complementary therapists is not politically viable and is probably undesirable. Our argument is that such a scheme does not require, and should not depend on, a statutory basis for its introduction. On the contrary, the mandate for introducing this scheme will come from an acknowledgement on the part of complementary therapies that ethics-led regulation is the most appropriate way of ensuring high standards.

A major shift of emphasis is required so that therapies come to realize that an ethical basis to practice is the key to protecting consumers and offering a genuinely professional service. If complementary therapies seize this initiative they will truly merit the support of the public they profess to serve. If they do not, and continue to operate ineffective, *ad hoc*, disciplinary mechanisms which are insufficiently accountable, they run the risk of the entire question of regulation being taken out of their hands and controlled either by central Government, or from Brussels.

D. Disciplinary functions

It would be both feasible and practical for a pan-professional body to assume disciplinary functions on behalf of all therapies other than those which are statutorily regulated. Again, we accept that not all therapies even have therapeutic organizations, but we feel that these will develop in the near future, driven by consumer demand. As we have already seen, there is almost a total absence of complaints of a therapeutic nature. There is no reason to expect that this state of affairs would necessarily change. As such, the bulk of complaints that a pan-professional disciplinary committee would be handling would be of an ethical nature. We would propose that the disciplinary committee should co-opt one or more representatives from the therapy in which the practitioner who is subject to a complaint practises. Such a body would not have to hear cases centrally, but could, where necessary, convene a local tribunal.

Whilst the emphasis on ethical instruction would come via its ethical training module, a pan-professional organization would still need to supplement this with ethical guidance to practitioners. Digests of disciplinary cases should be distributed to practitioners, and should be made freely available to the public.

E. Public information service

As well as functions relating to ethics, such a body could usefully provide information directly to members of the public and to other health professionals about different therapies.

15
Holistic Regulation

Looking ahead, we see the emergence of holistic based health care, combining the best of orthodox and non-orthodox approaches. We must recognize that the time schedule for change will be extremely gradual. This is inevitable, given what Capra calls 'the tremendous symbolic power of biomedical therapy' in our culture.

We need to accompany and facilitate this development with a holistic approach to regulation, recognizing the interplay of all existing regulatory mechanisms. Whilst we have focused on the centrality of ethics, we do not ignore the positive scope for using common law and statute law in ways which promote and facilitate a holistic therapeutic approach.

Having outlined our vision for voluntary self-regulation, let us conclude by looking at positive ways in which statute and common law could be used to promote a holistic approach to healing.

I. STATUTE LAW REVISITED

We acknowledge that a handful of highly 'medicalized' therapies will, in all probability require statutory control in order to protect patients from harm. This will only be the appropriate regulatory for the small number of therapies which carry *inherent* risks of harm, and whose technical skill base is such that patients are effectively excluded from taking an active part in their own treatment. By implication, these will be therapies which work predominantly on a physical level, even if practitioners attempt to provide those therapies in a patient-centred and holistic way.

To the extent that statutory regulation is pursued, it should be with a view to promoting the highest standards of practice, and not for the perceived benefits statutory regulation would bring. We have tried to demonstrate that, as far as complementary therapies are concerned, those benefits may well be illusory.

We are profoundly concerned that therapies may, none the less, seek statutory regulation in order to acquire professional power, rather than professional levels of competence. It would be unconscionable if statutory regulation were simply to create new professional monopolies for those so regulated. Should, for example, a revolutionary new manipulative technique evolve which differed from osteopathy and chiropractic, we would hope those professions would have the generosity to support and develop its development, rather than attempt to frustrate its growth.

Thus, we recommend that any further statutory regulation should embrace the comments made in relation to osteopathy and chiropractic. The importance of ethics applies no less to statutorily regulated professions than to voluntarily regulated therapies. If anything, the status that statutory regulation may confer makes it all the more important that this power is not abused and that therapeutic skills are employed for the benefit of patients.

II. A CONTRACTUAL MODEL

The common law, as we have stressed, operates independently of any other regulatory model which is in place. It is this area that radical changes could alter the basis of patient/therapist relationships. Rather than the one-sided legal relationship that characterizes existing tortious duties, we propose for complementary encounters, albeit cautiously, a contractual model, founded on the basis of mutual responsibilities. This, we believe, is more in keeping with the holistic relationship which depends, for its success, upon a genuine therapeutic alliance. We appreciate that this is a significant departure from the normal way of looking at the practitioner/patient relationship, but as we have stressed, the whole point about the complementary relationship is precisely that it is different from the doctor/patient relationship and is founded on substantially different values.

By a contractual model, we are not simply referring to the fact that because most therapists work in the private sector, the legal relationship between therapist and client is based on a contract. We are proposing that this model operate on a more profound level, namely, a level at which the patient's duty to exercise self-responsibility is actually incorporated into the legal relationship of rights and responsibilities. Suggesting this model has profound political implications. If we are to expect patients in this context to make responsible choices and to take steps to promote their own health, then this relies on the patient having access to a far greater amount of information than the law currently requires. In this model, the amount of disclosure could not be anything other than patient-centred, in much the same way as autonomy, rather than beneficence, would have to be the overriding ethical principle.

We recognize that there is a distinct danger that the notion of self-responsibility is capable of being used against the individual's own interests. After all, within the NHS we have already seen that the patients who do not exercise responsibility are being discriminated against in the provision of health services. The media have shown great interest in the increasing number of cases in which heavy smokers or obese patients are being refused surgical procedures, ostensibly on the grounds of clinical judgement, clearly bound up with an urgent need to keep down costs. Hypothetically, were these financial constraints removed, would these decisions, to the extent that they are genuinely based on clinical factors, be as objectionable? Could it not be argued, at least, that we should welcome this development, and see it as the medical profession firmly refusing to waste resources on patients who do not help themselves?

There are several obvious rejoinders. First, it begs the question of what we mean by 'wasting' resources, making considerable assumptions about entitlement theories. Secondly, it gives doctors an unprecedented authority to act as arbiters not only of our physical health, but also of our lifestyle choices. It could be argued that such discrimination is unjustified because it singles out easily identifiable targets, whereas everyone could do significantly more to reduce their chances of adverse health outcomes. Accordingly, to target specific groups arbitrarily is unjust. Thirdly, and most importantly, it presupposes that all members of society have equal opportunities, whilst smugly ignoring the sociological context of health, and the ample evidence linking, for example, poverty and disease.

On what basis, therefore, are we proposing that it is reasonable to impose more demanding standards on clients of complementary health practitioners? The difference resides, we would argue, in the fact that alternative practitioners are known and deliberately chosen by patients *precisely because they work within an alternative paradigm* and, in particular, in a way which will take account of the patients as 'whole' people, rather than as a collection of symptoms. Whereas NHS patients can expect to be treated almost uniformly within the 'medical model', patients who actively seek a complementary approach are making a conscious choice to explore a different path to good health. No one is making them do so. Neither, at present, does the Government facilitate this option. Yet, the patients are choosing to consult, and pay, alternative therapists working within a different conceptual framework.

What are the ramifications of this? We would argue that patients need to appreciate at the outset of treatment that they will not be permitted to be passive recipients, that there will be certain obligations upon them, and that the therapy will not work without their taking an active and ongoing role in the promotion of their own health. Certain therapeutic interventions, such as behavioural therapies, already make use of explicit contracts with their clients, setting out the basis of intervention, the goals sought by both parties, ways of evaluating and reappraising those goals, and mutual expectations. We would like to see these features defining not just the therapeutic relationship, but also the legal relationship. It is certainly arguable, at least, that a patient's responsibility to take an active part in his or her own health management, should find expression in the law.

The alternative, as we have seen, is a state of affairs where the concept of contributory negligence has no place, because the State does not feel that patients should be made to bear responsibility for their own health. Is this in patients' long-term interests or misplaced paternalism? If a quasi-contractual model were applied, patients would be expected to take steps to improve their own health.

Traditionally, the law has not seen fit to hold patients responsible on the basis that they are vulnerable and cannot be expected to act in their own interests. We would assert that this is not only inappropriate in the context of holistic medicine, but that it is also extremely disempowering to health service users as a whole, many of whom are not ill in the conventional sense. Should a patient who consults an unqualified, untrained practitioner not bear some responsibility if the person fails to deliver the same standard of care that a highly trained practitioner, working to a professional code of ethics, would be able to offer? We are not suggesting that such practitioners can be excluded from practice, nor that patients can be prevented, through legal mechanisms, from consulting them. Civil liberties and freedom of choice must preserve the right of an individual to seek succour from whatever source is felt appropriate, be it by crystal healing, transcendental meditation, or organized religion.

Indeed, it is only when we consider the arguments which have historically been applied against a contractual model in the area of health, that the value-laden assumptions underlying this position emerge. A primary argument would point to the unequal bargaining power of the parties, the social imbalance, and the relative imbalance of knowledge. It would be argued that vulnerable patients are not in a position to negotiate on equal terms since they are ill and thus not able to enter into a contract on favourable terms. The relationship of dependency would be adverted to, with the assumption that such dependence will create the potential for exploitation.

The first issue is that this line of argument automatically places the recipient of health care in a 'sickness' model, which may or may not characterize the alternative relationship. As with psychotherapy, many people consult therapists on account of a generalized emotional and spiritual malaise, rather than specific illness. They may be looking as much for an alternative way of looking at the same set of facts as a cure in the conventional sense. Indeed, many patients consult alternative practitioners for long-standing, chronic conditions precisely because allopathic medicine concentrates on their physical symptoms to the exclusion of emotional and spiritual dimensions and the consequence of that illness and what it means for them as a whole person. As to potential exploitation, it is true that exploitation can, and sadly does occur. But, as we have seen, statutory regulation does not provide a guarantee against exploitation.

But the most telling argument relates to power disequilibrium. It is true that this imbalance has characterized the doctor/patient relationship. But it does not necessarily define the therapeutic alliance between complementary practitioner and client. Furthermore, it is precisely this power disequilibrium that causes dissatisfaction with doctors and their patients, and it is the paternalistic provision of health care that is denounced by consumerists.

In terms of practical application, we recognize that not all complementary practitioners practice in an open, empowering way. For the law to be truly 'patient-centred' a commitment would have to be shown to the following:

(1) patient-centred standard of disclosure, with patients being given full information to make informed choices;
(2) the right to the best available treatment within available resources.

(3) explanations when things go wrong;
(4) compensation for mishaps.

As to a contractual model, could this work in practice? There are significant barriers to importing a wholesale contractual relationship into the health care setting. The parties do not have equal negotiating strength. Although the initiatives we have suggested throughout this book should go a long way towards reducing the power disequilibrium between practitioners and patients, patients are in a position of dependence and the nature of the relationship gives rise to special duties on the part of the practitioner.

None the less, some features of a contractual relationship could usefully be imported into the complementary therapist/patient relationship. In contract, for example, plaintiffs have a duty to mitigate their loss. This means that they must take reasonable steps to minimize the harm of any damage caused by the defendant. Extrapolating, is it fair to expect complementary therapists to bear full responsibility where patients have chosen not to consult an allopathic doctor, and harm results which could have been avoided or minimized had they done so? Could one not argue that therapists' duties on suspecting a medical condition are limited to advising patients that they should see an allopathic doctor? Once this duty has been satisfied, therapists should be free to treat patients. This seems to be a problem only around the issue of diagnosis. Once a patient has been diagnosed by a medical doctor, he or she is then at liberty to reject conventional treatment and seek out alternative approaches.

Similarly, one could argue that professional liability should also take account of the extent to which patients have a significant role to play in their own recovery. Thus, it would be unreasonable (save in the case of direct abuse) to allow a claim against a psychotherapist for failing to make the patient a happier or more integrated person. The robust, common sense response would surely be 'There's only so much I, the therapist, can achieve—the only person who can change your life is you'.

Conclusion

We have attempted to devise both practical suggestions for regulation in the immediate future, and a more visionary approach which will only become relevant as and when existing structures are broken down and 'whole person healing' becomes the central priority of all practitioners. We would urge policy-makers to proceed with caution. Change must be led by complementary therapists themselves, at a pace they feel comfortable with. Mobilizing practitioners is likely to take a considerable amount of time. We do not underemphasize the fact that this transformation will also require a huge amount of re-education of the public, and a realization that they themselves have the power, as well as the responsibility of influencing their own health. As Capra says: 'Transcending the biomedical model will be possible only if we are willing to change other things as well; it will be linked, ultimately, to the entire social and cultural transformation'.[1]

The implications of this book transcend complementary medicine. Current shifts in orthodox medicine demonstrate a growing awareness of the shortfalls of scientific, technological medicine being applied without reference to the patient as an individual. Meanwhile, as orthodox medicine struggles to put the humanity back into scientific medicine, so complementary medicine must learn to pay more attention to rigorous means of validation.

This is not to say that orthodox medicine and complementary medicine will ever be conceptually compatible. It has been the aim of this book to demonstrate that a degree of complementarity is required if health care is going to change with the times. Old hostilities should be laid to rest. The benefits of biomedical advances should be acknowledged, but appreciation must now be given to the need to provide allopathic medicine in a more holistic context.

Much of what is encouraged for the regulation of complementary medicine applies equally to orthodox medicine. Indeed, to many, the form of regulation called for may seem almost identical to the existing provisions for orthodox medicine. We make no apologies for this. Much of the existing regulation of medicine is to be commended, and in devising a new framework it would be pointless to throw out the good

[1] Capra, F., *The Turning Point*.

with the bad. On the contrary, the essential framework of a self-regulating profession, with the highest regard for ethical standards has characterized modern medicine, but regulatory failures have added to patient dissatisfaction, both as a consequence of defects in the regulatory provision and in the way they are implemented. We have tried to identify those areas of dissatisfaction and, where possible, suggest regulatory solutions. As stressed throughout the book, not all problems are regulatory, and improving health realistically requires a combined strategy, tackling health education, social welfare, housing, and environmental issues.

We conclude this book with a sense of optimism. Complementary approaches which put the whole patient first cannot but fail to infiltrate medicine as a whole. Healing should be the primary concern of any health professional. No one system of medicine or medical specialty has a monopoly. In practice, the boundaries between what is orthodox and what is alternative are not that clear. Indeed, wherever boundaries are drawn there will always be a fringe. As alternative therapies become incorporated into mainstream, so new alternatives will emerge, as part of a healthy challenge to orthodoxy. Doctors themselves now recognize that healing embraces more than the removal of clinical symptoms. To the extent that complementary medicine alleviates patients' suffering and is highly valued by patients, its use in a safe, and regulated, fashion should be welcomed and encouraged. We hope that the regulatory proposals suggested will avoid the ossification which would inevitably accompany attempts to place holistic therapies within the straitjacket of inappropriate regulation.

Index